DICKENS' WORKS IN GERMANY
1837—1937

BY

ELLIS N. GUMMER

B.A., B.Litt., Oxon.

OCTAGON BOOKS

A Division of Farrar, Straus and Giroux

New York   1976

First published by the Clarendon Press, Oxford, 1940

Reprinted 1976
by special arrangement with Oxford University Press

OCTAGON BOOKS
A DIVISION OF FARRAR, STRAUS & GIROUX, INC.
19 Union Square West
New York, N.Y. 10003

Library of Congress Cataloging in Publication Data

Gummer, Ellis Norman.
 Dickens' works in Germany, 1837-1937.

  Reprint of the 1940 ed. published by the Clarendon Press, Oxford, in series: Oxford studies in modern languages and literature.
  Includes bibliographies and index.
  1. Dickens, Charles, 1812-1870—Appreciation—Germany. 2. Dickens, Charles, 1812-1870—Influence. 3. German fiction—History and criticism. I. Title. II. Series: Oxford studies in modern languages and literature.

PR4588.G8 1976   823'.8   75-42386
ISBN 0-374-93323-5

Printed in USA by
Thomson-Shore, Inc.
Dexter, Michigan

OXFORD STUDIES IN MODERN LANGUAGES AND LITERATURE

General Editor
H. G. FIEDLER
Sometime Taylor Professor of the German Language
and Literature in the University of
Oxford

Die
Pickwickier
oder

Herrn Pickwick's

und der

correspondirenden Mitglieder des
Pickwick=Clubs

Kreuz= und Querzüge, Abentheuer und Thaten.

Nach den

Ueberlieferungen des Pickwick=Clubs

herausgegeben von Boz.

Aus dem Englischen

von

H. Roberts.

Mit Federzeichnungen nach Cruikshank.

Erstes Bändchen.

Leipzig,
bei J. J. Weber.
1837.

The title-page of Dickens' first novel in
German translation

PREFACE

AN attempt is made with this book to present a wide critical survey of Dickens' reception, popularity, and influence in Germany during the century following the appearance of his first novel in German translation. Some aspects of this subject have been examined by earlier investigators, but there existed nothing to which the English student of Dickens or of German literature could turn for a comprehensive survey of the field; the nearest approach to such a survey, a brief chapter on Dickens in L. M. Price's study of English literature in Germany, is restricted to an examination of Dickens' influence alone.

The evidence presented and discussed here has been collected over a wide field, but the primary work of research was lightened by the use of the bibliography compiled by Professor Price and of a list of Dickens studies drawn up by W. Dibelius and published in his book on Dickens in 1916; the latter provided a starting-point for the book-list appended to the third part of this survey. The main research was then carried out in the libraries of Oxford, London, Berlin, Bonn, and Heidelberg, and the work was presented in 1938 as a thesis for the degree of Bachelor of Letters of the University of Oxford. It has since been completely rewritten.

I wish to express my gratitude to the directors and assistants of the libraries in which I have worked, and more particularly to Dr. H. A. Krüss, Director-General of the Prussian State Library, Professor Dr. E. von Rath, of the library of the University of Bonn, who gave me special reading facilities, and Dr. L. F. Powell, Librarian of the Taylor Institution, Oxford; to Professor J. Boyd, for valuable advice on several details; and to Professor H. G. Fiedler, for his untiring help and encouragement throughout my work. I also acknowledge the help given me by my sister, Miss M. J. Gummer, in the preparation of the typescript, and a generous grant towards publication made by the Committee for Advanced Studies of Oxford University.

E. N. G.

OXFORD,
January 1940.

CONTENTS

INTRODUCTION 1

Part I. DICKENS' RECEPTION IN GERMANY

I. FACTS AND REASONS 7
II. CONTEMPORARY CRITICISM OF DICKENS' BOOKS, 1837–49 28
III. JULIAN SCHMIDT AND LATER CRITICISMS OF DICKENS, 1850–70 36

Part II. DICKENS' INFLUENCE ON THE GERMAN NOVEL

I. THE NATURE OF DICKENS' INFLUENCE IN GERMANY 55
II. DICKENS AND GUSTAV FREYTAG . . . 66
III. DICKENS AND OTTO LUDWIG 82
IV. DICKENS AND WILHELM RAABE . . . 94
V. DICKENS AND FRITZ REUTER 103
VI. DICKENS AND FRIEDRICH SPIELHAGEN . . 113
VII. DICKENS AND GUSTAV FRENSSEN . . . 124
VIII. SOME MINOR INFLUENCES 135

Part III. THE AFTER-FAME OF DICKENS IN GERMANY; LATER CRITICISM AND POPULARITY, 1870–1937

I. 1870–1900 142
II. 1901–16 150
III. 1919–37 163
IV. OTHER EVIDENCE 168

LIST OF GERMAN CRITICAL WORKS ON DICKENS, 1870–1937 175

APPENDIX I. List of Articles on Dickens in German Periodicals, 1837–70 180

APPENDIX II. Notes on Some Early German Translators of Dickens' Works 185

GENERAL BIBLIOGRAPHY 194

CHRONOLOGICAL LIST OF DICKENS' MAJOR WORKS . 198

INDEX 199

INTRODUCTION
DICKENS' PERSONAL RELATIONS WITH GERMANY

COMPARED with the interest he showed in America, France, Italy, and Switzerland, Dickens' relations with Germans and Germany were small.[1] He knew no German,[2] though he realized the importance of the language; he sent his eldest son (Charles) to study German at Leipzig after his schooldays at Eton, and later arranged for his third son (Frank) to visit Germany for the same purpose. He himself was only once in that country; that was in the early summer of 1846, when he travelled down the Rhine on his way to Switzerland. Forster gives an interesting account of this visit in his famous *Life*:

... the beauty of the weather showed them the Rhine at its best. At Mayence there had come aboard their boat a German, who soon after accosted Mrs. Dickens on deck in excellent English: 'Your countryman Mr. Dickens is travelling this way just now, our papers say. Do you know him, or have you passed him anywhere?' Explanations ensuing, it turned out, by one of the odd chances my friend thought himself always singled out for, that he had with him a letter of introduction to the brother of this gentleman; who then spoke to him of the popularity of his books in Germany, and of the many persons he had seen reading them in the steamboats as he came along. Dickens remarking at this how great his own vexation was not to be able himself to speak a word of German, 'Oh dear! that needn't trouble you' rejoined the other: 'for even in so small a town as ours, where we are mostly primitive people and have few travellers, I could make a party of at least forty people who understand and speak English as well as I do, and of at least as many more who could manage to read you in the original.' His town was Worms, which Dickens afterwards saw; '... a fine old place, though greatly shrunken and decayed in respect of its population; with a picturesque old cathedral standing on the bank of the Rhine, and some brave old churches shut up, and so hemmed in and overgrown with vineyards that they look as if they were turning into leaves and grapes'.[3]

[1] I dealt with this subject in detail in an article entitled *Dickens and Germany* in the *Modern Language Review*, vol. xxxiii (April 1938), pp. 240–7. The above is a brief summary, containing a few new points from the letters to Tauchnitz and from the new 'Nonesuch' letters.
[2] There is no evidence to support the assertion of the *Blätter für literarische Unterhaltung*, 1854, no. 48 (30 Nov.) that Dickens had recently begun to learn German.
[3] J. Forster, *Life of Charles Dickens* (numerous editions), Book 5, chapter 2.

This German was a Joseph Valckenberg, a wine-merchant of Worms; a letter written to him by Dickens a few weeks later is printed in the new edition of Dickens' letters in the 'Nonesuch' series.[1]

Dickens knew personally, or had correspondence with, several other Germans. Freiligrath, an admirer of his from the earliest years, sent him a copy of his poems through Longfellow, who was a personal friend of both;[2] J. A. Diezmann, the well-known translator, had correspondence with Dickens on the German versions of his books;[3] Emil Devrient, the German actor, met him at a dinner-party in 1852;[4] Dr. Flügel sent him a presentation copy of his German-English dictionary. Dr. Heinrich Künzel of Darmstadt wrote to him as early as 1838 to ask for particulars of his life for inclusion in the Brockhaus *Konversationslexikon*, and again in 1841 to ask his support for a proposed Anglo-German magazine which was to be called *Britannia*. Dickens' reply to this second request, though it is paradoxically only available in German translation, is of great interest, as it gives what is at least Dickens' early opinion of Germany in the warmest language. A contemporary translation in the *Magazin für die Literatur des Auslandes*[5] gives a pleasantly antique flavour:

13 September 1841.

... Was soll ich in Bezug auf die *Britannia* sagen? Daß meine besten Wünsche Ihnen gelten, daß meine herzlichste Sympathie und Theilnahme mit Ihnen ist? das wissen Sie bereits längst.

Glauben Sie mir, geehrter Herr, und ich äußere Ihnen das ganz unumwunden — daß ich nächst der Gunst und guten Meinung meiner eigenen Landsleute über Alles die Achtung der Deutschen Nation hochschätze. Ich ehre und bewundere sie mehr, als ich es auszudrücken vermag. Ich weiß, daß die Deutschen, bei ihren großen geistigen Gaben und deren Ausbildung das erwählte Volk der Erde sind; ich war nie stolzer und glücklicher als damals, wo ich zuerst erfuhr, daß meine Schriften von ihnen günstig aufgenommen wurden.

Ich kann gegen nichts gleichgültig seyn, was Englische Literatur mit Deutschland verknüpft. Der Zweck Ihrer neuen Zeitschrift ist auch mir eine Herzens-Angelegenheit, ja die jedes Engländers, welcher sich

---

[1] *The Nonesuch Dickens; Letters*, ed. W. Dexter, London, 1938 (3 vols.); vol. i; 25 June 1846. All subsequent references to Dickens' letters are to this, the most complete edition.
[2] S. Longfellow, *Life of H. W. Longfellow*, London, 1886, vol. i, p. 421.
[3] See Appendix II, Notes on Translators. [4] *Letters*, 29 June 1852.
[5] 1842, no. 8 (19 Jan.). There is a modern translation in the *Tägliche Rundschau*, 26 Feb. 1915 (*Unterhaltungsbeilage*, p. 190). I cannot hear of the original.

für den Fortschritt des menschlichen Gedankens interessirt und sich darüber freut. Gott segne Ihre Aufgabe und Sie. Ich wünschte beim Himmel, ich könnte Deutsch sprechen, wenn auch noch so schlecht. Könnt' ich's, ich würde in sechs Monaten bei Ihnen seyn. . . .

But the Prussian Government at least was not included in this testimonial, or, if it was originally, Dickens changed his mind within a few years; for, writing of Gottfried Kinkel's imprisonment in Prussia for political reasons, and of his subsequent escape, Dickens said:

. . . Since then we have heard nothing of him. I rather incline to the opinion that the damnable powers that be connived at his escape, but know nothing . . . . [1]

and in the following year, 1851, his article 'Whole Hogs', in the issue of *Household Words* dated 23 August, includes Germany in a list of countries where 'there are tyrants and oppressors . . . watchful to find freedom weak that they may strike, and backed by great armies . . .'.

The famous Leipzig publisher Bernhard Tauchnitz, and his son Karl Bernhard, were two other Germans who had personal relations with Dickens. The correspondence between Dickens and Tauchnitz runs from October 1843 until March 1870; the mass of it is unpublished, but extracts from a score or so of the more interesting letters are printed in a *Festschrift* of the firm of Tauchnitz.[2] All Dickens' books were published by this firm; Dickens arranged the education of his son Charles at Leipzig through Tauchnitz; he met Bernhard Tauchnitz in Paris about 1856[3] and his son Karl in England some time after 1863.[4]

Tauchnitz, of course, published Dickens' books in English. But all his books were translated into German immediately on their appearance in England; occasionally the German translation of a new book by Dickens would be on sale in Germany before the English publication arrived there, for arrangements were made very early in Dickens' career for the proof-sheets of his books to be sent to Germany immediately after correction, for the benefit of the translators. Several letters in the new 'Nonesuch' edition[5]

---

[1] *Letters*, 4 Dec. 1850.
[2] K. Otto, *Der Verlag Bernhard Tauchnitz, 1837–1912*, Leipzig, 1912, pp. 46 f.
[3] Ibid. p. 54.
[4] Ibid. p. 11.
[5] e.g., 9 Jan. 1844; 13 Sept. 1849; 23 Oct. 1850.

INTRODUCTION

show that Dickens took great interest in seeing that this was not overlooked. It appears, too, that he was so generous as to make no claim on the right of translation into German.[1]

Dickens' demonstrable acquaintance with German literature is very small,[2] and of no special significance. An inspection of his library list[3] (drawn up after his death) does, however, show that he at least possessed the means to make himself acquainted with some of the best productions of that literature; but little or nothing can be deduced from the presence of such books on his shelves, even though they are in English translation, for the date of acquisition is very seldom given, almost all the books in question are presentation copies, and in any case the furious tempo of Dickens' life left very little time for reading. It is nevertheless of interest to notice that he possessed a translation of Goethe's works (a selection, in five volumes, 1867) by John Oxenford; W. Ross's translation of Lessing's *Laocoon* (1836); Bohn's translation of Schiller's early dramas and tales (1849); T. Roscoe's well-known *German Novelists: Tales from Ancient and Modern Authors* (1826);[4] J. E. Reade's *Poems and Translations from Goethe* (1840);[5] and J. Gostick's *Spirit of German Poetry* (1845), which is an interesting collection of notes on, and translations from, Goethe, Schiller, Platen, Geibel, Freiligrath, and others, arranged in the form of a limited literary history. Dickens also had the German translations of nine of his earliest books, various accounts of travel in Germany, and his friend C. Stanfield's *Sketches on the Moselle, the Rhine and the Meuse* (1838), a collection of thirty lithographs.

These brief notes exhaust the evidence of Dickens' personal relations with Germany. Much of interest was probably lost to us in the bonfire Dickens made of all his personal papers and letters at Gadshill in September 1860, on which occasion he declared that he also proposed to destroy all his future letters except those on strictly business matters. We do at least know, however, that he

[1] *Letters*, 24 March 1870.
[2] On this subject see F. Fiedler, *Dickens' Belesenheit*, in *Archiv für das Studium d. n. Sprachen u. Literatur*, vol. 140 (1920), pp. 67 f.
[3] J. H. Stonehouse, *Catalogue of the Library of Charles Dickens, from Gadshill*, London, 1935 (a reprint of the early Sotheran catalogue).
[4] This includes the Faust legend, and stories by Gottschalck, Grimm, Fouqué, Musäus, Tieck, and Schiller.
[5] Translations from *Faust* (inc. the *Walpurgisnacht*, complete) and of Mignon's song from *Wilhelm Meister*.

was perpetually visited and worshipped by lionizing German travellers; Theodor Fontane, who was for a time a near neighbour of Dickens in Tavistock Square, wrote in *Ein Sommer in London* in 1852:

> Boz-Dickens ist mein nächster Nachbar und bewohnt zehn Schritt von mir einen reizenden, gartenartigen Einbau, der zwischen der Pancraskirche und unsrem Hause gelegen ist. Ich habe noch nicht den Mut gehabt, ihn aufzusuchen, und werd' es vermutlich auch in Zukunft nicht, um so weniger, als ich weiß, daß er von Deutschen überlaufen und mit den üblichen Bewunderungsphrasen gelangweilt wird. Nur den Park vor seinem Hause besuch' ich öfters und niemals, ohne den frommen Wunsch zu hegen, daß die frische Luft, die da weht, mir von dem Geiste leihen möge, der eben an dieser Stätte heimisch und tätig ist....[1]

In summary, then, all that can be said of Dickens' relationship with Germany is that he respected the strong intellectual life of the country, but disliked its politics; that he liked its people, counted some of them among his friends, and was delighted at his own popularity there, of which he had plenty of evidence.

But his popularity in Germany was far greater and more influential than Dickens ever knew. The reasons for this, and its details and effects, are examined in the following pages.

[1] T. Fontane, *Ges. Werke, Jubiläumsausgabe*, Berlin, 1920, 2te Reihe, vol. iii, p. 288.

PART I
DICKENS' RECEPTION IN GERMANY

I
FACTS AND REASONS

THE immediate and lasting success of Dickens' work in Germany is without parallel. As soon as the popularity of the *Pickwick Papers* became known in Germany, the publishers set their translators to work on that book, and the enthusiasm with which it was greeted very nearly equalled that shown in England.

The first German publisher to undertake this work was J. J. Weber of Leipzig; the translation of *Pickwick*, the first book he produced, was by H. Roberts.[1] The full work appeared in five small volumes from 1837 to 1838, and before it had completed publication the same translator was at work on a German version of the *Sketches*, which appeared as *Londoner Skizzen* in 1838. By 1842 Roberts' translation of *Pickwick* (*Die Pickwickier . . . von Boz*) had run to a third edition.

Its success attracted the attention of other German publishers, and F. Vieweg of Brunswick, as early as 1839, began his publication of *Boz's Gesammelte Werke* in his series *Bibliothek der Neuesten und Besten Romane der Englischen Literatur*; the first volume was *Pickwick* once more, in a translation by Otto von Czarnowski. The subsequent books of Dickens proved as successful; Georg Westermann, who had recently been in England and had firsthand knowledge of Dickens' fame, decided to produce one of his books as the first-fruit of his Brunswick publishing house, founded in May 1838; and by 1 June of that year his company was advertising as its first book *Leben und Abenteuer des Nicolaus Nickleby . . . von Boz, dem Verfasser der Pickwickier*. Westermann secured K. H. Hermes[2] as his first translator; he produced the German version of parts I and II of *Nickleby*, and the remaining five were translated by J. A. Diezmann,[3] who then continued with Westermann to prepare the translations of the *Sketches* and *Oliver Twist*, published in

---

[1] See Appendix II, Notes on Translators.
[2] See *Allg. Deutsche Biographie*, vol. xii, pp. 199–201.
[3] See Appendix II.

1838-9 and 1839, respectively the second and tenth productions of the famous Brunswick house.

Meanwhile at Leipzig H. Roberts continued his work for J. J. Weber on the translation of *Oliver Twist* and of *Nickleby*; the first of these was published by Weber in 1838-9, the second by C. B. Lorck, also of Leipzig, in 1838-40. This firm now took over the Weber publications of Dickens entirely until the year 1847, when the original work and the subsequent preparations of Lorck's firm reverted to Weber once more.

H. Roberts was now succeeded by E. A. Moriarty, surprisingly an Irishman but nevertheless an excellent translator,[1] who worked for C. B. Lorck during the following years on the German versions of *Master Humphrey's Clock* in its complete form (1840-1), *American Notes* (1842-3), *Chuzzlewit* (1843-4), the first two Christmas stories (1844-5), and part of *Dombey* (1846). In Brunswick during this period F. Vieweg had taken over Diezmann's work from Westermann and had published his versions of *Oliver Twist* and *Nickleby* in his own series in 1839, which allowed von Czarnowski leisure to work on *Master Humphrey's Clock*, published by Vieweg in 1840-1, and then on *American Notes* and the first parts of *Chuzzlewit* (1843).

While the general success was thus maintained, and as it became obvious that any translation of Dickens would be warmly received, the firm of Krabbe at Stuttgart began in 1841 to publish all Dickens' books in the translation of C. Kolb.[2] To make up for lost opportunity, Krabbe first published *Oliver Twist* and *Nickleby*, then added *Pickwick* and the *Sketches*; followed by the other books in approximately chronological order. Also at Stuttgart, the firm of F. G. Franckh published translations of the *Christmas Carol* and *Chuzzlewit*, by Erwin von Moosthal, in their series *Das Belletristische Ausland* in 1844.

There were numerous other independent publications and translations of smaller circulation. English editions in Germany should also be noticed; here the first in the field was F. Fleischer of Leipzig, who optimistically advertised the *Complete Works of Charles Dickens* as early as 1839. The best known by far, however, was to be the Tauchnitz edition; this famous collection was opened in 1841 with Bulwer-Lytton's *Pelham*, and continued in the same year with *Pickwick* in two volumes, followed in 1842 by *American*

[1] See Appendix II.   [2] Ibid.

FACTS AND REASONS

Notes. There was at that time no law of international copyright, and these books were simply reprints of English editions sent to Germany. In 1843, however, Bernhard Tauchnitz visited England, wrote to all the leading authors, and arranged to pay them a fee for authorization to reprint any future works of theirs in Germany. This proposal, most generous for the time, was welcomed; Dickens, whose opinions on the law of copyright are well known, was in full agreement with it, and from that year (in which his long correspondence with Tauchnitz began) the Tauchnitz publications of his books were expressly authorized by him. In the two years 1843 and 1846 alone ten of his books were so published.[1] It has recently been shown by a bibliographical study of the Tauchnitz edition of the *Christmas Carol*[2] that the early corrected proofs were sent to Leipzig by Dickens' publishers as soon as possible in order to allow simultaneous publication of the book in England and Germany; this method seems to have been adopted for all Dickens' books after 1843.

A survey of the position reached at this point shows that even if analysis be restricted to the four most important houses—Weber/Lorck, Vieweg, Westermann, and Krabbe—the figures of publication are impressive enough. During the first eight years all Dickens' works had been translated at least three times; and of *Pickwick* and *Oliver Twist*, for example, there existed five translations and publications each from these four firms alone. Weber, Vieweg, and Krabbe had all announced publication of the *Sämtliche Werke* already, and the first-named had produced *Ausgewählte Werke* of Dickens in 1839–44. The complete works in English had been advertised as early as 1839, and Tauchnitz had arranged for Dickens' personal authorization for the Leipzig reproductions of all future books by him. In the conditions prevailing at the time, this was an unparalleled success; and it was to be maintained until well after Dickens' death.

Further light is thrown on the popularity of Dickens' works in Germany at this time by a study of the numerous German imitations, especially of *Pickwick*, which soon began to appear. Sometimes, as in England, these imitations were published as actual

---

[1] There is a complete list of Dickens' books in the Tauchnitz edition in *Fünfzig Jahre der Verlagshandlung Bernhard Tauchnitz, 1837–1887*, Leipzig, 1887.
[2] J. Y. Southon in the *Dickensian*, 1912, pp. 181–3.

books by Dickens. The *Dresdner Abendzeitung*, mentioning one of these, says:[1]

> Es war zu erwarten, daß Humoristen sich des Namens Boz bedienen würden, um gleichsam die Gattung ihrer Schriften dadurch anzuzeigen, und so ist es auch im folgenden Büchelchen geschehen:
> *Mukkebold und Fridolin, Weltfahrten zweier Eisenbahnreisenden zwischen Dresden und Leipzig. Ein Geschenk für Eisenbahnreisende von Boz.*
> Erstes Heft: *Herr Mukkebold in Leipzig.* Leipzig, 1840.

Such 'Pseudo-Boz-Literatur', as the *Abendzeitung* calls it, was of short life and of no reputation. A few imitations, however, published by better-known authors under their own names, were more lasting. These were sufficiently examined by J. T. Geissendoerfer in 1915.[2] One such imitator was Ferdinand Stolle,[3] a long-since-forgotten author, but one who was popular in his day; his *Deutsche Pickwickier*, published at Leipzig in 1841, ran to a second edition in 1856 and to a third as late as 1878, while a continuation, *Deutsche Pickwickier auf Reisen*, appeared in 1864. His foreword to the first edition of *Deutsche Pickwickier* says:

> Fern sei dem Herausgeber dieser Blätter die Anmaßung, sich mit dem bekannten genialen englischen Autor in Vergleich zu stellen. Er hat die Aufschrift *Deutsche Pickwickier* aus keinem andern Grunde gewählt, als um den ungefähren Inhalt und die Art und Weise der Behandlung dieses komischen Romans anzudeuten, welcher letztere allerdings mit dem englischen Werke gemein hat, daß er mehre originelle vaterländische Stereotyp-Charaktere vorführt und ihr Leben und Treiben, so wie die verschiedenen Abenteuer derselben zu veranschaulichen bemüht ist.

That was certainly all that Stolle managed to do. The general criticism of his works, 'von denen die ersten meist an den nackten Tatsachen hängen bleiben und nirgends zu rechter Charakteristik von Personen und Ereignissen ansetzen',[4] applies in this particular case. There are long rows of scenes and stories, unskilfully

---

[1] In the supplement *Blätter für Literatur und Bildende Kunst*, 1840, no. 66 (15 August).
[2] *Dickens' Einfluß auf Ungern-Sternberg, Hesslein, Stolle, Raabe und Ebner-Eschenbach, Americana-Germanica*, no. 19, 1915, pp. 6–16.
[3] The future editor of the *Gartenlaube*. See *Allg. Dte. Biographie*, vol. xxxvi, Nachtrag, pp. 786–8.
[4] Ibid., p. 787.

arranged and badly connected; Dickens had no influence on the actual construction of the characters, which is poorly done, and the attempts at moralizing are direct and blatant. A few incidents are borrowed directly from *Pickwick*.[1] The words of his biographer give the most charitable criticism of both Stolle's imitations of Dickens:

Die 'komischen Romane', die den unsterblichen 'Boz' nachahmen wollen, ihm aber nicht das Wasser reichen, leisteten immerhin lobenswertes in ihrer bewußten spießbürgerlichen Sphäre.[2]

Another imitator of Dickens was Bernhard Hesslein,[3] whose *Berliner Pickwickier* appeared in 1854. The sub-title runs: *Fahrten und Abenteuer Berliner Junggesellen bei ihren Kreuz- und Querzügen durch das moderne Babylon*; and an enthusiastic publisher's note on the cover, which claims every literary virtue for the book, explains that it is 'eine humoristische Schilderung Berliner Lebens und Treibens in ähnlicher Weise, wie der geniale Boz in seinen *Pickwickiern* und anderen Werken das Leben der englischen Gesellschaft so meisterhaft dargestellt hat'. J. T. Geissendoerfer[4] devotes six pages to a comparison of this book with *Pickwick*; he shows that many characteristics of Mr. Pickwick have been copied in the figure of Joseph Eduard Meyer, the main character of Hesslein's book; that Bob Sawyer and Ben Allen have been copied in the Stud. Jur. Grunow; and that several scenes have been taken over directly from Dickens' book. A contemporary criticism of *Berliner Pickwickier* in *Europa*[5] calls the book 'breit und platt, als Satire plump, als Parodie trivial; ... der Diener ist eine matte Kopie des bekannten Sam Weller in den echten *Pickwickiern*'.

English imitations even were thought worthy of translation into German; thus G. W. M. Reynolds' continuation of *Pickwick*: *Pickwick Abroad* (1839), appeared at Brunswick in 1841 as *Pickwick in der Fremde, oder die Reise nach Frankreich*, the translator being L. Herrig. The *Memoirs of Joseph Grimaldi*, which were only edited by Dickens, were twice translated, once by C. Kolb for Krabbe's series, once by H. Roberts for Weber in 1839; Roberts' translation required a third edition in 1844. The *Picnic Papers*, another book which was no more than edited by Dickens, was also

[1] J. T. Geissendoerfer, op. cit., pp. 12–16.
[2] *Allg. Dte. Biographie*, vol. xxxvi, p. 788.
[3] See F. Brümmer, *Deutsches Dichterlexikon*, 1876–7, vol. i, p. 358.
[4] Op. cit., pp. 6–12. [5] 1854, no. 82 (5 Oct.).

translated twice; once, again, by the indefatigable C. Kolb, once by Amalie Winter[1] for Vieweg. Among other publications owing their existence to Dickens' popularity in Germany may be noticed Weber's *Bildergallerie zu Boz' Sämmtlichen Werken* (1842 f.) and M. Lefrank's *Geheimnisse London's, Englands und der Engländer* (Berlin, 1844), compiled from Dickens' books after the success of Eugène Sue's *Mystères de Paris* in Germany.

By the middle of the forties Dickens' popularity in Germany was well established, and from this point the translations, publications, and re-publications become extremely numerous. From the bookseller's point of view the Christmas stories were probably the most successful of Dickens' works at this time; they were published singly, they were published in collected editions, and they were published in almost every imaginable combination; and from the number of re-publications it must be concluded that the German public did not tire of them. This is true not only of the decade after the publication of the *Christmas Carol* (1843), but of much later years also; the sixties and especially the seventies, as is shown in another section of this book. In the forties also, Dickens' books began to appear in editions prepared for schools, a use to which they were very frequently put later in the century; thus in 1847, less than four years after its publication in England, the *Christmas Carol* was published at Leipzig as a school text in an edition by August Andreae. It proved to be one of the most popular of Dickens' books for this purpose; among later publications of it for school use may be noticed that of L. Riechelmann (Leipzig, 1864), of which a second edition was needed within nine years.

The best-known firms meanwhile continued their publication of Dickens' books in German. C. Kolb was the regular translator for the firm of Krabbe until the early fifties, at which time his work was taken over by the house of Hoffmann, also at Stuttgart. Hoffmann also had the services of such lesser-known translators as J. E. Wessely, Adolf Banner, Edmund Zoller, L. Dubois;[2] their combined work enabled the firm to commence publication in 1860 of a complete edition of Dickens, concluded in 1876 in 27 volumes,

[1] Pseudonym of Amalie, Baronin von Gross; 1802–79. She also translated De Quincey's *Confessions of an English Opium-Eater* in 1840.

[2] These translated respectively the four first Christmas stories; *Hard Times*; *Little Dorrit*; *Great Expectations* and *Our Mutual Friend*. J. E. Wessely is perhaps Ignaz Emanuel Wessely, author and translator of Leipzig: see W. Haan, *Sächsisches Schriftsteller-Lexicon*, Leipzig, 1875, p. 368.

incorporating all the earlier work of Kolb and a later translation by him of the *Tale of Two Cities*.

In 1847, as was mentioned above, the Lorck editions of Dickens reverted to J. J. Weber of Leipzig, who then continued the publication of the complete works which he himself had begun in 1839. He now had the services of one of the best contemporary translators, Julius Seybt,[1] who worked for him and for C. B. Lorck until about 1864, producing German versions of all Dickens' work from the *Cricket on the Hearth* (1845) to *Great Expectations* (1862). With the help of Seybt chiefly, but also, to a much smaller extent, of Moritz Busch, Marie Scott, and Emil Lehmann,[2] Weber continued his complete edition of Dickens without a break until 1870; volumes 123–5, which were the last, contained the translation of *Edwin Drood*. Meanwhile, C. B. Lorck of Leipzig had started a new complete collection in 1852. This well-known edition, introduced with a foreword by Julian Schmidt, the famous critic,[3] incorporated the early work of H. Roberts and E. A. Moriarty, and also many of Julius Seybt's translations, which thus occasionally appeared in two editions simultaneously. Lorck published twenty volumes in this series, which was then taken over and completed by the Leipzig firm of Wiedemann, also with the use of Seybt's work. The same house published a cheap edition of the complete Dickens in twenty-four volumes in 1861–2.

From the time of the Napoleonic wars until the middle years of the nineteenth century Germans showed a very lively interest in England, grounded for the most part on admiration of English political institutions and of the national pride and prestige of the country. It was an interest which made itself seen in the visits paid to England by German writers, in the books they wrote on the country, and in the numerous other publications of the time dealing with English life, language, literature, and politics. A surprising number of these can be discovered by a glance through the pages of the Leipzig *Literarischer Anzeiger*, for example, of any date between the two revolutionary years 1830 and 1848.

[1] See Appendix II, Notes on Translators.
[2] These translated respectively *Little Dorrit*; *Great Expectations* and *Our Mutual Friend*; *Edwin Drood*. The two last-named translations were expressly authorized by Dickens.
[3] See below: Part I, Chapter III. There is a very appreciative article by Julian Schmidt on this collected edition in his periodical *Die Grenzboten*, 1853, vol. iii, pp. 436–7.

There is no doubt that this strong interest in England generally, coupled with the news of the great success of *Pickwick* in England, formed the primary reason for its first translation into German. At that time English books were translated into German on the slightest pretext; with reference to this period E. Engel later wrote of what he called the 'Übersetzungsseuche in Deutschland',[1] and in 1895 another critic wrote of the 'Übersetzungsraserei' apparent in Germany during the whole second quarter of the century.[2] The fact that Dickens' first successful book appeared in German immediately after its publication in England has therefore little special significance.

What is at first sight more surprising is that this and the subsequent books gained for themselves such an immediate and lasting popularity in Germany that not only were three editions of the first (Roberts') translation necessary within four years, but also that at least three separate translations of all the earlier works were called for, which themselves sometimes ran to further editions. The reasons for this were many, and varied in some details with the successive books; but they show conclusively that Dickens' success in Germany was no mere transitory reflection of his popularity in England.

To open the examination of these reasons with a study of the German reception of *Pickwick*: it is clear that the chief ground for its success was what the Germans called its *Behaglichkeit*; that element, so clearly seen in the whole story, of generous good nature, of solid comforts and everyday joys, coupled with a warm and pleasant humour; a definite and positive expression of the view that life is well worth living. Freytag's personal experience of the reception of *Pickwick* was that it came like a burst of sunshine; he paints a dreary picture of conditions of life in Germany at the time, emphasizing the absence of this very warmth and good nature not only in the literature but in public and private life also.[3] There is no doubt that when in 1870 he wrote the generous article 'Ein Dank für Charles Dickens' he exaggerated this unpleasant detail, partly, it may be suggested, under the influence of Julian Schmidt,

---

[1] Quoted by L. Weizmann, *Dickens und Daudet in deutscher Übersetzung*, Berlin, 1880, p. 1.

[2] H. Hart, 'Charles Dickens', in *Tägliche Rundschau, Unterhaltungsbeilage*, 11–12 June 1895.

[3] 'Ein Dank für Charles Dickens'; first published in *Grenzboten*, 1870: rep. in *Gesammelte Aufsätze*, Leipzig, 1888, vol. ii, pp. 239–44.

who had drawn contemporary conditions in very much the same colours in his essay on Dickens of 1852.[1] But Freytag's account of the book's reception is the description of a personal experience, and carries more weight:

> Man muß jene Zeit in gebildeten bürgerlichen Familien durchlebt haben, um die schöne Wirkung zu begreifen, welche das Buch auf Männer und Frauen ausübte. Die fröhliche Auffassung des Lebens, das unendliche Behagen, der wackere Sinn, welcher hinter der drolligen Art hervorleuchtete, waren dem Deutschen damals so rührend, wie dem Wanderer eine Melodie aus dem Vaterhause, die unerwartet in sein Ohr tönt. Und alles war modernes Leben, im Grunde alltägliche Wirklichkeit und die eigene Weise zu empfinden, nur verklärt durch das liebevolle Gemüt eines echten Dichters. Hunderttausenden gab das Buch frohe Stunden, gehobene Stimmung.... [2]

There is much more in the same strain, not only in the essay of 1870 but also in the last volume of *Die Ahnen* and in Freytag's memoirs; this evidence will be considered below in a special chapter on Freytag and Dickens, and is mentioned here to illustrate the fact that even in the last years of his life Freytag remembered the pleasure which *Pickwick* gave to the German reader as soon as it appeared.

Although it has been said that Freytag exaggerated his dreary picture of ordinary life in Germany at the end of the thirties, it is nevertheless true that it was an unhappy period. The country had no national life, and was, indeed, as Italy was also at the time, little more than a 'geographical expression'. What national history there was had produced little to be proud of during the last decades; the Napoleonic wars had given a prospect of better things, a certain unity of purpose and method and an example of almost national action, but since then the old, almost medieval discords and divisions had reappeared. 'Der ganze stolze Freiheitsstrom verlief sich kläglich im Sande angestammter Untertanentreue'.[3] Public as well as private life 'had a strongly Philistine tinge'; the Direktor von Zehren in F. Spielhagen's *Hammer und Amboß*, in about the year 1834, speaks of 'die unglaublich nüchterne, geistes- und tatenarme, ideenlose, durch und durch epigonenhafte Zeit, in der wir leben...'.[4] Nor had the country any commonly acknowledged

[1] *Boz (Dickens), eine Charakteristik*, Leipzig, 1852.
[2] G. Freytag, op. cit., p. 241.
[3] F. Spielhagen, *Hammer und Amboß: Werke*, Leipzig, 1874, vol. ix, p. 373.
[4] Ibid., p. 373.

centre to give a lead or to act as a nucleus; there was nothing to correspond in importance to London or Paris, for Berlin, Leipzig, Munich were at best merely local capitals. The Zollverein had as yet produced but little tangible improvement; incipient industrialization had caused social unrest; and the general dissatisfaction had steadily increased since the news of the revolution of 1830 in Paris.

In contemporary literature the same discords could be seen. The age began to find its major interest in the everyday realities of life; it had no need to find an escape from the alarms and anxieties of the revolutionary and Napoleonic period in the dreamy, idealized Middle Ages loved by the Romantics; it began to demand more attention for the problems of the present day. There had been a great increase in the number of books published;[1] many of them were directed to a discussion of the needs of the hour, partly because of the spread of industrialism and its attendant unrest, partly because of the general interest felt in new social theories, symptoms of which were the attention paid in Germany in the thirties to the doctrines of Saint-Simon and, a few years later, the popularity with certain classes in that country of the novels of George Sand.

It was for these reasons that there had recently appeared in Germany that school of young writers known collectively as 'Jungdeutschland', whose work was so largely directed to the preaching of a new social order, much of it being frankly revolutionary and directed against fundamental precepts of order in Church and State, in public existence and private morals. This, coupled with their frequent tastelessness and occasional immorality, had led to the bitter attacks of Wolfgang Menzel and the subsequent banning of all the works, present and future, of the Young Germans by the Bundestag in 1835. The 'official' literature was a rather colourless continuation of the Romantic school, which gave little satisfaction to any one; otherwise the drama and particularly the novel were made the vehicles, very largely, for the diffusion of new ideas, political and social, and even the lyric was beginning to take on a political tinge.

It was into this Germany, into this atmosphere of social unrest and general dissatisfaction, of mixed doctrines which all inveighed against the way in which everyday life was lived, that the *Pickwick Papers* were introduced by translation in the last months of 1837

[1] Partly due to the invention of the steam printing-press by F. König in 1811.

and in 1838. It is necessary to realize how confused and dispirited the age was in order to understand Heinrich Laube's cry of pleasure on reading *Pickwick* for the first time; he writes in his memoirs, of his journey abroad early in 1839:

> Das letzte neue Buch, welches damals erschienen war, erheiterte mich unterwegs vortrefflich; es waren *Die Pickwickier* von Dickens. 'Es gibt also noch heitere Talente starker Kraft', rief ich, 'die Welt ist nicht versauert, wie's hinter uns aussah!'[1]

The fact is that the book was clearly written by a man who believed life to be thoroughly well worth living; who showed how, in ordinary everyday matters, there could be pleasure and good humour; and whose whole outlook was consequently positive, not directed against fundamentals of ordinary existence. Laube's remark has affinity with what Julian Schmidt wrote some years later; the book shows:

> ... handgreiflich vor Augen ...., wie viel Freude, Schönheit und Idealismus in dem ganz gewöhnlichen Leben zu finden sei. ... Hier haben wir die unmittelbarste Gegenwart mit all' ihren Schwächen, Torheiten und Verirrungen, und doch fühlen wir uns zu Hause und finden, daß das Leben schön ist. Die Poesie zeigt uns das Wunderschloß der Ideale nicht mehr in der Ferne, sie verklärt selbst die nebeligen Straßen Londons, sie läßt einen Strahl in die Wohnungen des Elends fallen, sie durchdringt die ganze Schöpfung .... Darin besteht der unerschöpfliche Reiz dieses Buches. Wir können es hundertmal gelesen haben, und gehen immer mit neuer Lust daran.[2]

Pickwick was, indeed, in this sense a direct opposite of the polemic literature of which Germany had seen so much, and which so many readers found either incomprehensible or, if they understood it, definitely bad.

The fact that many could not understand the contemporary literature was an additional reason for the success of English works, and especially of Dickens, in German translation. Julian Schmidt was later to demonstrate that in these years and for some time to come there were two distinct classes of German writer; the educated and imaginative type, whose work, of whatever sort, was usually far above the head of the general reading public, and the opposite type, which produced purely ephemeral literature of a very low standard, whose sole merit was that at least the average

---

[1] F. Laube, *Erinnerungen* (*Gesammelte Schriften*, Wien, 1875–82, vol. i), p. 358.   [2] J. Schmidt, op. cit., 1852, pp. 24, 26.

reader could understand it, and that it dealt with conditions and characters with which he was familiar. Between these types there was a great gap; and this the English writers, more particularly Dickens, filled admirably.[1] Robert Prutz gave the same explanation forcefully in his *Deutsche Literatur der Gegenwart*[2] a few years later:

Unser Publikum liest die Dickens und Thackeray, die Sue und Dumas nicht deshalb, weil sie Engländer und Franzosen sind, noch läßt es die deutschen Romane ungelesen, weil sie deutsche; sondern es liest die einen, weil sie unterhaltend sind, weil es das Leben der Wirklichkeit darin abgespiegelt findet, weil interessante Charaktere, mächtige Leidenschaften, spannende Verwicklungen ihm daraus entgegentreten — und wirft die anderen beiseite, weil sie langweilig sind oder doch wenigstens eine Sprache reden und von Dingen handeln, die das Publikum im großen entweder nicht versteht, oder für die es sich nicht interessiert.

This is not to say that Dickens' books were purely second-class; the significance of these remarks is rather that there was something in them for every one, of whatever standard of culture.

Contemporary German criticism supports this analysis of the success of *Pickwick*. Details of this will be given in the following chapter, which is devoted to a study of the reviews and articles on Dickens which appeared in contemporary German periodicals; but a few of the most interesting opinions may be included here. The *Stuttgarter Literaturblatt*[3] greets the book with the words:

... es ist sehr erfreulich, daß diese komische Manier wieder aufkommt. Man atmet gleichsam wieder frei, nachdem man sich an den breiten historischen Romanen tödlich gelangweilt und an den Gräßlichkeiten und Unflätereien der neufranzösischen Romantik geekelt hat. In diesem altenglischen Humor weht gesunde frische Luft.

The *Blätter für literarische Unterhaltung*[4] says:

... Ein Roman wie die Pickwickier, mit einem so durchgehenden Grundzuge von Gemütlichkeit und Humor, könnte in dem heutigen literarischen Deutschland nicht zustande gebracht werden.

The *Blätter zur Kunde der Literatur des Auslandes*[5] adds to this:

Wir nehmen die komischen Romane fremder Völker gern auf und

---

[1] J. Schmidt, op. cit., 1852, p. 9. [2] Leipzig, 1859, vol. ii, p. 75.
[3] 1838, no. 22 (28 Feb.) (supplement to the *Stuttgarter Morgenblatt*).
[4] 1838, no. 253 (10 Sept.). [5] 1838, no. 109 (Nov.), on *Pickwick*.

eignen sie uns soviel möglich an; wir belachen das allgemein Menschliche und machen uns auch das Nationale und Lokale einigermaßen verständlich; aber der deutsche Boden selbst scheint kein lebensfähiges komisches Produkt, das sich den Beifall eines großen Kreises erwerben könnte, hervorbringen zu wollen.

The important *Jenaische Allgemeine Literaturzeitung*[1] adds two further points on *Pickwick*:

Zwei seltene Vorzüge zeichnen das Werk vor vielen anderen seines gleichen aus: der Spott ist nicht hämisch und bösartig, er ist so froh und wohlgemut, daß gewiß mancher, der sich getroffen fühlt, . . . darüber lachen muß. Ferner wird der Verfasser, wo er das Gemeine schildert, nicht selbst gemein.

The humour of the book was, indeed, very strongly appreciated in Germany. To this statement the usual English reaction is one of surprise; the general English view is well expressed, for example, by P. Fitzgerald, who wrote in his *Pickwickian Manners and Customs* of 1897 that 'the difficulty of course was that none of the adventures could have occurred in a country like Germany, or if they did, would have become an affair of police. No German could see humour in that.' There is an element of truth in this judgement. But in Germany most of this appreciation went, not to the actual objects and details of the humour (which, as was soon realized, could only properly be enjoyed by Englishmen), but to the nature of it; the most frequent theme in contemporary German criticism was praise for the 'golden', 'sunny' type of humour in Dickens' books. As the Jena critic was so pleased to see, the humour was not bitter or spiteful. This was a most important detail, and contributed largely to Dickens' early success, for the age was beginning to be heartily tired of sharp criticism and biting satire, of which it had had such a surfeit; it was pleasant at last to find something so warm and generous as the humour of *Pickwick*. And there was something uproarious about it which put it close to the old Germanic tradition of the *Schwank*; as G. K. Chesterton has said, Dickens, in continuing 'the Old English legend of the coarse and comic novels of Smollett and Fielding', 'carries on a rank, rowdy, jolly tradition, of men falling off coaches'; and this, to some extent, struck a like vein in Germany. But whatever

[1] 1839, *Ergänzungsblatt* no. 28.

reason one chooses as an explanation, there is no doubt of the success of Dickens' humour, a success neatly described by the *Blätter für literarische Unterhaltung*,[1] which speaks of the

... herrliche Humor, den man in England vergöttert und in Deutschland mit Entzücken aufnimmt.

The word 'Germanic' has further implications. Towards the end of the century the 'Germanic' characteristics of Dickens' work were emphasized by the critics, and it is possible that these give a more subtle reason for his immediate and continued popularity in Germany, though they were not expressly pointed out until much later: by Heinrich Hart in 1895.[2] Without insisting on the relationships of blood and race, as does this writer, it may be noticed that he numbers among the essentially 'Germanic' traits of Dickens his deep sentiment of nature, of the sort which sees personal feelings reflected in natural phenomena, and can find sympathy in the trees and the waves; his strong feeling for the implications of the words *hearth* and *home*, and linked with this his tender sense for the family; his sense of justice; his piety, despising outward and empty show; and, not least of these, his stout pleasure in a good square meal, with plenty to drink. Very many of these traits (especially the last) can be seen already in *Pickwick*.

Enough has been said on the subject of Dickens' *Behaglichkeit* alone to show that with *Pickwick* only (a most happy beginning) he was assured of a welcome in Germany. There were, however, several other reasons for his success, which can be deduced from the nature of his earlier books taken together and a comparison with contemporary conditions and interests in Germany. Important among them is the fact that he possessed a quite definite moral code, which was not weakened by his humorous outlook; he drew a clear distinction between the good and the bad, and denounced the bad where he found it. Fifteen years later Julian Schmidt was to make the excellent suggestion that in this matter Nicholas Nickleby can well be taken as an embodiment of Dickens' attitude: for all his essential good humour and tolerance, he never hesitates to act when he meets the really bad.[3] This refreshing decisiveness was very welcome in Germany after the capricious variations of the

---

[1] 1842, no. 79 (20 March).
[2] Op. cit., *Tägliche Rundschau, Unterhaltungsbeilage*, 11–12 June 1895.
[3] Op. cit., 1852, p. 12.

Young Germans and the French romantics. This Freytag also saw, and wrote in his article of 1870:

> In jedem [Roman] fand der Leser einen oder mehre Charaktere, die ihm Menschennatur liebenswert und ehrwürdig machten, und in jedem einige gewaltige Schilderungen von Schuld und Strafe, von menschlichen Torheiten und Lastern, von dem innern Verderb, den diese in den Seelen hervorbringen, und von der gerechten Vergeltung, welche durch die Missetat selbst in die Verbrecher geführt wird.[1]

The poetic justice of his books was an element which a large class of his readers found acceptable. His whole standard of good and bad, especially as it appeared in the subsequent novels, was, indeed, of that solid type which is best named by the epithet 'middle-class'. The middle classes, particularly the lower middle class, in fact formed his ideal as well as the greater part of his actual public in both England and Germany; and in this detail it is once more apparent that Dickens had chosen a very propitious moment for his work. For it was the period of the rise of the middle class to a power in the state, as Immermann had shown so recently in his *Epigonen* (1836); a period in which, awakening to a sense of its importance, it began to demand more attention for itself and a better position in the economy of the state. From the end of the second decade onwards the middle class was a force of steadily growing importance; and the revolution of 1848–9 was to be a thoroughly middle-class movement. It was to this class that Dickens' books were chiefly addressed, and this class provided the majority of his readers.

Coupled with this was the growth of national feeling in Germany, which became especially noticeable, for example, partly under pressure of the occasionally warlike attitude of France, at the time of the accession of Frederick William IV of Prussia in 1840. Time and again the complaint is made that Germany has no national history, no national existence; and the example given of a country fortunate in possessing these things is usually England. This, as was mentioned, partly explains the interest felt in England by Germans at that time. In particular, it was for this reason that Dickens' works gained still more honour for themselves in Germany; a large amount of contemporary criticism in that country stresses the fact that they are the part products of a strong national

[1] Op. cit., p. 241.

sense and a pride in the native land, a thing to be envied and studied.

It was noticed above that another aspect of the age was its taste for liberal-social doctrines. German socialism at that time was 'still in its ideal and theoretical stage'; the ideas were still indefinite and at times compounded with more sentiment than sympathy required. The cause, chiefly growing industrialism, was evident enough, and of this the major element was the development of the new methods of transport. During these years the first steamship routes were opened between Bremen and North America. The first German railway, from Nuremberg to Fürth, was built in 1835; the first of any size, from Leipzig to Dresden, in 1837. Industrialization was causing unrest in various quarters of Germany, and in 1844 the weavers' revolt in Silesia (a theme not to be forgotten in literature) had to be quenched by force. East Prussia and the Rhineland, too, were 'hotbeds of political and social unrest'; the strong liberal tendencies of the latter district were expressed in the *Rheinische Zeitung*, whose editor, in 1842, was Karl Marx.[1]

This was a fruitful field for the spread of Dickens' successive works, preaching a mild and sentimental socialism not far removed from that expressed by George Sand, whose books also, significantly, gained some popularity for themselves in Germany. The immediate example is naturally *Oliver Twist*, but all the successive books, particularly the Christmas stories, showed the same spirit. The sympathy for the conditions of the working class was already present in Germany; Dickens felt this sympathy deeply himself, and, while not attempting to cover the fact that the conditions were bad, pointed out methods of betterment which were certainly vague, but which were in keeping with the sentiment of the period.

The fact that he did not attempt to hide the unpleasantness of the conditions leads to the mention of a less reputable detail of his German popularity; that is, that with such works as *Oliver Twist* he fed the interest in sensational themes, in the story of the criminal and the life of the underworld, which was noticeable in the reception, for example, of the books of Harrison Ainsworth in Germany—which were popular although contemporary criticism roundly denounced them. A far better example of this taste for the

---

[1] *Cambridge Modern History*, vol. xi (*The Growth of Nationalities*), Cambridge, 1909, pp. 52–4.

sensational was given by the immense popularity in Germany of Eugène Sue's *Mystères de Paris* in the years after its appearance in 1842.[1]

Those were the social and political reasons for Dickens' success in Germany. Considered from a literary point of view his works show further characteristics contributing to this popularity.

Certain details were fresh to that country, among them the excellence of his drawing of the London scene; but many elements clearly distinguished in his work were not the less enjoyed for being familiar. The most important of his forerunners in Germany was Jean Paul, whose work at this time was significantly at the height of its popularity. German readers sensed behind his books a warm and kindly nature, much closer to the ordinary man and woman than were the great classic writers, the deliberately secluded romantics and the too sophisticated, too 'emancipated' Young Germans. With Jean Paul there was already a taste for the quaint character, the eccentric but lovable person, the pleasant, ordinary, unimportant details of everyday life. With him, too, was the sympathy for the unfortunates of the world; in his books there was the gentle, sentimental, rather tearful humour with which their lives were viewed, a humour which sometimes turned, by sudden jumps, to the fantastic. Almost all these traits were to be found in Dickens, one of the differences, however, being that the Englishman's humour was more robust than that of the German. The other likenesses were frequently striking, and a reference to Jean Paul is a common detail of contemporary German criticism of Dickens. The general opinion of those critics whose articles appeared in the literary periodicals was that though Dickens was the better realistic painter, Jean Paul had greater powers of imagination; and it was not realized for some time that this, for Jean Paul, was not a merit but a defect. Dickens controls his imagination better, even though not always sufficiently. Theodor Mundt, in his history of contemporary literature published in 1842, wrote of 'Boz':

Vergleicht man ihn mit einem deutschen Dichter, mit dem er in der humoristischen Darstellung des volkstümlichen Kleinlebens einige Verwandtschaft behaupten kann, mit Jean Paul, so muß Boz freilich dagegen arm erscheinen, und hat nicht diesen großen und unerschöpflichen Springquell des Gemüts- und Gedankenlebens in sich[2]—

[1] See, e.g., E. Edler, *Eugène Sue und die deutsche Mysterienliteratur*, Diss. Berlin, 1932. [2] *Die Literatur der Gegenwart*, Berlin, 1842, p. 429.

a view with which Julian Schmidt was later to disagree; for him the exact opposite was true.[1] In any case, it was generally realized that Dickens stood close to Jean Paul in many things; Mr. Pickwick was occasionally mentioned as an almost Pauline figure in his 'Mischung von Edelmut, Gutmütigkeit und Lächerlichkeit',[2] and Tom Pinch (*Chuzzlewit*) was 'eine so Jean Paulisch angelegte Figur, wie es dem britischen Dichter nur möglich ist';[3] he is indeed in many respects close to Wuz, for example.

It should be noticed that some of the similarity of Dickens and Jean Paul can be explained by a reference to (probable) common literary ancestors. Dickens' relation to the English eighteenth-century novelists is well known. Jean Paul to some extent carried on the tradition of these same writers, Fielding, Smollett, Sterne, particularly the latter; one of the first books he had read was *Tristram Shandy*.[4] Sterne's influence was projected from the eighteenth century into the nineteenth, and was in any case much stronger in Germany than it had been in England; it can be traced in the Romantics, and seen in the Young Germans, and it was admitted in the case even of Wilhelm Raabe. Julian Schmidt saw that its most important detail was the rather tearful humour, and he traces the influence of this element in the work of many of the German humorists—Hippel, Jean Paul, E. T. A. Hoffmann—and sees it in the work of Arnim, Brentano, Heine, and Immermann.

The fantastic element in Dickens' work was a detail which also had a precedent in Germany, in the work of E. T. A. Hoffmann, though Dickens did not go so far towards the purely grotesque. Comparisons of their work were also occasionally made, though usually in very general terms; few went so far as to suggest detailed similarities, but R. H. Horne said of the *Christmas Carol* in 1844: 'The knocker which changes into Marley's dead-alive face, and yet remains a knocker, is taken from Hoffmann's *Golden Pot*.'[5] It is, however, unlikely that Dickens knew anything of Hoffmann's work, though it should be noticed that several of Hoffmann's

[1] J. Schmidt, op. cit., 1852, *passim*, and *Charakterbilder aus der zeitgenössischen Literatur*, Leipzig, 1875, p. 274.
[2] *Stuttgarter Literaturblatt* (supp. of the *Stuttgarter Morgenblatt*), 1839, no. 13 (4 Feb.).
[3] J. Schmidt, op. cit., 1852, pp. 51–2.
[4] See L. M. Price, *The Reception of English Literature in Germany*, Berkeley, California, 1932, p. 354.
[5] *The New Spirit of the Age* (1844), 'World's Classics' edition, Oxford, 1907, p. 35.

FACTS AND REASONS 25

stories had been translated into English before Dickens began to write, among them the *Goldne Topf* by Thomas Carlyle in 1827.[1]

It was the occurrence of such resemblances as these which produced Otto Ludwig's opinion, several years later, that Dickens' popular romanticism was a synthesis of Tieck, Jean Paul, Hoffmann, and Arnim, 'die Fratze Shakespeares in das Vaterland des schönen Originals zurückgekehrt, aber Fratze geblieben oder vielmehr erst recht Fratze geworden'.[2] In fact the mixture of the comic and the terrible, the grotesque and the tragic as seen in Dickens need not be bound to any special country or century; such a mixture, a popularized romanticism exactly, would have assured Dickens of some success with a certain class of reader at any time. But however popular he might have become, if his works had consisted of no more than this he would not have reached fame.

Other precedents are less important. The German humorists—Thümmel, Hippel—had not Dickens' genius, though the latter (a complete edition of whose works had just finished publication at Berlin) is frequently compared with Dickens in the *Blätter für literarische Unterhaltung* in 1838;[3] an appropriate passage runs:

In letzter Hinsicht erinnerte uns dieses Buch [*Sketches*] gar sehr an Hippel, dessen *Lebensläufe* [1778-81] uns das beste Buch scheinen, welches in dieser Art Deutschland jemals gesehen hat, wie es auch das einzige ist, was uns ein treues Bild von dem Leben der gelehrten und niedern Klassen der Gesellschaft ... jetzt vorhält. ... Hippel und ... Mr. Dickens haben beide scharf in das Menschenleben hineingesehen und ihre Anschauung von dem, was in der Welt vorgeht, dort gebildet, während Jean Paul in ein Nest sich verbarg ....

It may be noticed, too, that Immermann, at much the same time as Dickens' first appearance in Germany, had shown close affinities with Dickens' humour in parts of his *Münchhausen*. Rabener's gentle satires on the middle class, however, did not approach those of Dickens; and though cities such as Berlin and Vienna had recently appeared in German literature in E. T. A. Hoffmann's stories, for example, in A. Glasbrenner's popular sketches: *Berlin wie es ist und — trinkt* (1832 f.), and in I. Castelli's *Wiener Lebensbilder* (1828), London afforded far richer material for Dickens' successful handling of this type of sketch.

[1] In vol. ii of *German Romance; Specimens of its Chief Authors*, Edinburgh and London, 1827.
[2] *Epische Studien* (*Werke*, ed. A. Stern and E. Schmidt, Leipzig. 1891, vol. vi), p. 81.   [3] No. 14 (14 Jan.).

It was noticed above that the age was becoming more and more realistically inclined. This tendency was of course reflected in the literature of the time, most of all in the novel, the genre most fitted to the consideration of modern conditions and ideas, which became the prevailing literary type and was so for the whole middle third of the nineteenth century. It is not to be understood that realism was by any means a new element in German literature; but this age picked up the realistic traits in the work of earlier writers, and continued and enlarged their use. Immermann's prose works show this new tendency already quite distinctly. The insistence of the Young Germans (Laube particularly) on truth as an essential of literature was already a symptom; thus Laube wrote in the *Elegante Welt* on 23 May 1833:

> Warum dulden wir, daß immer noch die alten gestorbenen Interessen abgehaspelt werden; warum verlangen wir nicht vom Romanschreiber, daß die neue Welt sich abspiegele in den Erzählungen?[1]

Four years later the second and third parts of Laube's *Das Junge Europa* were published, named respectively *Die Krieger* and *Die Bürger*, the latter a most pregnant title; the second part of the trilogy showed the new realistic tendencies very clearly. The feeling of the period can be decided very well from a conversation reported by A. von Ungern-Sternberg in his memoirs[2] on the subject of his novel *Diane* of 1842:

> Warum da das Mittelalter belästigen, die abgenutzten Ritterfräulein, die Paladine, die tapferen Fürsten? Meine Welt ist die in der ich atme und wirke; aber freilich, da jeder Straßenjunge Kritiker und Kenner ist, muß ich so arbeiten, daß man mir keinen Fehler nachweisen kann. ... Welch eine Belohnung, wenn Jeder mit gesunden Sinnen sich in das Bild hineinlebt, sich selbst darin erkennt, und frisch aus der ersten Hand Moral, Belehrung und Amüsement bekommt.

It needs no special pleading to show how closely this could be considered as a definition of Dickens' work. His books well satisfied the new tendencies by their realism, just as they satisfied the remnants of romanticism by their phantasy and imaginativeness, and the socialist inclinations of the time by their sympathy for the poor and unfortunate. It was because they were set in the present day, and because they described it imaginatively but truly, that they gained still more readers in Germany; and that was why

---

[1] Quoted by S. D. Stirk, *Kritiken von H. Laube, 1829–1835*, Breslau, 1934, p. 27.   [2] *Erinnerungsblätter*, Berlin, 1855–60, vol. ii, p. 131.

Freytag could say in praise of the stories that 'alles war modernes Leben, im Grunde alltägliche Wirklichkeit und die eigne Weise zu empfinden, nur verklärt durch das liebevolle Gemüt eines echten Dichters'.[1]

Enough has been said to show that the great popularity of Dickens' work in contemporary Germany is not so surprising a phenomenon as it at first appears to be. The roots were there; many details of his work can be paralleled, though in rather weaker form, from that of earlier and contemporary German writers, the political background to his books happened to be just the one of most interest to the German at that time, and the liberal-social elements of his books arrived at the right moment for their full appreciation by the rising middle classes of Germany. The correct view of his reception in that country is probably that he brought comparatively little that was really new, except himself. That is to say that though many separate details of his outlook, manner, and matter can be paralleled from the native production of Germany, he himself was a focus, and something more besides, of all these diffuse but strongly appreciated lines of production. There was something in his work for every one to enjoy.

[1] *Gesammelte Aufsätze*, Leipzig, 1888, vol. ii, p. 241.

II
CONTEMPORARY CRITICISM OF DICKENS' BOOKS
1837–1849

TO complete the picture of Dickens' reception in Germany there remains to be added a study of the contemporary German criticism of his books. The history of this criticism falls naturally into two parts, divided by the revolutionary years 1848–9; after this date both the tone and the standard of criticism alter considerably. This chapter is devoted to the earlier criticisms, those of the books in the first half of Dickens' production: up to, but not including, *David Copperfield*. Seven representative periodicals were examined for these criticisms, of which a complete list (for the whole period 1837–70) is given in Appendix I.

The articles studied are of unequal length and importance; consequently their number in any one year does not give a true estimation of the standing of Dickens' fame in that year, quite apart from the obvious fact that an estimation based on criticism alone will generally be false. A better valuation can be based on the facts of translation and publication given in the preceding chapter, and on the remarks of the German critics on Dickens' great popularity with the German reader; very few of the articles examined below fail to mention this.[1] The number of articles can, however, be taken as giving some guide to the interest felt in Dickens. It is therefore interesting to see that from two articles in 1837 the number rises steeply to twelve and twenty-three in 1838 and 1839, drops to six in 1840, and thereafter maintains an average of seven in each year until the revolution. The high number of articles in 1839 is partly due to the really strong interest felt in Dickens at that time, and partly because the *Sketches*, *Oliver Twist*, and *Nickleby* were then all appearing, or were just completed, in German translation.

Further evidence is given by the fact that many of the contemporary periodicals found it profitable to reprint long extracts from Dickens' books in German translation. The collections of

[1] And the *Zeitung für die Elegante Welt*, 1839, no. 23 (not seen by me) said that if success was in fact the best criticism, no author of recent years had been so favourably criticized as Dickens (quoted by L. Sigmann, op. cit., p. 295).

CONTEMPORARY CRITICISM OF DICKENS' BOOKS 29

Dickens' earliest sketches were a favourite source for these magazines, and *American Notes* and *Pictures from Italy* provided useful material for the *Magazin für die Literatur des Auslandes*, which printed many chapters from both books in 1842–3 and 1846. A touch of comedy was provided in 1841 by *The British Museum: A Choice Selection from the Works of the Most Celebrated English Authors*,[1] a German weekly magazine printed in English, which, having published extracts from Dickens since 1838, rashly began to print the *Old Curiosity Shop* under the impression that it was to be a short story. To satisfy its readers, it persisted with the story, to the exclusion, eventually, of everything else in the magazine; published a long supplement at the end of the year to complete the tale, and then apparently went bankrupt.

The general tone of the criticism of Dickens' books during this period is varied, but, except in some reviews of the Christmas stories, praise and blame are usually mixed in fair proportions. Two major faults and one minor are frequently picked out by the critics: looseness of composition; too great an insistence on the darker side of life (especially in the case of *Oliver Twist*); and later, prolixity in the case of some chapters of *American Notes*, *Pictures from Italy*, and the *Cricket on the Hearth*. After a most appreciative beginning, the criticisms become more serious; the novelty of Dickens' books had worn off, there was a feeling that Dickens was writing too much, and *Oliver Twist* was not so pleasing in Germany as the irresistible humour of *Pickwick* or the balance and contrasted characters of *Nickleby*. The taste for Dickens was restored by the two main novels included in *Master Humphrey's Clock*, but the better critics judged the subsequent books by rather sterner artistic standards.

The pleasure with which *Pickwick* was greeted in Germany has already been described in this section. The critics agreed with this praise, though there now already appear the germs of the two major criticisms mentioned above; some felt that the book was too national to take place in the highest rank of literature, but that was an early criticism, and the final opinion praises the book in the warmest terms for its richness, diversity, and charm, its sparkling humour, and its good-humoured satire. Mr. Pickwick and the Wellers among the characters, Christmas at Dingley Dell among the scenes, are picked out for special praise, all of which is

[1] Bielefeld, 1837–41; 5 vols. (no more published).

summed up by the *Blätter für literarische Unterhaltung*[1] in the words:

> Ein solcher Humor, das ist ein solcher Scherz und Laune, dem ein gewisses Tiefe und Ernste unterliegt, herrscht in der ganzen Darstellung, eine so feine Ironie gegen manche Sitten der Engländer und eine solche Wahrheit in der Schilderung des Gemeinen wie des Erhabenen, daß von dem Inhalte bloß urteilen wollen, nichts anderes tun hieße, als aus einem lebendigen Wesen ein *caput mortuum* machen.

The *Sketches* were also well received; there is no adverse criticism on them in any of the periodicals studied, with the possible exception that one critic, not knowing that they represented Dickens' earliest attempts at writing, expresses the wish that Dickens would save his invention for full-length novels and not waste it on essays.[2] The other critics praise them for their freshness and their pleasant outlook on life, and for the amazing knowledge they show of the London scene. They are compared with the work of A. Glasbrenner, greatly to Dickens' advantage.

Nickleby, the next book published in Germany, generally received blame for loose composition and for a total lack of organic development; but the characters were found to be well contrasted, and almost all of them are praised; in particular for their lifelike nature, which makes them seem to be personal acquaintances of the reader. Nicholas and Kate, Mrs. Nickleby, the Crummles troupe, are praised by nearly all the critics. The *Blätter für Literatur und Bildende Kunst*[3] even preferred this book to *Pickwick*, for these reasons:

> Das Übertriebene, Karikierte, Geschraubte, was dem echten Humor dort Nachteil brachte, ist hier glücklich vermieden, die Charaktere sind nicht minder originell, aber naturgemäßer, die Ausmalung nicht minder kräftig und treffend, aber gemäßigter in Farbe und Haltung, kurz wir finden wohl englische Sitte und Eigentümlichkeit darin, aber dennoch nichts, was einem deutschen Geschmack geradezu entgegenträte, was nicht allgemein menschlich wäre und daher auch allgemein ansprechend.

The scenes in *Oliver Twist* which the German critics found most praiseworthy were those of the murder of Nancy, the flight and death of Sikes, and the condemnation and last hours of Fagin, the masterly psychology of which descriptions was almost universally

---

[1] 1838, no. 13 (13 Jan.).
[2] *Stuttgarter Literaturblatt* (supp. to the *Morgenblatt*), 1839, no. 14 (6 Feb.).
[3] Supp. to the *Dresdner Abendzeitung*, 1838, no. 73 (12 Sept.).

admired. Opinions were divided about Oliver himself, but the other good characters were found colourless; and there was almost universal condemnation of the plot, and especially the denouement, as consisting of the outworn themes and the common tricks of the lower class of novelist. One critic, in the *Blätter für literarische Unterhaltung*,[1] denounced the scenes of crime and evil in the book; he realized that they were there for a purpose, and that Dickens never conceals his own disgust for them, but he nevertheless felt that their publishing would do more harm than good (a typical judgement of the time) and maintained that they had no place in art.

Taste for Dickens was restored, it was noticed above, by the *Old Curiosity Shop* and *Barnaby Rudge*. There is, indeed, remarkably little adverse criticism to be found of these two books; in the case of the latter, practically none, in the case of the *Curiosity Shop*, besides the usual regrets at the poor composition of Dickens' books, only the opinion that Quilp is an unfortunate inclusion, though another critic, four years later, added his opinion that Nell is too oppressively good. This book was praised for its pathos and humour, its lifelike, almost visible characters (among which the travelling entertainers are singled out for appreciation), and the amazing powers of observation which it shows: one critic wrote on the appearance of the fourth part of the book:

nach seiner Anlage können noch vier Teile folgen, ja, es kann ein Buch ohne Ende werden, ohne daß wir müde würden, ihm zu folgen.[2]

Barnaby Rudge was found to have a richer variety of scene and tone, and to show Dickens a master of the historical novel as well. The characters of Barnaby himself, of the locksmith and those in his household, and of the circle of friends at the Maypole Inn, are given special praise.

The *American Notes* were generally considered to be well written and natural, benevolent and yet sternly looking for the truth; but too verbose in some parts, and containing some superficial judgements. Little attention was paid to *Chuzzlewit*, but the question of loose composition is raised once more, and it is doubted whether the chief characters of the book always act and develop

---

[1] 1839, nos. 285–8 (12–15 Oct.): 'Boz und die gegenwärtige Gestaltung des Volksromans'.
[2] *Blätter für literarische Unterhaltung*, 1841, no. 244 (1 Sept.).

logically. Tom Pinch is considered the best character of the story, and Dickens is praised once more for his powers of observation and description. A later critic,[1] however, finds the book to be more firmly composed than any of the earlier ones, and its characters to have substance; he considers Mark Tapley to be a true humorist himself, not merely a collection of humorous ideas. The book, in his opinion, gives promise that Dickens is giving more attention to artistic standards.

This critic was Wilhelm Danzel,[2] the future author of *Gottsched und seine Zeit* and of *Lessing*; he was from February 1845 a *Privatdozent* at the University of Leipzig, and began in that year to contribute articles to the *Jenaische Allgemeine Literaturzeitung* and to the *Blätter für literarische Unterhaltung*; among these was a long article on Dickens, entitled 'Über Dickens' Romane',[3] which is worthy of special attention. In this, like so many of the other critics of the time, he is more concerned to show Dickens' faults than his virtues, which were already sufficiently well recognized.

Danzel attributes Dickens' success to the fact that he deals with matters which are at the centre of public interest, and in particular with the condition of the working class. He does not deny him great advantages over many other writers, and allows him especially a *gesunde Lebensgrundlage*; but he has several stern criticisms to make. He attacks the looseness of composition to be seen in so many of the novels; the use of old and outworn romantic tricks, such as the motive of the ring which discloses Oliver Twist's parentage; a certain carelessness in details in the case of Master Humphrey (a criticism Julian Schmidt was to make later in the case of Pecksniff); and the fact that the story does not develop logically from the characters because they themselves have no development. The whole characterization is poor; it is not always a psychological unity that is set before us, and the common trick of characterization by repetition is too frequently employed. Danzel admits, however, that there is usually a sound basis to the better characters—Pickwick and the Cheerybles, for example, and Chester and the whole gallery of rogues. He parallels some elements of Dickens' work with others in that of Jean Paul and

[1] *Blätter für literarische Unterhaltung*, 1845, no. 225 (13 Aug.).
[2] See *Allg. Dte. Biographie*, vol. iv, pp. 753-4.
[3] This appeared in 1845 in the *Blätter für literarische Unterhaltung* (nos. 221-5, 9-13 Aug.) and is reprinted in Danzel's *Gesammelte Aufsätze*, ed. O. Jahn, Leipzig, 1855, pp. 99-117.

CONTEMPORARY CRITICISM OF DICKENS' BOOKS 33

E. T. A. Hoffman, pokes fun at some of Dickens' more painful moral scruples and'allows him only *Ansätze zum Humor*, but praises most highly his description of psychological conditions; characters in states of extreme emotion, especially fear. He condemns the tendencious nature of Dickens' books; however good the purpose, he feels that this leads to exaggeration, and thus characterization becomes caricature; so, aesthetically, intention spoils production. He sums up his remarks on comedy, humour, and satire in Dickens with the words: 'In der Tat ist Dickens nur da Humorist, wo er mit oberflächlichen und leicht zu überwindenen Torheiten zu tun hat', and quotes as an example of this the 'Child-bed-linen-monthly-loan Society' of the *Sketches*.

Danzel explains Dickens' exaggerated and superficial characters by the fact that the great town is usually the scene of his stories and is in any case Dickens' natural environment. In a large town there is no opportunity to study every character deeply: one can only notice certain clear traits, and is forced to guess at the rest, and so, he thinks, Dickens' usual methods are explained. Other faults of the characters spring from the fact that they are developed, not from general conditions, but from momentary situations; and consequently have a true existence only for a moment of time.

Dickens' faults, Danzel feels, have their root in the fact that he is too close to his subjects for proper observation; he hopes that the journey to America, away from his usual surroundings, may help him to a clearer and wider vision. In this connexion he passes the criticism on *Chuzzlewit* mentioned above.

Dickens' Christmas stories were variously judged by the German critics. The *Blätter für literarische Unterhaltung* saw in them a general decline, the nadir being represented by the *Battle of Life*; the other periodicals have little but praise for them. There was no adverse criticism of the *Christmas Carol*; it was praised for its fantasy, its philanthropy, and its quality of *Gemütlichkeit*, Scrooge was found to be a true and lifelike character, and the tale generally was ranked higher than *American Notes* and *Chuzzlewit*. The *Chimes* was felt to be one of Dickens' best pictures, an idyll of pathos and cheerfulness together; but the *Blätter für literarische Unterhaltung*[1] felt that, entertaining though the fantasy was, Dickens could have attained his object even better without it. The *Cricket on the Hearth*, in the opinion of the same paper,[2] though it

[1] 1845, no. 204 (23 July).   [2] 1846, no. 115 (25 April).

was poetic and romantic in Wordsworth's manner, would not increase Dickens' fame; its elements were simple, and by no means new, and Tilly Slowboy was the only original character. Other critics, though they notice a certain wordiness in the introduction, are reminded by it of Achim von Arnim and E. T. A. Hoffmann, and find excellent and moving scenes in the tale. The *Battle of Life* was roundly condemned by the *Blätter für literarische Unterhaltung*[1] as being *geradezu ein Bettel*; Dickens' purpose was good, the paper said, but his means in this tale were poor; the plot is very improbable, and the denouement threadbare. Other critics, however, again found much to praise; poetic beauty in the introduction, a good development of the tale, clear and sharp characterization, and a good blending of humour and seriousness. The *Magazin für die Literatur des Auslandes*[2] added the following remarks:

Die Herrn Dickens so eigentümliche Fähigkeit, auch den gewöhnlichsten Gegenständen neue und schöne Seiten abzugewinnen, die Gabe, auch in den niedrigsten Gestaltungen des Lebens Reize zu entdecken, der Aufschwung, den der Dichter stets von der Alltagswirklichkeit in die Regionen des Gedankens und der Phantasie nimmt — alles dieses findet sich auch hier und trägt zu dem schönen Eindruck bei, welchen das Werk hinterläßt.

On the *Haunted Man* the only criticism to be discovered in the selection of periodicals studied is that of the *Blätter für literarische Unterhaltung*,[3] which paper gives an apparently favourable summary of the tale, and says that though it teaches wholesome truths it may lose in popularity because it is not easy to understand.

Only one paper gave a criticism of *Pictures from Italy*; that was the *Stuttgarter Literaturblatt*,[4] which said that the book contained nothing deeper than *Genrebilder*, that it tended to verbosity, and that its views on art, for which it showed little interest in any case, were heretical. The *Genrebilder* as such were, however, masterly; and the description of the Roman carnival was in no way inferior for liveliness and richness to that given by Goethe.

Dombey and Son, the last book of Dickens within the scope of

---

[1] 1847, no. 145 (25 May).
[2] 1847, no. 15 (4 Feb.).
[3] 1849, no. 61 (12 March).
[4] Supp. to the *Morgenblatt*, 1846, no. 65 (12 Sept.).

CONTEMPORARY CRITICISM OF DICKENS' BOOKS 35

this chapter, had a notice only from the *Dresdner Abendzeitung*,[1] which described it as of absorbing interest, and as 'der Höhepunkt dessen, was dieser Autor sowohl in poetisch gemütreicher, als in humoristisch ergötzlicher Weise bis jetzt geschaffen hat'.

It is clear, then, that although Dickens' books from *American Notes* onwards were judged by the German critics according to more severe aesthetic standards, they were still given high praise for their real qualities.[2] The adverse criticism of Dickens is sufficiently described in the preceding pages, but the praise of Dickens is less clear-cut because of its quantity and variety; the consensus of opinion appears to be the following.

Dickens' sphere was realized to be the life of the town, and particularly the lower classes in the towns, their mother-wit and broad humour; it was understood that it was not within his power to show, with any depth and comprehension, country and unspoilt nature; good people and cultured people were seen to be rare and not very successful in his books, and his attempts at sustained pathos were felt to fail.[3] With these limitations, however, he could still produce masterpieces. The highest praise is given to his sharp observation and his remarkable use of it in his description of places (especially of London) and his characterization of people, which were found so clear and lifelike, and where he recorded with such skill the small and cleverly chosen detail, that they seemed to become personal acquaintances of the reader. His humour, with its serious undertone, his good-tempered wit and satire, his charm and *Gemütlichkeit*, and the spirit of philanthropy in his books were all frequently praised: and despite the criticisms of *Oliver Twist* it was generally considered a praiseworthy detail that the descriptions of evil in his books did not produce disgust.[4] He was soon, and frequently, called the 'ingenious', the 'unique', the 'incomparable'

[1] 1848, no. 1 (6 Jan.) in the *Feuilleton*, s.v. 'London'.

[2] This result should be compared with that of Luise Sigmann in *Die Englische Literatur 1800–1850 im Urteil der zeitgenössischen deutschen Kritik* (Heidelberg, 1918), pp. 294–304, on German criticism of Dickens within these limits. She declares that the general tone of the criticisms from 1843 onwards shows either indifference or distaste. I feel she has been too much influenced to this opinion by T. W. Danzel's adverse criticisms and the coldness of the *Blätter für literarische Unterhaltung* alone towards the Christmas stories.

[3] Summed up in the *Blätter für literarische Unterhaltung*, 1839, nos. 285–8 (12–15 Oct.).

[4] So in the important *Jenaische Allgemeine Literaturzeitung*, 1839, no. 138, and *Ergänzungsblatt*, no. 28.

Boz. Two short summaries of his praise may be noticed, both of which appeared in the early forties:

Dickens hat seinen europäischen Ruhm besonders durch die naturgetreue Auffassung und Darstellung der Gegenwart mit allen ihren komischen Auswüchsen begründet.[1]

Was Boz's Arbeiten recht eigentlich in seinem Vaterlande hat volkstümlich werden lassen, gewinnt ihm auch der deutschen Freunde viele; es ist neben seiner lebhaften und prägnanten Art zu schildern, der eigentümlich wehmütig-heitere Humor, den er seinen Gestalten als Mitgift und Reisegeleit gibt.[2]

But whatever the critics felt about Dickens, there is no doubt of his great and continued popularity with the German people. One exiled member of the German race summed up the feelings of his nation to Dickens himself several years later. In 1867, during his second visit to America, Dickens wrote to W. H. Wills from the Westminster Hotel, New York:[3]

'Mr. Digguns', said the German Janitor (the invariable name for the Hall Keeper) 'you are gread, meinherr. There is no ent to you!' That was his parting salutation as he locked me out into a hard frost. 'Bedder and bedder', he re-opened the door to add, 'wot negst!'

[1] *Blätter für literarische Unterhaltung*, 1842, no. 45 (14 Feb.).
[2] *Europa, Chronik der Gebildeten Welt*, 1841, vol. iii, p. 183.
[3] *Charles Dickens as Editor: Letters to W. H. Wills*, ed. R. C. Lehmann, London, 1912, p. 374.

III
JULIAN SCHMIDT AND LATER CRITICISMS OF DICKENS, 1850–1870

LUISE SIGMANN, whose book *Die Englische Literatur von 1800 bis 1850 im Urteil der zeitgenössischen deutschen Kritik*[1] contains a brief summary of contemporary German criticism of Dickens within the limits given by its title, concluded that summary with the rash statement that at the end of the forties Dickens, too, passes into the ranks of the forgotten writers. The only possible reason for such a conclusion is the fact that the German critics had little to say about *Dombey* and *Copperfield*; not because Dickens' popularity was on the wane, but because political events in Germany at the time demanded pride of place in most of the periodicals.

If Sigmann had continued her researches a little further, and especially if she had included the *Grenzboten* among the periodicals studied, the work of Julian Schmidt would have come to her notice, and such a statement would then have been impossible. Julian Schmidt, soon to become the most representative, and one of the best known and most influential, of German critics, had contributed articles to the *Grenzboten* since 1847, and in July 1848 became co-editor of that magazine with Gustav Freytag. In it appeared much of his work on Dickens: articles which he occasionally remodelled and published in book form. It was in this way that a 74-page essay on Dickens was composed, which appeared in 1852 as an introduction to the Lorck edition of the *Works*, and separately in the same year. In the same way was prepared Schmidt's *Übersicht der englischen Literatur im 19. Jahrhundert*,[2] in which there are ten pages of criticism of Dickens, and also his *Studien über Dickens und den Humor*, which appeared serially in *Westermanns Monatshefte* from April to July 1870, and which, rearranged and slightly expanded, were reprinted as an essay of 118 pages in his *Bilder aus dem geistigen Leben unserer Zeit, Neue Folge* in 1871. Schmidt's fourth published essay on Dickens—in his *Portraits aus*

[1] *Anglistische Forschungen*, Heft 55, Heidelberg, 1918. Dickens, pp. 294–304.
[2] In Romberg's *Die Wissenschaften im 19. Jahrhundert*, vol. ii, 1856; and separately, Sondershausen, 1859, where Dickens stands at pp. 160–70.

dem 19. Jahrhundert of 1878—falls beyond the scope of this chapter, and will be considered in its place in Part III.

The policy of the *Grenzboten* under its new editors was very different from that which it had professed under Kuranda; especially in its literary criticism, which proceeded for the most part from Schmidt. Its chief detail is clearly expressed by Freytag, who writes in his *Erinnerungen* of:

... eine feste und strenge Kritik aller der ungesunden Richtungen, welche durch die jungdeutsche Abhängigkeit von französischer Bildung und durch die Willkür der alten Romantik in die Seelen der Deutschen gekommen waren.[1]

As a corollary to this the new *Grenzboten* 'admired English life and character as expressed in English literature, and saw therein the most adequate means of opposing those tendencies of German literature which it held to be unsound. It favoured especially a moderate realism, such as prevailed in the contemporary English novel'.[2]

It was with these premisses that Julian Schmidt studied Dickens' work, and it is for this reason that there are to be found in these studies frequent excursions on the superiority of English political and social life as demonstrated by Dickens' books. In opposing not only the remnants of romanticism but also the work of 'Young Germany', especially that of Karl Gutzkow, Schmidt always pointed to English literature as the best contemporary source of what he considered to be true and healthy tendencies. The surest source was, for him, Charles Dickens. Thus Freytag writes in his memoirs:

Indem Schmidt verurteilte, was in unserer Literatur krank war, wies er auch unablässig auf die Heilmittel hin, und wurde dadurch in Wahrheit ein guter Lehrer für die Jüngeren. ... Er hatte an allem wohl Gelungenen eine tief innige Freude ... vor allem fesselte ihn die originelle Zeichnung der Charaktere, nächstdem die Grazie in Schilderung und Sprache. Die Darstellungsweise der englischen Dichter war ganz nach seinem Herzen, den Zauber der wundervollen Färbung bei Dickens empfand er so voll, wie nur ein Engländer jener Zeit. ...[3]

[1] *Erinnerungen*, Leipzig, 1887, p. 225.
[2] L. M. Price, *The Attitude of Freytag and Schmidt to English Literature, 1848–1862*, Hesperia series, no. 7, Baltimore, 1915, p. 4. This book gives an excellent analysis of Schmidt's attitude to English literature and of his criticism of unhealthy tendencies in contemporary Germany generally.
[3] Op. cit., p. 238.

JULIAN SCHMIDT AND LATER CRITICISMS

But Schmidt did not hesitate to criticize what he admired, and his appreciation of Dickens is, as will be apparent, far from being one-sided.

The essay of 1852, *Boz (Dickens): eine Charakteristik*, opens with a survey of the historical and political reasons for the superiority of the English novel. Here Schmidt once more emphasizes the unfortunate fact that so much of contemporary German literature is 'polemisch gegen die öffentlichen Zustände und gegen die öffentliche Meinung', and shows that there were two distinct types of German writer to be found at this time; there were, he says, 'zwei vollständig von einander geschiedene Bildungsformen', and nothing that Germany produced could fill the gap between the two, not even the 'Dorfgeschichte', for example, which was at best an escapist type of literature, having little or nothing in common with the life of the wider public. Since the revolution of 1848 had produced nothing but disillusion, matters were if anything worse.

In these circumstances it will be readily understood (he writes) that foreign literature, especially English, had such a ready reception in Germany. The foreign writers

waren uns vornherein verwandter. Mit Walter Scott und Dickens empfindet jedes unverdorbene Herz in den allerverschiedenartigsten Bildungsstufen.[1]

They in fact filled the gap which existed between the two extreme types of German work, and they could be readily appreciated by all. In the particular case of Dickens Julian Schmidt finds:

einen dichterischen Wert, der weit über alles hinausgeht, was unsere poetischen Landsleute in der letzten Zeit geleistet haben.... Er ist auch viel deutscher, als unsere gesamte romantische Literatur von Tieck und Schlegel herunter bis auf Hebbel und Gutzkow.[2]

For the true writer Schmidt insisted upon a sound moral sense, and also an optimistic view of human existence. This is made clear in the first pages on Dickens in this essay, and it is shown that Dickens possessed both these requisites. One can see clearly in his work:

... neben jener allgemeinen Menschenliebe, die auch das Unbedeutende und Unscheinbare hegt, weil jede Erscheinung des Lebens ihre ideale Berechtigung hat, einen sehr sichern, festen und unerschütterlichen

[1] p. 9.   [2] p. 11.

Idealismus, der das wirklich Schlechte und Verabscheuungswürdige mit leidenschaftlichem Zorn verfolgt.[1]

In this sense, he feels, we may perhaps take Nicholas Nickleby to be a representative of Dickens' own outlook; he is tolerant and good-natured, but can act decisively when faced by real evil.

This insistence on an optimistic view of human existence explains Schmidt's appreciation of such characters as the Cheeryble brothers in *Nickleby*—their contrast with the evil characters of the book is, he says, 'sehr wohltuend'—and of the conclusion of *Chuzzlewit*, where Jonas and Tigg both get their deserts—'und so macht der Schluß der Geschichte einen durchaus befriedigenden Eindruck'.[2] It also explains his criticism that the evil character of Uriah Heep is given too much attention.

This general appreciation of Dickens, and of English literature at large, occupies fourteen pages. The following sixty are devoted to an examination of each book by Dickens, in approximately chronological order, up to *Bleak House*, which was not complete at the time Julian Schmidt composed his essay. The *Sketches* are briefly noticed as showing already that Dickens possessed great narrative powers, a wonderfully sharp eye for detail, a complete mastery of language, and a marvellous gift for the fantastic animation of lifeless objects. Coupled with this is a discussion of his subjective descriptions ('es kommt ihm nur darauf an, durch die Gegenstände die angemessene Stimmung zu erregen'), his introductory characterization, and the sunny warmth and *Behaglichkeit* of his pictures of everyday life.[3]

The *Pickwick Papers* are much more fully examined. Schmidt describes the historical and literary background to the book's reception, and explains the enthusiasm with which it was greeted in both England and Germany. He emphasizes once more the positive, the happy and optimistic nature of the work, and writes: 'diese Lust am Leben macht den ganzen Wert des Buches aus. Die Komposition hat keinen Teil daran'. The character of Pickwick, though not a unity, is well done; his friends are not so successful, but Sam Weller and the host of minor characters are excellent. The weakest part of the book is the satire. Here there appears a criticism which Schmidt was to repeat on two later occasions:

Hier geht in der Regel der Zorn so mit dem Dichter durch, daß nicht

[1] pp. 11–12. [2] p. 51. [3] pp. 14–19.

JULIAN SCHMIDT AND LATER CRITICISMS 41

nur der ästhetische Eindruck abgeschwächt wird, sondern daß auch die Erfindung aus den Grenzen der Wahrheit tritt.[1]

In *Oliver Twist* Schmidt praises the masterly drawing of the murder of Nancy and the flight of Sikes, but feels that the grim theme of the book gave Dickens little opportunity to display his real talents. The fact that the book was written with a definite object caused bad exaggerations, necessary but not artistic. Schmidt makes use of this passage to demonstrate the difference between the reforming zeal of Dickens and that of the Germans: Dickens' zeal is practical and particular, not general, as is that found in Germany, where the would-be reformers search for one formula to cure all evils.[2]

Nickleby gives Schmidt an opportunity to show the disadvantages of publication in serial form; but he finds high praise for the character of Nicholas, and for the figures of Ralph, the Crummles, the Cheerybles, and Mrs. Nickleby. He dislikes the picture of Dotheboys Hall, a description which, however true, 'ist empörend, und geht über die Grenzen der Ästhetik hinaus'; but in the case of Ralph Nickleby he points out the strength of Dickens' talent in the analysis of the mental processes which take place in states of strong emotion—a theme picked up again in many of Dickens' later works, but not with the same success as here.[3]

He considers the *Old Curiosity Shop* the most moving story Dickens has written, and defends the sentiment in it as legitimate, for Dickens' tears 'strömen aus dem Herzen, nicht, wie bei den meisten Schwelgern der Empfindsamkeit, aus dem Hirn'; and the conclusion, though it moves us once more to tears, is not finally depressing. Swiveller, he says, is one of Dickens' best inventions, second only to Sam Weller; the wanderers and vagabonds are good, but Quilp is an unbelievable figure. The composition of the tale is weak even for Dickens. The Christmas stories are also briefly considered: Schmidt finds that they begin well, but fade into rather commonplace moralizing. In *Barnaby Rudge* he discovers a better composition, and praises the humorous middle-class scenes and the masterly description of the crowd scenes. But he feels neither Chester nor Haredale to be a successful character, for the analysis of their personalities is incomplete.[4]

[1] pp. 20–33. Quotation from p. 32. [2] pp. 39–40. [3] pp. 34–8.
[4] *Old Curiosity Shop*, pp. 41–4. *Christmas Stories*, p. 44. *Barnaby Rudge*, pp. 44–8.

The fate of Pecksniff, the 'modern Tartuffe' of *Chuzzlewit*, demonstrates for Schmidt the inborn feeling for justice of the English; but he is unsatisfactory as a character, being too entirely one-sided. His daughters are better drawn; they have some development. Young Martin, lightly sketched, is an excellent figure nevertheless; Tom Pinch, Mark Tapley, and Ruth are also good, while among the secondary figures that of Sarah Gamp is outstanding, and of the famous 'Mrs. Harris' Schmidt says that such an inspiration comes only to Dickens.[1]

At this point, apropos of Dickens' short editorship of the *Daily News*, there is a brief discursion on Dickens' politics. Schmidt finds him to be a true democrat in the best sense of the word, very different from most of the other popular English writers, who are aristocratic in outlook and have only a bird's eye view of the suffering of the lower classes:

> Dickens erhält die Berechtigung zu seinen Ideen vorzugsweise durch die Wärme und die Wahrheit, mit denen er sie vertritt. Es ist in seiner Liebe zum Volk keine Spur von Phrase; was er sagt, hat er angeschaut und tief empfunden. ...

Dickens had little to do with the dry reasoning of ordinary politics and soon returned to his own colourful romantic world. But one can always trace in his books, Schmidt declares, the struggle against aristocratic exclusiveness and its source, pride and egoism—clearly, for example, in his next work, *Dombey and Son*.[2]

Of this book Schmidt says that the drawing of Dombey's personal pride and that which he had in his firm is excellently done; but that his eventual change of mind is unmotivated, and spoils the effect. His daughter Florence is hardly characterized except by the impression she makes on other characters, but this is done with masterly skill. Carker is an advance over Pecksniff, but too much a mixture of motives to be a clear and convincing character; Edith too is not made psychologically clear—Dickens here leaves too much to his readers' imagination. There is in the book once again an astounding diversity of episodic figures; Paul's relations to his father and sister are shown with fine poetry of description, and only Dickens could have created such a character as Captain Cuttle.[3]

With the English view that *David Copperfield* is Dickens' masterpiece Schmidt does not agree. It is an excellent book, but its

---

[1] pp. 49–52.   [2] pp. 53–6. Quotation from p. 56.   [3] pp. 56–9.

JULIAN SCHMIDT AND LATER CRITICISMS 43

matter does not fit Dickens' essential manner. Such a mixture of truth and invention is dangerous; chiefly because the writer's recollections of people he once knew is apt to be limited to a few outstanding details, and if, on that insecure foundation, he attempts to build up characters for a book, the result will probably be bad. As for the chief character, Schmidt supposes that Dickens possibly felt David might be taken as a self-portrait and so took pains to make him as modest as possible, with the result that he is a rather colourless figure. (It should be remembered that in 1852 Schmidt had no opportunity of knowing to what extent *Copperfield* was autobiographical.) Of the episodes of the story those descriptive of middle-class life and the scenes with the Peggottys are excellent, but those which show Mr. Creakle's school are unfortunate. For the characters Schmidt has full praise in the case of Dora and Agnes, Traddles and his circle, Littimer, and Betsy Trotwood, though the gentleness and subtlety of feeling which the latter eventually shows are hardly in keeping with our other impressions of her character. Micawber is not quite so good, being largely an incoherent collection of excellent ideas; and the truthful but repulsive drawing of Heep's character is given too much prominence. The prison visit at the close of the book was a good inspiration; in this scene Dickens packed his whole hatred of hypocrisy.[1]

Schmidt closes his survey with a mention of *Bleak House*, then appearing, of which the first numbers already contained some fine descriptions; and of Dickens' periodical *Household Words*, which should be taken as an example by the German producers of such papers; there is in it no affectation or condescension, as in the German equivalents. Finally, Schmidt draws a further comparison of German religious, political, and social life with the English, and once more points out the unsound elements in German life and praises the sound and concrete nature of English methods.[2]

In this essay, then, a large part of Schmidt's praise went to Dickens' positive and optimistic outlook and the exhilarating humour of his characters and scenes. Schmidt was writing while Dickens was at the height of his powers and fame. Unfortunately the subsequent books—particularly *Bleak House* and *Hard Times*—were not at all so well suited to Schmidt's principles of criticism, and he passes some very stern judgements on them in the *Grenzboten*.[3]

[1] pp. 59-64.   [2] pp. 65-74. *Bleak House, Household Words*, p. 65.
[3] e.g. 1854, vol. i, pp. 178-86 on *Bleak House*, where he expresses sorrow

It can consequently be understood that though the chapter on Dickens in the *Übersicht der englischen Literatur im 19. Jahrhundert* (1856) still praises Dickens' work and his earlier books as highly as ever, and declares that during the last generation:

... ist eine so reiche übermütig sprudelnde Quelle poetischer Phantasie, eine so tüchtige, von innerer Herzensgüte getragene Natur nicht wahrgenommen worden

—Schmidt feels compelled to write:

Leider müssen wir hinzusetzen, daß in der letzten Zeit auch diese schöne Erscheinung durch fremdartige ungesunde Elemente getrübt wird.[1]

Much of this earlier criticism was taken up once more in the long essay printed in *Bilder aus dem geistigen Leben unserer Zeit* in 1871. Here Schmidt has space to examine the various books in full detail and to quote long passages in illustration. There is much stern criticism side by side with full appreciation; but Schmidt says of his subject:

Es läßt sich Vieles und Ernstes gegen ihn einwenden, aber wer es unternimmt, an ihm Kritik zu üben, muß es tun mit dem Hut in der Hand: denn er steht einem Mann gegenüber, auf dessen Stirn die Natur den Stempel des Genius geprägt.[2]

The brief introduction to the essay was written two days after Dickens' death, and shortly summarizes his powers and his weaknesses. Dickens, Schmidt says, had command of the whole range of the novelist's technique, and was 'the first poetic power of our generation': but he was not always completely true, and his optimism was not steady and continuous: 'es kommen in seinen Werken Züge so grenzenloser Verstimmung und Verbitterung vor, dass man sie mit der schönen Physiognomie seiner Dichtung schwer in Einklang zu setzen weiß'.[3] The original essay, which dates from the preceding year, continues with a further demonstration of the weak points in Dickens' work: the mixture of humour and satire, the unsatisfactory, one-sided figures of the hypocrites, the exaggerated satires of English law, government, and politics.

that Dickens ever wrote the book; 1854, vol. iii, pp. 129–30, and vol. iv, pp. 401–3 on *Hard Times*, where he regrets that Dickens is debasing his work in such a way; 1856, vol. iii, pp. 77–8 on *Little Dorrit*, which he thinks the poorest book of Dickens so far, and where he hints at a failure of Dickens' inventive powers.

[1] *Übersicht*, &c., ed. of 1859, p. 160.   [2] p. 6.   [3] p. 4.

JULIAN SCHMIDT AND LATER CRITICISMS 45

Dickens' power of arousing sympathy for the unfortunate is praised, but his biassed attacks on the methods used by other reformers, political and social, are shown to have been short-sighted.[1]

The discussion of the separate works, in essence the same as that which had appeared in 1852, is interrupted freely with general examinations of Dickens' productions. Thus there is linked with the study of the *Pickwick Papers* a long analysis of Dickens' powers as a creator of characters. Here Schmidt finds very much to praise: the eccentrics and the vagabonds, the astonishingly funny characters of the type of Mrs. Nickleby, the excellent types of Sam Weller and of Traddles, the children, the young women; and in all these figures, as Schmidt re-emphasizes, a full joy in life. But Schmidt also shows that not infrequently Dickens' forceful imagination runs away with him, with the result that he produces impossible or incomplete characters; and there is occasionally to be found in his work what amounts to an unhealthy preference for the extreme and the monstrous.[2]

Dickens' technique of tension is studied, with reference to Fagin's trial and the flight of Sikes in *Oliver Twist*, and to the daemonic in *Barnaby Rudge*; in which book, Schmidt says, the crowd scenes are wonderfully effective, but might have been more forceful if they had been a little more soberly drawn; Dickens lacks Scott's sense of historical perspective. The nature descriptions in *Chuzzlewit* are quoted to show that Dickens only used his pictures of reality in order to create the correct atmosphere for his story: 'die Realität der Natur dient nur dazu, die Stimmung des Gemüts zu illustrieren'. In composition *Dombey* marks an advance, according to Schmidt, but there are some bad and disconcerting changes of plan to be found in it.[3]

Next to *Pickwick*, Schmidt declares, *Copperfield* gained the most readers for Dickens, not only in England but on the Continent also. He illustrates the popularity of this famous book in Germany in the well-known sentence:

Als Copperfield erschien, 1849, harrte in Deutschland Mann, Weib und Kind sehnsuchtsvoll auf jedes neue Monatsheft, und so stark uns damals die Politik im Kopf lag, es wurde im Ganzen über Dora und Agnes mehr disputiert als über Radowitz und Manteuffel.[4]

[1] pp. 5–27. [2] pp. 27–50. [3] pp. 51–97. [4] p. 111.

But Dickens' later works were not at all so successful. For this Schmidt gives several explanations, at first referring to *Bleak House*, but extending his judgments equally to the following books. It is clear that the ugly and the polemic nature of these works offends against his own standard of optimism; thus he writes of *Bleak House* that in this book:

drängt sich eine solche Masse von Ungeheuern und Mißgeburten zusammen, daß es scheint, als ob alle Irrenhäuser und Lazarette ihre wüsten Bewohner in diesen engen Raum ausgespien hätten; die *Mysterien von Paris* sehen bescheiden aus neben dieser Häufung von Greueln.[1]

This was severe censure indeed for Julian Schmidt. He writes further that Dickens' power to express benevolence seems to have deserted him, that he no longer appears to possess his belief in the essential goodness of life; and Schmidt receives much the same impression from the subsequent productions of Dickens.[2]

But apart from these later works, he feels, Dickens has produced the most valuable books of all that have appeared for a generation. He is no longer quite so popular as he was, but there is always something fresh to be found in his novels; he is of historical value; his good influence continues; and above all it is true to say of him that:

im Wesentlichen hat er doch den Schatz unsrer geistigen Genüsse vermehrt, indem er mit der Aufmerksamkeit für alles Lebendige auch die Freude am Leben gesteigert hat.[3]

Julian Schmidt's criticism of Dickens is not only an important section of the history of Dickens' reception in Germany; it has added significance in the fact that, as L. M. Price sums the matter up: 'Schmidt was the spokesman of a popular movement of wide political, social, and literary bearing. . . . He formulated most clearly the average opinion of that industrious middle class which . . . was now with the rise of the liberal party about to become dominant'.[4] With such a position Schmidt could pronounce opinions which were more than purely personal; his views on Dickens, in particular, were not only those of Freytag (to a large extent) also, but those of the majority of the German public generally. The *Grenzboten* stood, for the middle years of the

---
[1] p. 114.
[2] pp. 114–16.
[3] pp. 116–18. Quotation from p. 117.
[4] L. M. Price, op. cit., 1915, pp. 107–8.

century, 'in the position of the Greek chorus'; and it had, moreover, a certain influence on the literature of the period, for 'by assuming the literary sponsorship for the works of Ludwig, Reuter, Auerbach, and Freytag, Schmidt put himself in an advantageous position for influencing them in their products'.[1]

It is not suggested that Schmidt added to Dickens' popularity in Germany. That was already firmly established, as has been shown, well before his first articles appeared. But it is not too much to propose that his wholehearted advocacy of the methods and general outlook of that author prepared the way, to some extent, for an influence of Dickens on those writers mentioned in the preceding paragraph, who were Schmidt's literary associates. This, though it is by no means definite in the case of Reuter, is most probable in Freytag's case, as will be shown below in a special chapter on Freytag and Dickens; and though such a deciding influence from Schmidt on Ludwig's studies of Dickens cannot be proved, it is at least known that the two men were in complete agreement in their appreciation of Dickens' books. Schmidt writes of Ludwig's *Epische Studien*:

... er zeichnete damals eine Reihe von Romanstudien auf, über Scott, Dickens, u s w., ... und ich war ganz erstaunt, wie vollständig wir in unserm Urteil zusammentrafen.[2]

Auerbach, however, in any case expressly denies an influence from Dickens on his own work.[3]

Articles in German periodicals on the books of this second period are less numerous, and, beside the criticisms of Julian Schmidt, of less significance. The interest shown by German magazines and literary reviews in each new book by Dickens was no longer so apparent after the revolutionary years: this was partly because *Bleak House* and the following books were of poorer quality than was expected of Dickens, and of a very different style from that of his earlier works; chiefly, however, because politics now became a main interest of many of the periodicals, which thenceforward gave their time to educating their readers for a greater Germany and so had less occasion to examine foreign literature. This preoccupation with politics was, indeed, the main-

[1] Ibid., p. 109.
[2] *Charakterbilder aus der zeitgenössischen Literatur*, Leipzig, 1875, p. 186.
[3] *Briefe an Jakob Auerbach*, Frankfurt a/M., 1884, vol. i, p. 409.

spring also of Julian Schmidt's articles and essays on Dickens, in whose books he pointed out to the German people his model of what a nation's political and social institutions should be.

The other German critics left this to Schmidt, and contented themselves with notices of Dickens' new books which were always brief, and, after *Hard Times*, rare. *Copperfield*, despite its popularity in Germany, they hardly noticed, probably because the events of the day were of so much more importance; the *Blätter für literarische Unterhaltung*[1] has only half a column on the book, and that is translated direct from the *Athenaeum*; so that its preference of *Copperfield* above all Dickens' other books cannot be taken to show enthusiasm. The *Magazin für die Literatur des Auslandes*[2] confines its praise to Hablot K. Brown's illustrations. The same paper was the only one of the selection studied to provide an article on *Bleak House* three years later,[3] and this, too, is tinged with politics; the critic considers the book less as a piece of literature than as a social document, and sees in it:

... der siegreiche Feldzug des tätigen großen englischen Bürgertums gegen die historische Heiligkeit der privilegierten Stände und ihrer sittlichen und sozialen Standpunkte, von denen der juristische und politische Hierarchismus in den Vordergrund gestellt sind. ...

What literary criticism he does present shows more enthusiasm than sense:

... man wird gestehen, daß Dickens vielleicht mit mehr Genie, Noblesse und Poesie die hohe Welt eines Dedlock zu schildern weiß, als die dunklen Höhlen der Armut und Verwahrlosung. Die drei Hauptdamen in *Bleak House* gehören gewiß zu den schönsten Charakteren, die jemals von Dichtern konzipiert und geschildert wurden.

More attention was given to *Hard Times*, though the critics, like Julian Schmidt, found in it more to blame than to praise. Hermann Marggraf of the *Blätter für literarische Unterhaltung*[4] did indeed qualify his adverse criticism with the words:

... doch treten alle diese Mängel zurück gegen die Energie der Zeichnung, gegen die mächtige Auffassung der Leidenschaften und Seelenzustände, gegen die malerische Schilderung der Lokalitäten. ... Ungemein reich ist auch dieser Roman an tiefen Blicken in den düstern Abgrund menschlicher Verhältnisse, an gesunden Lebensmaximen und

---

[1] 1851, no. 46 (22 Feb.).
[2] 1850, no. 15 (2 Feb.).
[3] 1853, no. 115 (24 Sept.) in the monthly *Literaturbrief aus England*.
[4] 1854, no. 49 (7 Dec.).

treffenden Bemerkungen nach allen Richtungen hin. Die satirische Bloß-
stellung menschlicher Irrtümer kann oft gar nicht eindringlicher sein....

but the general opinion of the contemporary critics is definitely adverse. In the same article Marggraf says of *Hard Times* that the reader cannot feel enough sympathy with the characters to share their sorrows fully; that the dialogue is too prolix; and that Dickens' well-known mannerisms are beginning to pall. The characterization he describes as 'sowohl moralisch als ästhetisch verderblich wirkende steckbriefartige Personalbeschreibungen'. A correspondent of the *Magazin für die Literatur des Auslandes*,[1] examining *Hard Times* as an attack on the 'Manchester School', says that Dickens:

hat sich, mit einem Worte, die Sache zu leicht gemacht und mehr auf seine individuelle Ausmalerei gegeben, als auf wirkliches Aufsuchen des Feindes in seiner Demoralisation und Feigheit.

F. G. Kühne's *Europa*, in an article which can hardly be taken seriously, passed the most severe judgment on *Hard Times*.[2] Condemning the naturalism of the tale, and declaring, of all things, that Dickens cannot use his eyes, the writer says:

Dickens... ist vollständig versunken in sein Thema; diese Hingebung an die stickichte Schwüle in der Atmosphäre des englischen Fabrik-
pöbels, sein Fatalitätsglaube an die Unverbesserlichkeit dieser Ver-
tierung grenzt an Kretinismus....

and he declares:

wir staunen über... die stupide Treue des gesamten europäischen Pub-
likums in der Bewunderung dieser poesie- und humorlosen Travestien der bürgerlichen Verwahrlosung des englischen Winkellebens....

This article was so obviously unjust and bad-tempered that the *Magazin für die Literatur des Auslandes* felt that it called for a published reproof; the book in question, it said,[3] had obvious faults, but Dickens deserved none of the blame poured out by *Europa*:

Der Humor seines guten Herzens erheitert immer wieder die düsteren Sittengemälde seiner massiven Hand, und die allgemeine Lebenswahrheit seiner Darstellung entschädigt für einzelne Fehlgriffe in der Charakteristik. Wenn man ihm aber 'poesielosen Kretinismus' und langweilige Nachahmung der Wirklichkeit vorwirft, ohne auch nur

---

[1] 1854, no. 112 (19 Sept.) in the *Literaturbrief*.
[2] 1855, no. 5, pp. 53–4.   [3] 1855, no. 27 (3 March).

einen einzigen seiner unbestreitbaren Vorzüge anzuerkennen, so ist das unverkennbar eine Äußerung deutscher Mißgunst gegen den vielgelesenen englischen Schriftsteller...

Despite this antidote, however, the final impression given by German criticism, not forgetting the severe censures of Julian Schmidt, is that *Bleak House* and *Hard Times* must have done much harm to Dickens' reputation in Germany, with the general reader as well as with the critics. A fact which perhaps supports this conclusion is that the *Blätter für literarische Unterhaltung*, until then so interested in Dickens, did not notice a single one of his books after *Hard Times*, in which it, and probably its readers, were apparently disappointed. A retrospective paragraph on Dickens' books in *Europa* in 1861[1] probably sums up the final feeling on *Hard Times*:

In *Harten Zeiten* geriet der Verfasser auf Abwege, die schon früher da und dort ihn anlockten: auf das Spannende um jeden Preis; auf das Schauerliche und Schreckliche ohne den wohltuenden Humor, ohne die versöhnende und befreiende Poesie.

Little Dorrit seems to have passed practically unnoticed, except, of course, for Julian Schmidt's criticisms. The *Magazin für die Literatur des Auslandes* apparently only studied the first number, and could only say of it:[2] 'der Anfang ist vielversprechend'. A later article in *Europa*, however, the one mentioned above which appeared in 1861,[3] briefly notices the book as a whole, and says of it:

In *Klein Dorrit* lenkte Dickens wieder ein in die frühere, vortreffliche Art seines Schaffens, aber er wurde breit, redselig....

From now on only *Europa* of the periodicals studied contains anything of value on Dickens' new books. The ownership of this magazine had passed in 1859 to C. B. Lorck of Leipzig, one of the best-known German publishers of Dickens, and a distinct change of tone is consequently visible in the articles appearing after that date. Not that they now present only praise; but they achieve much better balance than was shown, for example, by the magazine's criticism of *Hard Times*.

The article on the *Tale of Two Cities* which appeared in *Europa* in 1860[4] describes the book as a not very successful historical novel:

Das Auge, das so scharf und humoristisch die Verhältnisse und

[1] 1861, no. 51, cols. 2045-6.
[3] 1861, no. 51, cols. 2045-6.
[2] 1855, no. 149 (13 Dec.).
[4] 1860, no. 10, col. 327.

Persönlichkeiten des kleinbürgerlichen Lebens aufzufassen versteht, wird durch die größeren Dimensionen geschichtlicher Charaktere ganz und gar irre und begnügt sich, weil es den feinen Blick verloren hat, mit den gröbsten Effekten zu malen. ... In diesem historischen Genre findet der Autor nur da seine alte Kraft wieder, wo er mit glutvollen Farben das Toben des Aufruhrs, die fieberheiße Atmosphäre der chronisch gewordenen Revolution schildert.

As examples the critic mentions St. Evrémonde, *der reine Theaterbösewicht*, and the scenes of conspiracy in the Defarge wine-shop, which *gehören in einen Räuberroman*; but against these he praises the crowd scenes, the description of Darnay's ride under escort to Paris and of the maddened men and women round the grindstone, sharpening their weapons. He has further praise for Jerry Cruncher and Miss Pross, and speaks of the 'feingemalte Seelenbild des Arztes von Beauvais', Dr. Manette. The book as a whole shows, he considers, Dickens' talent 'wieder in frischerer Kraft, als in seinem letzten Romane'.

Europa's article on *Great Expectations*[1] places that book between *Dombey* and *Hard Times*, which the critic takes as the highest and lowest peaks of Dickens' production. It shows, he says, the faults both of *Hard Times* and of *Little Dorrit*; in the first part it strains after the sensational, in the following parts it becomes prolix. Dickens:

... erschöpft ein ganzes Arsenal von Schauerlichem und Fürchterlichem, von Wahnsinn und Verbrechen, um Erregung und Spannung zu erwecken und zu erhalten, und wenn er damit auch ein noch viel größeres Publikum als mit seinen edlen, keuschen Meisterwerken gewinnt, so verletzt er damit doch um so mehr die Freunde dieser.

But, the article continues, it is easy to point out these faults; it is not so easy to enumerate all the beauties and truths of the book, all its variety of scene and character, 'kurz die ganze Gewalt und den Zauber seines Humors'. And it is pleased to find:

auch hier wieder jene scheinbar absichtslose, wie am Faden des Zufalls sich künstlerisch entwickelnde und doch so laut und ernst redende sittliche Idee.

The first volume of *Our Mutual Friend* was briefly discussed by *Europa* in 1864;[2] the article describes Dickens as a painter who in

---

[1] 1861, no. 51, cols. 2045–6.
[2] *Europa-Chronik* (a supplement), 1864, no. 22, col. 324.

his early days used more bright than dark colours, but who has gradually turned into a Rembrandt, and whose latest book promises the same deep colours and shadows. The second chapter is, however, 'im guten alten Stil der *Pickwickier*', but the style of the whole volume 'ist nicht immer natürlich und wird im Streben nach Originalität mitunter dunkel'.

This brief criticism can be supplemented by the opinion of Berthold Auerbach, which appears in his correspondence with Jakob Auerbach. He wrote of *Our Mutual Friend* that Dickens suits the opening very much to his own convenience:

... Wie bequem macht er's sich! Er legt sechserlei und mehr Anfänge hin, die er dann verknotet, indem er die Fäden zusammenzieht, und dabei bewegt er sich stets im Faktischen, auch wo er Gemütsstimmungen exponiert ... er macht auch mit keckem Pinsel die Figuren lebendig.[1]

His opinion of the first number of *Edwin Drood* may also be included, as none of the periodicals examined has any criticism of that book.—

Der Mann spielt stets seine alte Drehorgel, und es fehlen Stifte auf der Walze, so daß sie quiekst. Ein junges zierliches Paar, incommensurable Originale drum und dran, das geht so fort. In jedem Kapitel fängt die Geschichte neu an, aber er weiß doch zu packen und läßt den Zusammenhang ahnen.[2]

Fortunately Auerbach did not venture to predict the conclusion of the book.

Other critics of Dickens during this period are very few, and deserve only brief notice. Dr. Bohnstedt's *Life and Writings of Charles Dickens*,[3] an essay in English of 22 pages, need not be specially considered; it is a fairly accurate, but long-drawn and overladen criticism of Dickens' work (the description of his life covers one page only), almost all praise, often where it is not deserved. A lecture on Dickens given in 1869 by Professor H. Behn-Eschenburg of Zürich[4] is worthy of rather more attention; it is a short, clear account of Dickens' life, work, and methods, too compressed to be of any great value, but containing a few interesting decisions. The lecturer was another of those many readers who

[1] *Briefe an Jakob Auerbach*, Frankfurt a/M., 1884, vol. i, p. 409.
[2] Ibid., p. 23.   [3] Prog. Siegen, 1854.
[4] Pub. 1872 in *Öffentliche Vorträge gehalten in der Schweiz*, Bd. I., Heft 6.

appreciated Dickens' sound sense and his sparkling humour; and he, too, emphasizes Dickens' essential optimism.

Of the many articles and essays which Dickens' death called forth, mention may be made of one by 'Corvin' published in *Europa*,[1] which considers Dickens as an artist in literature, a great humorist, and a benefactor to the common people. This essay speaks with rather more authority than most, for 'Corvin' had actually worked for Dickens on the staff of *Household Words* and of *All the Year Round* in 1855–7 and from 1858 to about 1861; in which year he wrote an article on one of Dickens' public readings for the Leipzig magazine *Die Gartenlaube*.[2]

Dickens' death was as deeply mourned in Germany as in England, and many prominent Germans have left record of the deep sorrow they experienced on hearing this news in June 1870. Julian Schmidt, for example, wrote in the first lines of his essay of 1871:

> Ich kann nicht leugnen, daß die Nachricht von Dickens' Tod mich heftig ergriffen hat, und ich glaube, daß dies Gefühl wie an einer elektrischen Kette sich durch die ganze Welt ziehn wird;[3]

and Professor E. Engel, several years later, added to this in his history of English literature:

> Ältere Leser erinnern sich noch der Trauer, die bei der Nachricht seines Todes im Juni 1870 auch durch Deutschland ging. Man empfand ihn wie den Verlust eines teueren Gliedes der großen geistigen Familie, die trotz sprachlichen Schranken durch alle Länder reicht.[4]

Professor Carl Lehmann-Haupt recently told how 'vividly he recalls the deep and sad impression created in his family circle in Hamburg upon the receipt of the news that Dickens was dead'.[5] Berthold Auerbach wrote to Jakob Auerbach of the same sad impression;[6] and Freiligrath wrote to his daughter Käthe on 18 June 1870:

> Wie tief Dickens' Tod auch mich erschüttert hat, brauche ich dir

[1] 1870, no. 33, cols. 1045–56. For 'Corvin' (= O. J. B. von Corvin-Wiersbitzki) see *Allg. Dte. Biographie*, vol. xlvii, p. 531 f. There is another article on Dickens in *Über Land und Meer*, 1870, no. 42 (not seen by me).
[2] 1861, no. 39 (pp. 612–14): 'Eine Vorlesung von Charles Dickens'.
[3] *Bilder aus dem Geistigen Leben unserer Zeit, Neue Folge*, Leipzig, 1871, p. 1.
[4] *Geschichte der Englischen Literatur*, Leipzig, 1906 (6te. Auflage), p. 387.
[5] *The Dickensian*, 1929, p. 159. He was then only nine years old.
[6] Op. cit., vol. ii, p. 33.

nicht zu sagen, liebes Kind. . . . In solchen Momenten ist's, als legte sich ein dunkler Schleier über alles, was uns eben noch so hell und strahlend ansah. . . . Dickens' Tod ist in der Tat mehr als bloß 'a national calamity'.[1]

The finest compliment paid to Dickens at this time, however, was the more subtle for being unexpressed. Forster quotes in his *Life of Dickens*[2] a letter from Paris of 25 September 1870, which shows, in his words:

. . . a scene that made itself part of history not four months after his death, which, if he could have lived to hear of it, might have more than consoled him. It was the meeting of Bismarck and Jules Favre under the walls of Paris. The Prussian was waiting to open fire on the city; the Frenchman was engaged in the arduous task of showing the wisdom of not doing it; and 'we learn', say the papers of the day, 'that while the two eminent statesmen were trying to find a basis of negotiation, Von Moltke was seated in a corner reading *Little Dorrit*'.

[1] *Briefe*, hrsg. L. Wiens, Stuttgart, Berlin, 1910, pp. 187–8.
[2] Book 8, chapter 1 (on *Little Dorrit*).

PART II
DICKENS' INFLUENCE ON THE GERMAN NOVEL

I
THE NATURE OF DICKENS' INFLUENCE IN GERMANY

THE great popularity of Dickens' books in Germany did not only mean that they were much read, much liked, and discussed at length by the critics. It meant also that they exerted an influence, and not on the literature of the country only, which demands a full examination.

Of the social influence of Dickens in Germany it is difficult to say more than has already been set down by Freytag and by Julian Schmidt. Unfortunately, however, although both write from personal experience, it is hard to know how much weight should be allowed to their opinions; any examination of social influences is a dealing with intangibles, and there are no means to check the dicta of the *Grenzboten*, which may exaggerate through enthusiasm. This reservation made, however, it may be noticed that Julian Schmidt, to choose one from several such remarks, says of the effect of Dickens' books on the German reader:

Tausend und abertausend Leser sind es, die durch Dickens eine reine und heitere Freude, Stärkung und Läuterung des Gemüts gefunden haben . . .[1]

Gustav Freytag confirmed and extended this opinion in his article *Ein Dank für Charles Dickens*,[2] written on Dickens' death in 1870. It was noticed in the first chapter of the preceding section that Freytag gave much the same description of the pleasant and cheering influence of *Pickwick* on its publication in Germany; extending this to all Dickens' books, he wrote in 1870:

Überall kündeten seine Bücher, daß eine ewige Vernunft und Weisheit in den Schicksalen der Menschen sichtbar wird, und daß der Einzelne nicht nur unter den eigenen Fehlern, auch unter der Verbildung seines Volkes krankt . . . . Fast aus jedem Roman blieben rührende oder lebensfrische Gestalten fest in der Seele des Lesers, welche ihm unmerklich selbst die innige Auffassung alles Lebenden, das ihn umgab, und die gute Laune im eigenen Kampf mit dem Leben

---
[1] *Die Grenzboten*, 1853, vol. i, p. 436.
[2] G. Freytag, *Gesammelte Aufsätze*, Leipzig, 1888, vol. ii, pp. 239–44.

steigerten . . . Solche bildende Gewalt über die Zeitgenossen erhält freilich nur der wahre Dichter, der aus dem Vollen gibt und wie mühelos seine Schätze spendet. Und er bildet am kräftigsten an der Jugend und an denen, die verhältnismäßig wenig lesen.

Daß diese kräftige Einwirkung des englischen Dichters uns Deutschen gerade in den Jahren half, wo die eigene schöpferische Kraft schwach, das nationale Leben krank; das Einströmen der französischen Oppositionsliteratur, sozialistischer Ideen und frecher Hetärengeschichten übermächtig zu werden drohte, das ist sehr Vielen der jetzt tätigen Generation ein Segen geworden, für den wir dem Toten recht innigen Dank schulden.[1]

A contemporary opinion of the social value of Dickens' books may be added. It has recently been said of Dickens that 'his popularity with all classes was, in itself, a means of bringing rich and poor into sympathy . . . an enjoyment in common must prove a bond'.[2] It is interesting to notice that a German periodical of good standing, the *Blätter zur Kunde der Literatur des Auslandes*, made the same valuation of the social influence of Dickens as early as 1839:[3]

Wenn die komische Ader und die Empfänglichkeit für das Komische und Humoristische einerseits Beweise von tüchtiger Gesundheit sind, so liegt auch eine gewisse versöhnende Kraft darin . . Solche Schriften, wie die von Dickens, emanzipieren das Lachen, welches vom Pathos und von den heißen Leidenschaften ganz verschlungen und unterdrückt zu werden drohte, setzen dies charakteristische Merkmal der menschlichen Natur wieder in seine Rechte ein, schmelzen eine Menge Seelen von verschiedenen Tendenzen und Farben, wenigstens für eine kurze Zeit, in eine fröhliche Gemeinde zusammen, machen die verschiedensten Menschen für eine Weile ihre Parteileidenschaften, ihre individuellen, sie spaltenden Interessen vergessen. . . .

It is not to be suggested that this conciliatory influence of Dickens was as great in Germany as it was in England. But these extracts help to define what was in any case a noticeably cheerful atmosphere spread by the great popularity of Dickens in that country. A casual note in a contemporary English magazine perhaps sums this up fairly for both lands:

There is no doubt that this sudden taste for crowding upon the sunny side of the road was originally generated by a facetious gentleman who, for some months, escaped detection under the name of 'Boz'.[4]

And this must be given its fullest implication; the taste for the

[1] Op. cit., pp. 241–3.
[2] A. Cruse, *The Victorians and their Books*, London, 1935, pp. 147, 154.
[3] No. 84 (24 July).   [4] *Court Magazine*, vol. x, p. 185.

sunny side of the road means a new and wider acceptance of the belief that life should be cheerfully lived, is in essence good and reasonable; and implies an extension of kindliness, goodwill, and sympathy. All these points were insisted on by Freytag in *Ein Dank für Charles Dickens* in 1870.

That was the social influence of Dickens. A political influence is more doubtful, though Freytag felt that, by his books, Dickens produced in Germany a more friendly feeling for Englishmen and a more kindly attitude to England.[1] The literary influence, however, was marked, and extended over a wide range of types.

Dickens' use of the ordinary man and woman, of the details of everyday life, as the subject-matter of his books, was the first influential detail of his work. In the German novel any person but the ordinary man, any sphere but that of everyday life, had too frequently been chosen. The hero was more often than not an aristocrat, or at least a man of extraordinary powers and influence, and the sphere of the novel was mostly high society. Partly under the influence of Dickens, however, mingled in this case with that of Balzac, Eugène Sue, and some others, and running parallel with the change in social values throughout the nineteenth century, a change in the social standing of the hero and other characters of the German novel became apparent before the middle of the century; the trend was downward, and the classes thought fit to supply the main characters of the novel very soon included all shades of the middle class, and later of the proletariat.

The fact that Dickens had at his disposal such a storehouse of material as the great capital London, and that he used it so brilliantly, was a matter of admiration and of envy to the German of the period. Time and again the complaint is made, in connexion with Dickens' pictures of London, that Germany has not only no national existence but no centre of national culture, no focus of modern life such as is given by a great town. She had many minor centres, small towns and the typical *Residenzstädte*, but nothing to raise her contemporary realistic novel above the level of the provincial. Freytag and Julian Schmidt, Spielhagen and Otto Ludwig, among many others, make this complaint. Auerbach's expression of it may be taken as an example of the general feeling:

Dickens . . . hatte das Glück, ein Engländer zu sein. Was sind wir? Immer und immer Provinzialmenschen. Wir haben kein Zentrum, das

[1] Op. cit., pp. 243-4.

Jeder kennt, wir haben keine Nationaltypen .... Was hat Freytag, und was habe ich gemacht? Doch nur provinziales Leben. Wir müssen von der Peripherie ins Zentrum.¹ ...

Besides producing this often-expressed envy, Dickens' books also produced a desire to follow their example as far as German conditions would allow. There had already appeared a slight tendency in this direction in Germany; it was noticed in an earlier chapter that E. T. A. Hoffmann had chosen Berlin as the scene of some of his tales, and that Adolf Glasbrenner, the *Erzieher des Berliner Witzes*, was already at work at his sketches—*Berlin, wie es ist und— trinkt* (32 Hefte, 1832–50), for example, in which there is 'eine ganze Reihe typisch gewordener Figuren aus dem Berliner Volksleben mit höchster Treue geschildert'.² These sketches were very popular, and called forth innumerable imitations in many German towns. This interest in the everyday life of the townsman was accelerated by the appearance of Dickens' books, products of the essential townsman and almost all placed in London; the theme was continued in Germany in various ways, for, as Julian Schmidt wrote later (in 1870) of the *Sketches*:

> Wenn unsre deutschen Schriftsteller sich beklagen, daß unser Leben ihrem Griffel wenig geeignete Charakterköpfe biete, daß ihnen der Hintergrund des großen Londoner Lebens fehle, so können diese Skizzen sie belehren, daß man auch mit geringen Stoffen haushalten kann. Figuren und Ereignisse, wie man ihnen hier begegnet, könnte man allenfalls auch in Berlin auftreiben.³

Glasbrenner, who had the good fortune to come in on the tide of this interest, increased his popularity and continued his work with such publications as *Alt-Berlin, Buntes Berlin* (1835–52), *Berliner Volksleben* (1846). A further good example is provided by A. von Ungern-Sternberg, who, under Dickens' influence (as he himself admits) placed the action of his novel *Diane* (1842) chiefly in Berlin.⁴

Close to this interest in the townsman is the growing interest in the condition of the working classes; Dickens' influence is again

---

[1] B. Auerbach, *Briefe an Jakob Auerbach*, Frankfurt a/M, 1884, vol. ii, pp. 33–4. It is interesting to compare the present position of Hollywood, as explained by J. B. Priestley in *Midnight on the Desert*, London, 1937, pp. 182–3.

[2] *Allg. Dte. Biographie*, vol. ix, p. 214.

[3] J. Schmidt, *Bilder aus dem Geistigen Leben unserer Zeit*, Neue Folge, Leipzig, 1871, p. 28. But see the *Athenaeum*, 2 Nov. 1844, p. 998, for a very cold criticism of Glasbrenner's use of this material.   [4] See below, Chapter VIII.

mingled with that of Eugène Sue in accelerating this interest in Germany, though the influence of the latter is probably predominant as the formative inspiration, for example, of E. Willkomm's *Weiße Sklaven* of 1845; the theme was continued by R. Prutz in 1851 with *Das Engelchen*, and three years later by F. Hackländer in *Europäisches Sklavenleben*.

The mention of Friedrich Hackländer leads to the consideration of a further new interest stimulated by Dickens; that in the sketch as a literary genre, generally humorous, but not necessarily dealing with the townsman. Hackländer, more than once called the 'German Dickens', began to write in 1840, three years after the first appearance of Dickens in Germany. His *Bilder aus dem Soldatenleben im Frieden* (1840—eighth edition by 1873) were extremely popular. In his light daguerreotypes—by which title one of his books is significantly named—he avoided discussion of any deep problems or the portrayal of strong emotions; he limited himself to the representation of a few sides of life in an interesting and simple manner and to the humorous or purely whimsical drawing of characters and contrasts. Of him Julian Schmidt said: 'er würde ein deutscher Dickens werden, . . . wenn das deutsche Leben nicht so unendlich spießbürgerlicher wäre, als das britische',[1] and thereby showed the exact nature of Dickens' influence in this case; Dickens' example was followed as far as German conditions allowed. To Hackländer may be added the example of Karl von Holtei, the 'schlesische Boz'; his broadly-sketched pictures of travelling comedians and showmen fall in the same category, and his well-known *Die Vagabunden* of 1853 and his *Letzter Komödiant* of 1863 have frequently been compared with Dickens' description of actors and showmen in the *Old Curiosity Shop* and *Nicholas Nickleby*. Here, too, may be mentioned J. D. H. Temme, a former judge, who was partly dependent on the interest in the life of the proletariat inspired by Dickens as well as Eugène Sue; his stories of crime and criminals began to appear in 1852.

It should also be noticed that Dickens' periodical *Household Words* (1850 f.) had some influence on the development of similar periodicals in Germany. England had given a lead in this matter before; the *Penny Magazine* (1830 f.) became in Germany the *Pfennig-Magazin* (1843 f.) and the famous *Gartenlaube* owes something

[1] Quoted by L. M. Price, *The Reception of English Literature in Germany*, Berkeley, Cal., 1932, p. 422.

to English models. *Household Words* gave the formative inspiration for the publication of Gutzkow's similarly-named *Unterhaltungen am häuslichen Herd* from 1852.

These were all subsidiary lines of influence. It is more important to examine the influence Dickens' work had on the first-rank novel, especially that of the middle decades of the century.

The beginnings of literary realism in nineteenth-century Germany were briefly noticed in an earlier chapter, together with some reasons for its development. Significant of its growth was the decline in the popularity of Byron, one of the heroes of Young Germany, after the late thirties, and the publication in 1842, for example, of Ungern-Sternberg's *Diane*, as was shown above, and of A. von Droste-Hülshoff's *Die Judenbuche*, in which starkly realistic passages are mingled with something of the Romantics' symbolism. Though views of this realism, the predominant literary style in the middle years of the century, frequently differ from one another, and though it was never reduced to anything like a system, it is fairly well explained by the term used to describe it by Otto Ludwig: 'Poetic Realism'. It was a realism which stopped short of photography, and still painted; and it was in general a positive view of life, incorporating frequent touches of humour, and being in the main optimistic, though this (despite Julian Schmidt) was not a necessary ingredient.

An important forerunner of this was the *Dorfgeschichte*, a genre to be much cultivated from the beginning of the forties onwards; clearly a revulsion from the pessimism, the uncertainties, and the 'problematic natures' of the Young Germans, though the new interest was helped by the pioneer work of the romantic school and spurred on by the great acceleration of travel introduced by the railways, which brought sympathy for what seemed to be a fast-disappearing world.[1] The village tale gave a description of a firm and positive way of life in realistic outlines. It could not, however, be a proper substitute for the true novel of modern life; it was at best no more than an escape. But, as Julian Schmidt recognized, it bore in it the germ from which could grow exactly what was wanted.

Die Dorfgeschichten werden nur dann einen dauerhaften, segensreichen Einfluß auf unsere Literatur ausüben, wenn wir uns aus der

[1] See F. Altvater, 'Wesen und Form der deutschen Dorfgeschichte im 19. Jahrhundert', *Germanische Studien*, no. 88, Berlin, 1930, pp. 43–54.

Anschauung einfacher und plastischer Gestalten die Kunst aneignen, überhaupt bestimmte und lebendige Gestalten zu zeichnen; und diese Kunst, die uns durch die zersetzende Reflexion der letzten Jahre verloren gegangen ist, alsdann auf Gegenstände übertragen, die unserm Denken und Empfinden näher stehen, als das Stilleben entlegener Hinterwäldler.[1]

The method and style of the village tale, in fact, were to be enlarged and applied to the treatment of wider themes and of subjects with which the ordinary reader could feel more sympathy than he could, for example, with the existence of the Schwarzwald peasant. In this way the true modern novel was to be formed; and this, Schmidt felt, was what Freytag had done to produce his *Soll und Haben*, that book of great importance in the history of the German middle class and of German nineteenth-century literature.

The following chapter, on Freytag's relations to Dickens, will show how much *Soll und Haben* is under Dickens' influence. The characters, the scenes, the humour, the whole tone of the book are all strongly reminiscent of Dickens' work, which has here been applied to German conditions by an author who fully appreciates both. If, therefore, in the opinion of the best judge, Julian Schmidt, *Soll und Haben* was produced by an enlargement of the methods of the village tale to suit the handling of modern conditions and wide interests, to this must be added the fact that Dickens' methods were also employed, and to no small extent. *Soll und Haben*, the first example of the 'poetic realist' novel, thus appears as a blend of the manner of Dickens and of that of the *Dorfgeschichte*, applied to modern German conditions.

This fact established, it becomes of the greatest interest to study a brief essay by Otto Ludwig, one of the theorists, as Schmidt was the proclaimer and Freytag the practitioner, of this middle-class, middle-century realism; it is incorporated in his fragmentary *Epische Studien*[2] and is entitled *Dickens und die deutsche Dorfgeschichte*.

Ludwig first defines the *Dorfgeschichte* as being:

wie ein einzelnes Glied des Dickensschen Romans zu einem Ganzen geschlossen; ein Charakterbild aus jener Menge herausgenommen, eine Stimmung aus jener Mannigfaltigkeit von Stimmungen, eine Reflexion aus jenem Reichtum; sie ist der Geist jenes Romans in Form der Anekdote.

[1] Quoted by L. M. Price, *The Attitude of Freytag and Schmidt to English Literature*, Hesperia series, no. 7, Baltimore, 1915, p. 103.
[2] *Werke*, ed. A. Stern and E. Schmidt, Leipzig, 1891, vol. vi, pp. 74–80.

He shows that a difference lay in the more careful composition, *große Innigkeit, Zusammenhalten, saubre Ausführung* of the German village tale, which balanced the lack of richness and diversity which it shows on comparison with the Dickensian novel. To this, however, must be added the fact that:

das englische Behagen wurde in deutsches umgesetzt, aber ein Hauptteil der Wirkung blieb immer die Übertragung des Behagens und des stillen Vergnügens, mit dem der Dichter seine Gestalten anschaute, auf den Leser.

And now the really important section; Ludwig proposes that the way to the true novel of modern German life lies in the widening of the *Dorfgeschichte* to approach the fullness of the Dickensian novel. There was, in fact, to be a synthesis of all that was best in the two; all the good points of Dickens' work were to be retained, and all those details which had shown themselves in the village story during its evolution as properly fitted to the German character were equally to be continued.

Ludwig then examines the details of this proposed synthesis, which shall produce a novel he defines as:

... der Dickenssche Roman, aber beschränkter in der Extensität und dies durch die Intensität ersetzt, die Komposition und Ausführung nicht so salopp, die Charaktere nicht so grillig oder bloß äußerlich durch karikierende Übertreibung des charakteristischen Zuges bewirkt. Mehr das Gemüt als die Phantasie beschäftigt und durchaus nicht jenes Behagen vergessen. Dazu das Mittel, das wir schon im Dickensschen Romane finden — der Humor.... Was der Dickenssche Roman von Shakespeare hat, die Beziehlichkeit der einzelnen Stämme, das Herausheben der Charaktere durch Kontrast, die Gruppierung aller Stämme solchergestalt um eine Idee oder Hauptanschauung, die innern Entwicklungen, das stete Anwachsen nach dem Ende bis zu allgemeiner Katastrophe, die poetische oder vielmehr sittliche Gerechtigkeit, ... müßte natürlich möglichst beibehalten werden ....

This essay is of prime importance for the comprehension of the nature of Dickens' influence on the development of the German novel of the period. The extension of the *Dorfgeschichte*, which Schmidt advocated, was carried out by Freytag in *Soll und Haben* by the addition of some of the best and most helpful details of Dickens' work: exactly the method which Otto Ludwig was later to suggest as the best way of producing a novel properly suited to contemporary demands. It is not suggested that all the points in the synthesis of Dickens and *Dorfgeschichte* advocated by Ludwig were ever fully carried out; but the following chapter will demonstrate that Freytag did fulfil many of these demands, and did, as has been said, produce in *Soll und Haben* a mingling of the best in both; and consequently formed a book which is generally accepted as the best example of the art of the poetic realists.

Something of the same blend can be seen in many of the other contemporary novelists. Continuing from the literary tradition of Germany those details which were most fitted to the conditions and demands of their age, they added to them points from Dickens' work which proved to be of value. Thus they made full use of Dickens' rich technique of characterization, especially of humorous or purely comic figures; this is seen perhaps most clearly in Fritz Reuter's books, and can also be found in the earlier works of W. Raabe, in some of Otto Ludwig's stories, and more recently in the novels of Gustav Frenssen. His wonderful psychological descriptions, as seen in *Oliver Twist*, for example, were of interest to Ludwig particularly, and perhaps had some influence on like descriptions in *Zwischen Himmel und Erde*. Another detail of Dickens' manner which proved to be of influence at this time was his humour, so much enjoyed in Germany from the earliest years. His work here was again to sustain and to accelerate; a tendency to a gently humorous view of life's contrasts lay very much in the nature of 'poetic realism', but the German tradition of humour in the first half of the nineteenth century had not been strong; Dickens' example showed new methods of its application and representation, and it is certainly owing to him, to no small extent, that there is so much warm humour in the works of the poetic realists. Their use of his actual methods will be considered in detail in the following chapters.

In this matter books like *Pickwick* were most influential. All the novels of the first half of Dickens' work, that is up to (and including) *Copperfield*, had some influence of manner or matter on different German books, as will become apparent. The first and last of this part of his production, *Pickwick* and *Copperfield*, were, indeed, the most liked and the most influential of all his books. The influence of *Copperfield*, chiefly in plan but partly also in characters and scenes, can be traced surprisingly clearly from Freytag's *Soll und Haben* in 1855 through Raabe, Reuter, and Spielhagen down to some of the recent novels of Gustav Frenssen, such as *Otto Babendiek* of 1926; this will be shown in detail for each author in the following chapters. It is, in fact, doubtless owing largely to the great popularity of this book that there are to be found in German literature from the middle of the century onwards so many novels devoted to the tracing of a young man's development from early years to maturity; *Soll und Haben, Der Grüne Heinrich, Der Hungerpastor, Hammer und Amboß*, the largely autobiographical novels of Fritz Reuter, and later Gustav Frenssen's *Jörn Uhl*. This great influence of *Copperfield* is explained by the fact that with its much stronger plan and its breadth and clarity of description it formed a most welcome supplement to the chief German model of the novel of development: Goethe's *Wilhelm Meisters Lehrjahre*, so that, when both novels were used as models for a new *Bildungsroman* or *Entwicklungsroman*, the framework of Dickens' book tended to predominate.

It was, indeed, the framework of Dickens' books which found most use in Germany. The internal structure of the German novel, the thoughts and sentiments of the characters, the characters themselves, remained purely German; Dickens' influence was perhaps most seen in the general structure, the grouping, relation, and contrast of the characters, their presentation, and the plan and grouping of the scenes.

This influence was not of long duration, except for the repeated use of the plan of *Copperfield*. Slight traces of an influence of Dickens have been noticed in many of the minor novelists of the late nineteenth and early twentieth centuries, but these are of very small importance, and because of the late date and the confusion of influences it is difficult to point to any one definite connexion. Many small points of Dickens' technique have passed into the common stock, and have become part of the ordinary heritage of the modern writer; it is of small value to trace back all such minor influences to their source. Here once more Julian Schmidt had already summed the matter up seventy years ago:

> Man mag Dickens loben oder schelten, seinem Einfluß kann sich Keiner der Neuern entziehen. So wenig es möglich ist, zu der einfacheren musicalischeren Technik des vorigen Jahrhunderts zurückzukehren, nachdem durch glänzende Virtuosen jeder Art die Instrumentation, alle Kunstmittel ins Unendliche gesteigert sind; so wenig es möglich ist, die bescheidne Farbe der Düsseldorfer Zeit wieder aufzunehmen, seitdem man Gallait und ähnliche niederländische Kolo-

NATURE OF DICKENS' INFLUENCE IN GERMANY 65

risten kennt: ebenso wenig kann man der glänzenden Farbenpracht von Dickens gegenüber in der Poesie sich des ältern schulgerechten Stils bedienen ....[1]

After a few decades, indeed, the influences become very mixed, and it is a useless task to attempt to unravel the tangle of connexions. Gerhart Hauptmann, for example, certainly adds, with *Hanneles Himmelfahrt*, a new extension to the theme of the unfortunate child;[2] Dickens equally certainly had stimulated interest in this very theme some decades earlier; but after such a time it is almost impossible, and in any case of very little value, to decide how the Dickensian treatment of the theme (with Smike, or Little Nell) has been continued in Hannele.

These remarks are equally a restriction, to a less extent, of the conclusions reached in the following chapters, where the probable influences of Dickens on German writers are pointed out in detail. It must not be forgotten that it is not always possible to decide which is the true source of certain points; Dickens: the English writers of the eighteenth century, who were Dickens' literary predecessors and who still had some influence in Germany: Jean Paul, with whose work, as was shown, Dickens has something in common: or in a few cases E. T. A. Hoffmann, whose phantasies are sometimes close to those of Dickens. The point is not of first importance, and Dickens has usually had the benefit of the doubt, for it will be shown that all the writers considered had read and enjoyed his works, and had in most cases studied them deeply; so that it is fair to grant him, in nearly every case, a deciding influence. His great example in particular was thus usually what it has been shown to have been in general; where not entirely fresh, almost always stimulating and accelerating.

[1] J. Schmidt, op. cit., p. 117.
[2] A. E. Schönbach, *Über Lesen und Bildung*, Graz, 1900, 6. Aufl., pp. 253-4.

II
GUSTAV FREYTAG

FREYTAG's theoretical attitude to Dickens, which was, generally speaking, close to that of Julian Schmidt, was considered in the preceding section, where reference was made in particular to his very cordial article of 1870: *Ein Dank für Charles Dickens*. The details of the *Grenzboten*'s attitude to English writers in general and especially to Dickens need not be repeated here; this chapter will be concerned with a discussion of the conditions for, and evidences of, Dickens' influence on Freytag's work.

Freytag's English was never very good; it has been pointed out[1] that in 1865 he had difficulty in understanding a review of his *Verlorene Handschrift* in *The Times*.[2] It must be concluded, therefore, that he read Dickens' books in German translation, and there is other evidence to show that it was, in all probability, Seybt's translations that he used. The same applies to the other English authors he knew: Scott (whose books delighted him during his schooldays at Oels), Cooper, Shakespeare, Byron; later Macaulay.

It was as a student at the University of Berlin that he first became acquainted with Dickens' work—almost immediately on its first publication in a German version. A passage in his *Erinnerungen* describes the effect this reading had. The exact year is not given, but it can be taken with some certainty to refer to 1838. The sons of the Koppe family took him frequently to visit their home at Wollup in the Oderbruch; the party was usually large, and included four daughters of Amtsrat Koppe. Freytag says:

... Und uns umkreist geschäftig ein guter Geist, welcher wohlwollende Annäherung vermittelt, und dieser Geist ist Herr Pickwick. Wir erkennen, daß wir uns in einem Reiche bewegen, in welchem Boz als König herrscht, auch wir werden von den jungen Damen schelmisch darauf angesehen, ob wir mit den Begleitern des lieben Herrn Pickwick einige Ähnlichkeit haben. Aber wir haben keine andere als die, daß wir Sam Weller für die Krone aller Bedienten halten; wir fangen an, uns behaglich zu fühlen, und erweisen uns im Ganzen als leidlich und menschlich . . . .[3]

[1] By R. Freymond, *Der Einfluß von Dickens auf Freytag*, Prag, 1912, p.14.
[2] It appeared on 23 April 1865.
[3] *Erinnerungen*, Leipzig, 1887, pp. 129–30.

'Wohlwollende Annäherung'; that is the keynote of Freytag's opinion of Dickens' earliest influence in Germany. He struck that note on three separate occasions; once, as here, in his *Erinnerungen*, once more, as has been shown, in his *In Memoriam* article of 1870, and a third time in 1880, in the last of all his novels: *Aus einer kleinen Stadt*, the sixth volume of *Die Ahnen*. In this book, as he writes in his memoirs,[1] 'sind Eindrücke, welche dem Schlesier in seiner Jugendzeit kamen, sorglos und reichlich benutzt. . . . Auch bei Schilderung einzelner Menschen und des gesellschaftlichen Treibens in der Stadt sind Nachklänge aus der Wirklichkeit nicht vermieden'. It may be that in writing the following passage he had his stay at Amt Wollup in mind; but the frequency with which he mentions this effect of Dickens' first books leads rather to the conclusion that it was more than once a personal experience of his. In the following extract from *Aus einer kleinen Stadt* Viktor is in the company of Valerie and Käthe:

Er frug sie nicht ohne Bosheit nach dem Dichter, den sie am meisten begünstige. Aber diese Frage hatte auf beide junge Damen eine ähnliche Wirkung, als wenn man bei Champagnerflaschen Draht und Schnur zerschneidet. 'Boz' klang zugleich aus beider Munde, und die Worte strömten ohne Ende heraus; Lob und Freude, Lachen und Rührung. Da nun Viktor denselben Dichter in hoher Ehre hielt, so beteiligte er sich tapfer bei dem Erguß und die drei vergaßen den Lärm des Marktes und fanden in ihrer Begeisterung kein Ende, bis die Sonne völlig unterging. . . . Dennoch hatte dieser Abend Folgen. Denn Viktor behandelte seitdem das Fräulein mit einer Herzlichkeit, welche Käthchen beglückte.[2]

Here it is interesting to recall that Freytag was more than once accused of describing himself in this book. The charge has certainly been carried too far, and he attacks it stoutly in his memoirs; but there is no doubt that many personal experiences went to make up the body of the story; and there are several definite resemblances between Viktor König and Freytag himself, not the least being that Viktor is a Silesian, of Freytag's own generation, who eventually turns to journalism at the time of the revolution of 1848. In any case, as it has been shown that the experience of Viktor quoted above was also an experience of Freytag's on at least one occasion, it is very likely that in this instance particularly Viktor is Freytag himself; and consequently it is of

[1] *Erinnerungen*, p. 367.   [2] Leipzig, 1880, 2nd ed., pp. 359–60.

special interest to see, in the discussion of 'Boz', that 'Viktor hielt denselben Dichter in hoher Ehre'.

With such pleasant experiences and with so good an opinion of Dickens' first books it is to be expected that Freytag should have read several more with interest. But the direct evidence of his further reading is small. He certainly read *Oliver Twist*, but there is no direct proof of this; he knew *Martin Chuzzlewit*, as a reference in the 1870 article shows;[1] *David Copperfield* he certainly studied, though here again there is little direct evidence. In 1856 he sent a copy of *Nicholas Nickleby* to the Duchess of Coburg, writing: 'Möchte dieser frühere Roman des vortrefflichen Mannes Ew. Hoheit nicht weniger guten Eindruck machen als sein *Copperfield*'.[2] He had certainly read it himself, for he refers in his memoirs[3] to the 'Gebrüder Wohlgemut [Cheeryble] im *Niklas Nickleby* von Boz'.

In later years he still read Dickens. A list of the books he ordered from Hirzel in Leipzig between 1854 and 1894 is given by P. Ulrich;[4] for 1875 the entry includes 'Übersetzungen der Romane Dickens' '. And of a still later period, his last years in Wiesbaden, Alfred Dove writes in the *Allgemeine Deutsche Biographie*:

Am liebsten kehrte er in ruhigen Stunden 'zu den alten Bekannten, fast sämtlich Engländern' zurück: Scott, Dickens, Macaulay, selbst Cooper nicht ausgeschlossen.[5]

There are several reasons why Dickens had such a lasting appeal for Freytag. In many ways he fits Freytag's ideal of a novelist extremely well. A comparison between the two men shows many points of contact, together with the expected divergencies, which have been sufficiently well worked out by J. Dresch[6] and by R. Freymond.[7] Divergencies do not concern the theme of this chapter, but attention must be given to those points in Dickens' work which must have interested Freytag, especially after 1848.

[1] *Gesammelte Aufsätze*, vol. ii, p. 243.
[2] *Gustav Freytag und Herzog Ernst von Coburg im Briefwechsel, 1853–1893*, hrsg. E. Tempeltey, Leipzig, 1904, p. 355 (6 Feb. 1856).
[3] *Erinnerungen*, pp. 171–2.
[4] *Freytags Romantechnik*, Marburg, 1907 (*Beiträge z. dtn. Literaturwissenschaft*, vol. iii), p. 126 f.
[5] Vol. xlviii, p. 764.
[6] *Le Roman Social en Allemagne, 1850–1900*, Paris, 1913, pp. 116–19.
[7] Op. cit., sections 1, 2*a*, and 2*b*.

GUSTAV FREYTAG

A well-known passage in Freytag's works demands of the true creative writer of narrative works:

Ein starkes und freudiges Gemüt, voll von gutem Zutrauen zur Menschheit, nie verbittert durch das Schlechte und Verkehrte, dazu die Kenntnis des Lebens und menschlicher Charaktere, welche durch reiche Beobachtungen gefestigt ist.[1]

It has been noticed that with this sentence Freytag characterizes himself and, perhaps better still, Dickens.[2] The exact nature of the parallel is well summed up by Dresch, who remarks:[3]

Dickens et Freytag avaient des points communs.... Dickens a dans la peinture humoristique du milieu bourgeois, des petites gens surtout qui lui étaient si sympathiques, quelque chose d'ensoleillé, d'heureux, de confiant; il n'a guère représenté le quatrième état, le prolétariat, déjà si développé en Angleterre par l'usine et la grande industrie; il est, comme Freytag, un peu 'archaïque', en ce qu'il 'peint avec délices dans ses romans les choses qui vont disparaître'.[4]

It was that 'quelque chose d'ensoleillé, d'heureux, de confiant' which must have appealed most strongly to Freytag and was most in accordance with his own views. Dresch also quite rightly points out that the sympathies of both are with the middle class; the slight but not unimportant difference being that Dickens portrays chiefly the lower middle class, while Freytag tended at least towards a rather more cultured upper middle class (especially in *Die Verlorene Handschrift* of 1864). Both, again, have little good to say for the aristocracy of their period, while, as Dresch also mentions, neither has much to say about the 'fourth estate', the badly treated working class; though both knew something of its condition. Politically both represented a kind of moral liberalism, though Dickens was more radical than Freytag: and in general, as E. Kohn-Bramstedt recently has summed up the matter[5] 'In his black-and-white delineation Freytag has a strong affinity with Dickens ... both describe the triumph of honesty and goodness over dishonesty and egoism'. Both, too, enjoy the very detailed

---
[1] *Ges. Aufsätze*, Leipzig, 1888, vol. ii, p. 218.
[2] R. Freymond, op. cit., p. 10.
[3] Op. cit., p. 115.
[4] Dresch here quotes L. Cazamian, *Le Roman Social en Angleterre*, Paris, 1904, pp. 217–18.
[5] *Aristocracy and the Middle Classes in Germany; Social Types in German Literature*, London, 1937, p. 136, n. 2.

painting of the everyday life of their people. Freymond remarks well:

> Dickens wie Freytag sind außerordentlich feine Beobachter physischen und psychischen Lebens bis ins Kleinste und Geringste, beide gute Kenner menschlicher Charaktere . . . . Beide legen besonderen Wert auf die Beschreibung des Details; bei beiden wachsen die vielen Milieuschilderungen aus dem Kleinleben hervor.[1]

This was certainly a point in Dickens' work of great appeal to Freytag, though it would be dangerous to stress it, for his own technique in this matter may have been learned from Dickens. Finally a second dictum of Freytag, on the essentials of the novel, may be quoted as showing a further affinity with Dickens' outlook. Freytag requires that the novel should be so planned:

> . . . daß der Leser eine einheitliche, abgeschlossene, vollständig verständliche Geschichte empfängt, die ihn erfreut und erhebt, weil ihr innerer Zusammenhang dem vernünftigen Urteil und den Bedürfnissen des Gemütes völlig Genüge tut.[2]

Some of Freytag's directly expressed opinions of Dickens' works should be noticed. One concerns the serial method of production: Freytag writes in his memoirs[3] that this is 'ein Unrecht gegen die Kunst . . . . Auch die neueren Romandichter der Engländer, vor allen Boz, sind durch die bruchstückweise erfolgten Veröffentlichungen ihrer Geschichten zum Schaden ihrer Kunst beeinflußt worden'. A final appreciation of Dickens by Freytag places him, as a novelist, only just below Scott. As L. M. Price points out,[4] Freytag's contrasting opinions of Scott and Dickens are found together in a *Grenzboten* article of 1851,[5] where Scott is called 'ein großer Dichter . . .', Dickens not 'ein großer' but 'ein glänzender Dichter'; further, it is Dickens' merit 'einen gewissen größern Kreis von Personen und Schicksalen mit ausgezeichnetem Humor zu empfinden'. There is elsewhere in the same article a slight criticism of Dickens' purely selective method of characterization, but Freytag points out that the restrictive influence of this method 'bei der sehr glänzenden Darstellung . . . in der Regel verdeckt wird'. Finally, the memoirs speak of the 'Zauber der wundervollen Färbung bei Dickens'.[6]

[1] Op. cit., p. 11.   [2] *Ges. Aufsätze*, vol. ii, p. 218.
[3] *Erinnerungen*, p. 296.
[4] *The Attitude of Gustav Freytag and Julian Schmidt to English Literature, 1848–1862*, Baltimore, 1915 (Hesperia series, vol. vii), p. 91.
[5] Vol. iv of the year, p. 264.   [6] p. 238.

The story of Freytag's change of mind in the later years of the forties, his break with 'Jung-Deutschland', and his eventual link with Julian Schmidt and the *Grenzboten* has been well told by O. Mayrhofer[1] and by Price[2] among others: it need not be studied afresh here. The important fact is that from 1848 onwards Freytag was co-editor of the *Grenzboten*, of which the attitude to English literature, and in particular to Dickens, was so cordial. Here doubtless Julian Schmidt was the leading spirit, but on Dickens and others he voiced an opinion which was to a great extent also that of Freytag. The Anglophile attitude of the literary section of the paper was very pronounced for the first six or seven years after 1848; and in the five years prior to the publication (in 1855) of Freytag's *Soll und Haben* the interest in Dickens was paramount. *David Copperfield* had appeared in Germany in 1849–50, and Schmidt's own description of its immense popularity has already been noticed. In 1852 Schmidt was preparing his excellent pamphlet *Dickens: eine Charakteristik* for the Lorck edition; a little later Jakob Kaufmann, another of Freytag's collaborators on the *Grenzboten*, was preparing a translation of the *Old Curiosity Shop*, and Julius Seybt,[3] whom Freytag knew well, was occupied during this time on his German renderings of *Bleak House* and *Hard Times*. It is not surprising that during these years, while the plan and characters of *Soll und Haben* were slowly evolving in his mind, Freytag should also have turned to Dickens, in particular to the book of the moment, *David Copperfield*, and that something of its matter and manner should have flowed into the composition of his own future masterpiece.

Some proof of his own occupation with Dickens during this period is given by the results of a slight investigation carried out by W. Fehse in 1927, embodied in an article: 'Dickens "Pickwickier" und Freytags "Journalisten" '.[4] Fehse draws attention to the neat compliment paid to Dickens in the opening scene of the play; the retired Colonel Berg and his daughter Ida are on the stage, and the appropriate lines are:

> *Oberst.* Hier, Ida, sind die neuen Sorten der Georginen, welche unser Gärtner gezogen hat, du sollst Namen für sie erfinden....

---

[1] *Freytag und das Junge Deutschland*, Marburg, 1907 (*Beiträge z. dtn. Literaturwissenschaft*, vol. i), chapters 5 and 6.
[2] Op. cit., chapter 5. [3] See Appendix II.
[4] *Die Neueren Sprachen*, vol. xxxv, pp. 138–40.

Ida. Eine soll heißen wie Ihr Lieblingsdichter, 'Boz'.
Oberst. Vortrefflich, und das muß eine recht prächtige sein, hier die gelbe mit violetten Spitzen....

Fehse finds exact parallels between the election scenes at Eatanswill and those in *Die Journalisten*—the parties, colours, newspaper propaganda and last-minute decision; compares Pickwick and Piepenbrink in name and nature (*bieder, lebensheiter, gelegentlich kratzbürstig*), and also the names Boz and Bolz. Bolz is a true humorist in Dickens' manner, and Fehse suggests that the character is meant partly as a *Denkmal für den Briten*, who was also a journalist, a member of that despised profession which is rehabilitated in the play.

Die Journalisten, written in 1852, appeared two years later; and it was at this time also that Freytag was occupied on the production of *Soll und Haben*. Generally speaking his method in the preparation of a novel was to build up the whole plan in his mind first; to brood quietly over this plan, to work out the details of his characters, and find suitable names for them; to divide the whole into books and sections, and only then to begin writing, slowly and, according to mood, where he liked. In this pre-natal period, as Freymond has pointed out,[1] the work was specially susceptible to outside influences; more particularly in the case of Freytag, whose imagination was not great, 'so daß er sehr wahrscheinlich oft von anderen Schriftstellern aufnahm, ohne es selbst zu wissen'. In this connexion it is important to remember what Freytag himself has to say about Dickens' influence in the article of 1870. The particular passage is as follows:

Wer da meint, daß die Traumgebilde eines Dichters nur wie flüchtige Schatten durch die Seelen der Leser gleiten, der verkennt die beste Wirkung der Poesie. Wie Alles, was wir erleben, so läßt auch alles Wirksame, das wir gern lasen, seinen Abdruck in unserer Seele zurück. Aus der Sprache des Dichters geht in unsere über, seine Gedanken werden unser Eigentum, auch der Humor lebt in uns fort, er färbt immer wieder unsere Betrachtung der Menschen und erhöht uns zu heiterer Freiheit, so oft die empfangene Stimmung in uns lebendig wird.[2]

'Klingt das nicht wie ein Selbstbekenntnis?' asks Freymond, to whose excellent work this extract serves as a motto.

On the publication of *Soll und Haben* it was not long before the

---

[1] Op. cit., section 1, part 4. [2] *Ges. Aufsätze*, vol. ii, p. 242.

GUSTAV FREYTAG

influence of Dickens was noticed in its composition; in England, for example, it was pointed out as early as 1856, when a critic writing in the *Westminster Quarterly Review* for October of that year submitted Freytag's book to a very cool examination, and said: 'There are many faults in *Soll und Haben*, among them a tiresome imitation of Dickens'. The first serious attempt to work out Freytag's debt to Dickens on the basis of this book was made in 1908 by Vera Völk, whose essay[1] considers chiefly the technique of humour; and in 1912 Roland Freymond, whose careful and most interesting book has already been referred to in this chapter, produced what is almost a final investigation into the question, concentrating on *Copperfield* and *Soll und Haben*.

The very aim of the book was reminiscent of that of Dickens' work. Summed up by Freytag in the often quoted words of Julian Schmidt, it is: 'Der Roman soll das deutsche Volk da suchen, wo es in seiner Tüchtigkeit zu finden ist, nämlich bei seiner Arbeit.' Although this was nothing really new for the German novel, the attitude is significant, for as A. Banning points out:

> Wenn Freytag in seinem Roman . . . sich von dem Grundsatz hat leiten lassen, 'das deutsche Volk in seiner Tüchtigkeit, nämlich bei seiner Arbeit' zu beobachten und dementsprechend zu schildern, so gilt dies noch im erhöhten Maße von Dickens.[2]

In the same way as Dickens does for his country, Freytag here shows, with rather more emphasis, what is good and lasting in his people's culture; and just as Dickens condemns the evil in England, so Freytag also points out specific wrongs and misuses in Germany, but with rather less emphasis than Dickens allows himself.

In the technique of *Soll und Haben* several probable influences from Dickens can be noticed. Freymond has studied this question well; he points out that though P. Ulrich[3] emphasizes the importance of Scott as a model for Freytag's composition, Dickens may have had a greater influence than has been supposed, especially since 'als Freytag seine sozialen Romane schrieb, dürfte ihm Dickens näher gestanden haben als Scott'.[4] Dickens' books are

---

[1] *Dickens Einfluß auf Freytags' 'Soll und Haben'*, Salzburg, 1908. (Salzburger Mädchenlyzeum, 4. Jahresbericht.)
[2] *Dickens Beziehungen zu Carlyle;* Teil I, Prog. Hagen i. W., 1895, p. 2.
[3] *Freytags Romantechnik* (cit.).   [4] Op. cit., pp. 13–14.

much more carefully composed than they appear to be at first glance, and in general they well fulfil Freytag's demands for the right building-up of a story—demands which were not easy to meet, for, as is well known, in Freytag's case the technique was apt to be 'painfully exact'. The major points were an insistence on a clear and complete opening, the requirement of a clear defining line between exposition and action, and the demand of a complete and credible conclusion; and in the particular case of *Copperfield* Dickens does all these things well. To illustrate his contention that *Copperfield* is well composed, Freymond prints comparative graphs of its development and of that of *Soll und Haben*.

A further section of his work refers to Freytag's use of specially contrasted characters, and shows that Dickens also made good use of this technique; there are again plans to illustrate his thesis, but here it seems to be unnecessary to propose an influence from Dickens specifically, for the method is common. He points out, however, that both took great care in the naming of their characters, and in this connexion mentions (without undue emphasis) the similarity of the names Hippus and Heep, Rosa (Dartle) and Rosalie (Ehrenthal); the two last named play similar parts in the respective stories. Vera Völk draws attention to the probability that Freytag was influenced by Dickens in his method of introductory characterization: in both authors 'geschieht dies in der Weise, daß man zunächst allgemein Auffallendes zu sehen bekommt und erst nach und nach die den ersten Gesamteindruck ergänzenden oder korrigierenden Einzelheiten';[1] the characters, moreover, are usually set; they develop little if at all during the course of the story, just as those of Dickens remain what they were.

Vera Völk's chief service was to compare the humour of Dickens and Freytag, to show what are the methods they use to produce it, and to give colour and weight to her contention: 'am meisten von Dickens gelernt hat Freytag wohl in Bezug auf den von beiden Dichtern in reichlichem Ausmaße verwendeten Humor'. She finds in all eleven methods used by both writers; her results are important enough to be given in full. Humour is achieved:

1. durch drollige Vergleiche.
2. durch Übertreibung.
3. durch Umschreibung.

[1] Op. cit., p. 15.

GUSTAV FREYTAG

4. durch erläuternde oder das Gesagte korrigierende Nach- und Zwischensätze.
5. durch Wortspiele und Wortspielerei.
6. durch Zusammenstellung disparater Gegenstände oder Begriffe, den Gebrauch oximorischer Wendungen, und durch Kontraste.
7. durch leicht-spöttische und gutmütig-ironische Bemerkungen.
8. dadurch, daß der Dichter seine tatsächliche oder vorgegebene subjektive Meinung über das objektiv Berichtete ausspricht und sein überlegenes Wohlwollen für die Personen seiner Erzählung äußert.
9. durch Nennung eines Teiles statt des Ganzen.
10. dadurch, daß Personen oder Sachen mit den Namen der Dinge, mit denen sie früher verglichen wurden, bezeichnet werden, oder nach einem charakteristischen Merkmale ihrer äußeren Erscheinung.
11. durch launige Beifügungen.

Examples of all these types are given, and some may be repeated: 4 and 10 in particular need illustration. A good example of the fourth method is in the *Pickwick Papers*: '"He sleeps" murmured the spinster aunt. (His organs of vision had been closed nearly twenty seconds)'—and of the tenth in *Oliver Twist*: 'Mrs. Corney protested . . . that Mr. Bumble was indeed a dove. . . . The dove turned up his coat collar. . . .'.

It would be pointless to insist on all these types; they are of unequal value, and it is very difficult to draw a clear distinction in practice between those which Völk numbers 1, 2, 7, and 11. Again, there must be no suggestion that these methods could only be found in Dickens' work; the sixth, to take one example, is a well-known method of Jean Paul. For the rest, however, there are striking resemblances, and there can be little doubt that there was here an influence of Dickens' manner, though its extent is doubtful.

The best summary of the influence of Dickens on the technique of *Soll und Haben* is found in H. Mielke:

> Man spürt den Geist des Engländers Dickens in den reizenden Genrebildern, in der Art, wie die Besonderheiten der Nebenfiguren in eine humoristische Beleuchtung gezogen werden, in der eindringlichen Kraft, mit der düstere Stimmungssituationen entworfen sind. Hier zeigte der Deutsche eine verwandte Ader, aber sie war leider nicht so reich und unerschöpflich wie die des Engländers. Worin er ihn übertraf, war das künstlerische Gewissen, mit dem alle Typen zueinander

abgestimmt sind, war die mustergültige Komposition, die einen festen, gechlossenen Bau errichtet hat.[1]

If the thread of the story, the interrelation of the characters, and the actual scenes are examined, further influences from *Copperfield* can be traced, some of them quite definite, but all certainly unconscious. In the first place the large outlines are the same; both stories follow the life of a young man from birth to maturity. The parents die early in the boy's life, and he is brought up by a friend or a relation of his parents (Betsey Trotwood, Schröter). From that point the more important action begins, which is well summarized by Vera Völk:

> Sie werden durch einen ihnen gesellschaftlich und geistig überlegenen Freund (Steerforth, Fink) stark beeinflußt, stehen lange Zeit unschlüssig zwischen zwei liebenswerten Frauen (Dora, Agnes: Lenore, Sabine), bekämpfen erfolgreich im Dienste eines der geliebten Wesen (Agnes, Lenore) einen nichtswürdigen Jugendgenossen (Heep, Veitel) und laufen nach verschiedenen Fährlichkeiten glücklich und zufrieden mit dem ihnen kongenialen Mädchen in den Hafen der Ehe ein.[2]

There are, of course, large differences. Freytag's book, more firmly composed than that of Dickens, restricts not only the changes of scene and the number of characters, but the life-story of the hero also; we learn very little about Anton's early years, nothing of him after his marriage with Sabine; and there is no parallel in his life to David's marriage with Dora, which plays so large a part in Dickens' book—to take only a few more important points of dissimilarity. But a further comparison of the nature and experiences of the characters in *Soll und Haben* with those in *Copperfield* shows some surprising likenesses. This was the task Freymond carried out with considerable success,[3] though at times he was apt to carry the search for parallels rather too far. The following is a short summary of his results.

The most obvious, and most interesting, parallel is that between Steerforth in *Copperfield* and Fink, in whom several have seen the real hero of *Soll und Haben*. Freymond demonstrates how much this type of clever, distinguished, but too self-centred young man was a favourite of Freytag; with small variations it had already appeared as Saalfeld, Waldemar, Bolz.[4] It can be expected that

---

[1] *Der deutsche Roman*, Dresden, 1920, 7. Auflage, p. 186.
[2] Op. cit., p. 5. [3] Op. cit., section 2.
[4] In *Die Valentine* (1847), *Graf Waldemar* (1848), *Die Journalisten* (1852).

this character in *Copperfield* made an immediate appeal to Freytag's taste, and it is not surprising that it should have had considerable influence on the portrayal of Fink, who is (as Robert Prutz had long before pointed out),[1] a continuation of the Waldemar-Bolz type. Fink treats Anton much as Steerforth treats David; first in a very casual manner, later with condescension, after some time as a friend. Fink's privileged position in the Schröter household is like that of Steerforth in Creakle's family. Fink attempts to impress the Ehrenthal family in exactly the same manner and for the same reasons as Steerforth makes himself pleasant among the Peggottys. The major difference is in the sequel; there is no parallel in the German story to the seduction of Emily, for Fink, on Anton's reproof, declares that his interest in Rosalie was merely superficial. These are the main outlines of similarity, but Freymond has carefully shown how closely many of the smaller details of Fink's share in the tale parallel those of Steerforth's life in *Copperfield*.

Equally clearly Veitel Itzig here takes the place of Uriah Heep. Their appearances tally, both wear black, they have the same original position of office-boy and errand-boy. Veitel's ambition to rise in the Ehrenthal firm makes him take special lessons; Uriah spends his spare time in study for the same purpose. Both achieve a growing influence over their masters; each eventually proposes to marry his master's daughter (Rosalie, Agnes). The schemes of both are eventually discovered. For Veitel's schooldays, shortly described, Ralph Nickleby may have had some influence; and it is clear that the murder of Nancy by Sikes in *Oliver Twist* has lent a large amount to the murder of Hippus by Veitel Itzig in *Soll und Haben*. Both murderers at first escape, are haunted by their action, are eventually discovered and chased, and at last are sent to death by an illusion born of fear or conscience.

It has already been shown that in general outline Anton's story resembles that of David; but there are very few influences of detail, and those few that Freymond has discovered are not always convincing. Much the same must be said for his attempt to show an influence of Dora on the drawing of Lenore and her mother the Baroness Rothsattel; but it is at least clear that a few traits from Dora's character have their parallels in Lenore, particularly

[1] *Deutsche Literatur der Gegenwart, 1848–1858*, vol. ii, Leipzig, 1860, 2te Auflage, p. 106.

the butterfly spirit she shows in her inability to concentrate on a difficult task. Both lack the patience to manage a household with success, both prefer amusement to study. A few special details from Dora's life-story may also have influenced Freytag, in particular the description of her illness and death, which shows many similarities with his description of the same events in the story of the Baroness. A more satisfactory parallel is that between Agnes and Sabine, though the latter is a rather colourless figure. Both help their fathers (Wickfield, Schröter) as young housekeepers in place of the mother; both become friend and adviser of the hero (David, Anton); both warn him against what may be the bad influence of his distinguished friend (Steerforth, Fink); both represent for him the good influence in the background of his life, and he at last assures himself of that influence permanently by marriage.

In a few details Schröter may be compared with Wickfield, chiefly in his love for his daughter; while Ehrenthal, who may also have been formed partly under the influence of a study of Wickfield's story, shows rather more clearly in his attitude to his son, Bernhard, a reminiscence of the feeling for her son of Mrs. Steerforth. There are faint traces of Rosa Dartle in Rosalie Ehrenthal's attitude to Fink and to Sabine, of whom she loves the first (Steerforth), but hates the second (Emily) for an apparent attempt to win the man's love. The quiet scholar Dr. Strong may just possibly have lent his chief characteristic to Bernhard Ehrenthal. The clerks in Schröter's office (Purzel, Pix, Specht, Liebold) have gained a little from Freytag's reading of *Nicholas Nickleby*, in which appears the figure of Tim Linkinwater, genial, careful, precise in his methods and appreciated by his firm. As has been pointed out: when Ulrich[1] compares Pix and Specht with the clerks of Nelson's bank in *A Tale of Two Cities*, there can be no question of influence from this book by Dickens, since *Soll und Haben* preceded *A Tale of Two Cities* by four years; but his remark has a certain interest, if only as demonstrating how close relationship between the methods of Dickens and Freytag could be. The chain Linkinwater–Schröter's clerks–Nelson's clerks is significant. Finally there are vague traces of Mr. Peggotty in the figure of Auflader Sturm.

These parallels between *Soll und Haben* and *Copperfield*, not all convincing if taken separately, are clear when they are considered

[1] Op. cit., p. 80.

GUSTAV FREYTAG

in context. But no part of this chapter should be held to be a belittlement of Freytag's originality. *Soll und Haben* came at the right moment, and deserved its success; much of its framework undoubtedly came from Dickens, but the material and detail supplied by Freytag was properly fitted to the time and the needs of his country: for that he deserves his praise. The conclusion reached by Rudolph Borchardt[1] gives a true balance:

> Der letzte große Ausländer, den das deutsche Publikum, unbeschadet aller Herzlichkeit, mit Haltung aufgenommen hat, ist, soviel ich sehe, Dickens gewesen. Der geschichtliche Ausdruck für beides, die Herzlichkeit wie die Haltung, ist, daß im Momente des lebhaftesten Interesses ein Deutscher sich der fremden Gattung und ihres Stiles versicherte, ein nach den vorliegenden kopiertes Schema mit deutscher Zuständlichkeit erfüllte, und so, mit *Soll und Haben*, ein unendlich gelesenes Buch von kaum zu erschütternder Geltung schuf, neben dem die Originale langsam wieder zurückgesunken sind.

For Freytag's other novels the result of Ulrich's research[2]—that the important influence was that of Scott—holds good, except for a few details of technique already noticed, and with the further possible exception that, as Freymond demonstrated, Dickens may have had some influence on the structural method employed by Freytag.

Some points in *Die Verlorene Handschrift* (1864) should, however, be noticed. It is undoubtedly true to say, as Freymond does, and (by implication at least) Ulrich, too, that the influence of Dickens on this book was very small; so true, indeed, that it is not even possible to agree with Ulrich when he declares[3] that 'Gabriel ... scheint ein direkter Abkömmling des treuen Sam Weller des Herrn Pickwick zu sein'. But there is one character in the book which may possibly have been built up on ideas supplied by a character of Dickens; that is Magister Knips, who occasionally resembles Uriah Heep sufficiently closely to warrant an examination. Apart from a slight similarity in the sound of the names (which may be pure coincidence, for *Knips* has a definite meaning in the dialect of Thüringen, for example), both characters have much the same appearance; both are thin, almost emaciated men with bony figures, and in each case attention is drawn to their specially hard and protruding knees. (Knips, for example: '. . .

---

[1] *Rede über Hofmannsthal* (1902): 2nd ed., Berlin, 1918, p. 19.
[2] P. Ulrich, *Freytags Romantechnik* (cit.). [3] Op. cit., p. 80.

seine Kniespitzen, welche in ungewöhnlicher Glätte und Abgestoßenheit glänzten . . .'.) Knips squirms almost as much as Heep ('. . . "Deuce take the man!" said my aunt, ". . . don't be galvanic, Sir!"'), and though he does not perpetually profess 'Umbleness' he is always described as *andächtig, unterwürfig*, above all *demütig*. He too is angry that no one will recognize his worth—'mich ehren nach meinem Wissen tut Niemand'—and he attempts to swindle his employer as well. His brother, Knips junior, is put in the same position of trust as Heep, and gaining the confidence of his employer in the same way misuses the funds of the business and eventually robs the house of almost everything.

These are the points of resemblance. There are, of course, major differences; the bearing of Knips when he is found out is very different from that of Heep in the same circumstances, and his part in the tale is much smaller than that played by Heep in *Copperfield*. The points of parallel are comparatively few, but not inconsiderable.

There are also a few traces of a type of humour very close to that of Dickens; a good example is given by the apostrophe to the moon in the first book;[1] 'you are reminded that your value is assessed by the solid burgers only—"genau nach den Summen, die du der Stadtkasse an Gaslicht ersparst"'. An even better example is given by the description of the family's joy at receiving Fritz's first book:[2]

> Herr Hahn aber nahm . . . das Buch . . . und trug es in den Garten. Dort legte er es auf den Tisch des chinesischen Tempels, las mehrere Mal die Widmung und umkreiste darauf den Pavillon, immer wieder hineinsehend, um zu beobachten, wie sich der Baustil in Verbindung mit dem Buch ausnehme.

Dickens' influence on Freytag was of such a nature that it can be said to have been very nearly typical of his influence in Germany generally. As in German thought and literature, so in Freytag the seed existed already, and had already borne some fruit; Dickens had an influence which was strengthening and stimulating, but which did not cause any radically new growth. This is true both generally, of the attitude to life, and particularly, of the methods of technique displayed by Freytag especially in *Soll*

---

[1] Book I, chapter 1.   [2] Book II, chapter 5.

und Haben; the book accepted with such enthusiasm by the German people because it summarized so nearly their own aspirations and their own valuation of the world and the age. Freytag was talented enough not to need to follow any literary dictator; but he found Dickens a useful guide.

III
OTTO LUDWIG

THE long and detailed examination of Dickens' work in Ludwig's *Epische Studien* affords good reason for a close study of Ludwig's narrative works with the object of discovering if they demonstrate any influence of Dickens on the German's material and technique.

The *Epische Studien* themselves are full of interest. Written in fragmentary form and in very concentrated language, they are a kind of enlarged diary of Ludwig's readings and musings; they were never intended for publication, being the product of Ludwig's careful but essentially personal search for clarity in his own mind on the nature of the novel in general, and of the contemporary novel in particular. The books by Dickens mentioned in the Studies are the *Pickwick Papers*; *Master Humphrey's Clock* (which includes *The Old Curiosity Shop* and *Barnaby Rudge*); *Chuzzlewit*; *Dombey*; *Hard Times*; *Little Dorrit*; the *Tale of Two Cities*; and *Great Expectations*; it can probably be assumed, however, that Ludwig had read most of the other works, even though they remain unmentioned in his Studies. The most thoroughly examined are the four latest books—*Hard Times, Little Dorrit, Two Cities, Great Expectations*, while only two of the earlier works (*Dombey* and *Barnaby Rudge*) are studied in detail. This fact makes it seem likely that Ludwig set out to avoid a mixing of old and new impressions in his study of Dickens; commencing his *Studien* in 1855, after writing *Zwischen Himmel und Erde*, he paid little attention to earlier conclusions and began, with his critical sense fully alert, on the latest work, *Hard Times*. He then continued with each new book by Dickens, of which the last he knew was *Great Expectations* (1861); he died in February, 1865, and Dickens' penultimate novel, *Our Mutual Friend*, finds therefore no place in his Studies. The question of whether he read these books in English or in German translation is of some importance for the study of his technique; F. Lüder[1] says briefly, but without reference, 'Ludwig las Dickens übersetzt'; J. Betz,[2] however, very rightly refers to Kramer's

---

[1] *Die epischen Werke Otto Ludwigs und ihr Verhältnis zu Charles Dickens* (Diss. Greifswald), Leipzig, 1910, p. 50.

[2] *Otto Ludwigs Verhältnis zu den Engländern* (Diss. Frankfurt), 1929, p. 10.

report of Ludwig's life during the winter of 1841–2, where there is the information that during this time he studied English 'regelmäßig abends von 8 bis 11 Uhr'.[1] From this she concludes that Ludwig subsequently read Dickens' books in the original. The question is still undecided, but the balance is slightly towards the latter conclusion; for the rich variation in language, the skilful dialogue, 'das Stammeln, Stottern, u.s.w. der Verlegenheit, die Salbung des sich gern reden hörenden, der sich an seinen rhetorischen Wendungen einen Schmaus gibt'—all those points which Ludwig praises in Dickens in the Studies[2] lose much of their force, necessarily, when transferred through the medium of a foreign language.

A brief summary of Ludwig's criticism is of interest, though on many points the final judgement must remain subjective, since frequently a detail of criticism is altered by a second on another page, and both may then be further qualified by a third expressed elsewhere. A fault to be found occasionally is one of overgeneralization; a criticism which may be legitimately applied to one of Dickens' books will be extended to cover the whole of his work. In sum, however, Ludwig's criticism is excellent, and of great penetration.

Most of his remarks concern Dickens' methods of characterization. He first makes the point that Dickens excels at showing the limitations of the minds of his characters:

> Bei Boz ist die Inslichtsetzung der Borniertheiten, gutmütige und bösartige, die Borniertheit der Personen nach Stand, Bildungsgrad, Hantierung, Alter, Affekt und Leidenschaft die Hauptsache.[3]

He finds the methods used to display these limitations of great interest; one method he notices in particular:

> ... Wie er dann seine Personen wie mit fixen Ideen behaftet, wie ihnen irgend ein Assoziationshaken gegeben wird durch die Rede eines andern, auf ihr Lieblingsthema zuzustürzen, was übrigens in der Natur begründet ist.[4]

---

[1] Betz here quotes A. Stern, *Otto Ludwig, Ein Dichterleben*, Leipzig, 1891, p. 145. Lüder (op. cit., p. 50), however, gives the information that he found no books of Dickens in Ludwig's library.

[2] *Epische Studien*, in vol. vi of the complete Works (ed. A. Stern and E. Schmidt), Leipzig, 1891, p. 159. This is so far the only complete edition of the *Studien*.

[3] *Epische Studien*, pp. 65–6.   [4] p. 71.

The dramatic qualities of Dickens' composition and especially of characterization interested him perhaps most strongly of all. He writes, for example:

> Der Bau seiner Romane hat Ähnlichkeit mit Dramen. Seine Romane sind erzählte Dramen mit Zwischenmusik, ... Seine meisten Figuren sind verkleidete Schauspieler. Alle haben eine treffende Maske und sind Virtuosen im Gebärdenspiel. ... Die Bozischen Romane sind wahrhafte Schauspielerschulen .... Das Drama selbst erlaubt dem Dichter nicht so schauspielerisch zu sein, als der Bozische Roman....[1]

Of these points the one to be stressed is the mimic element, the *Gebärdenspiel*, which Ludwig describes as of 'truly astonishing variety'. This, supported by the dialogue (the handling of which is a *Hauptkunst* of Dickens),[2] is the reason for the visual clarity of Dickens' work. The very dialogue, says Ludwig, is visible, not only audible. H. Lohre, interpreting Ludwig's conclusions on this point, writes:

> Für Anschaulichkeit sorgen schon die Dickensschen Vorbemerkungen, in denen er die Aufstellung der Sprechgruppe angibt, und die oft ganz die kupierte Sprache von Regieanweisungen annehmen .... Inmitten des Gesprächs wird Stellung und Gebahren oft in kurzen Parenthesen angedeutet, ganz wie der Theaterdichter dem Schauspieler seine Winke gibt.[3]

Ludwig's criticisms, however, are not all praise or appreciative observation. There are points in Dickens' work which he blames sharply. A very well-known criticism, for example, reappears in the Studies:

> Die komischen Personen sind auf dem Weg der Karikatur erzeugt: das charakteristische Moment ins Ungeheure vergrößert, das innerliche wie das äußerliche. Es sind Menschen, wie man sie von jeder Straße aufgreifen kann, mit irgend einem Merkmal, das sie eben nur von allen unterscheidet, dieses wird nun ins Ungeheure getrieben. Eine Äußerlichkeit in Gestalt u.s.w. eine Gewohnheit u.s.w.[4]

and later, in a discussion of *Hard Times*:

> Seine Figuren sind Abstraktionen ... die meisten haben eigentlich kein Innres, sie sind poetische Automaten, die eine gewisse Anzahl von Bewegungen nach dem Uhrwerke abspielen....[5]

[1] pp. 66–7. [2] p. 69.
[3] *Otto Ludwig und Charles Dickens* (in *Archiv f. d. Studium d. n. Sprachen u. Literatur*, vol. cxxiv, 1910, pp. 15–45), p. 30.
[4] *Epische Studien*, p. 68. [5] p. 69.

and these become, consequently:

> Weniger wirkliche Menschen, als ein seltsames Geschlecht von Wechselbälgen der Phantasie.[1]

Here the dangerous generalization mentioned above is clear. Ludwig's remarks can be applied with justice to certain of Dickens' minor, tendentious, and less successful characters, but certainly not to all his figures. The two quotations preceding are taken from discussions of *Hard Times* and *Little Dorrit*, not the best of examples. Lohre sums up Ludwig's attitude, and remarks:

> Alle Ludwigschen Ausführungen über Einseitigkeit, Karikatur, Mechanismus in der Dickensschen Charakteristik gründen sich zwar auf scharfe Beobachtung, treffen aber nur zu für einen engeren Kreis von Gestalten[2],

and he shows that there are signs that Ludwig was preparing to modify his rather over-sensitive criticism. Lohre holds that the harshness of Ludwig's judgement may be partly caused by his ignorance of the English literary tradition of odd and eccentric characters; but his explanation must be accepted with reserve, in view of Ludwig's acquaintance with the work of Fielding and Smollett.[3]

A point in Dickens' creation of the correct atmosphere for an event was of special interest to Ludwig. He writes:

> Lichtputzen, Schatten, alles muß agieren, über alle Hausgeräte kommt eine Wut zu agieren, über die Uhren, charakteristisch zu sprechen, in einer gewissen angenommenen Rolle zu extemporieren. In der Tat, alle Bozischen Charaktere, so Menschen als Dinge, sind eigentlich Rollen, durchgespielte Rollen[4]

and:

> Tisch, Stuhl, Wände, Häuser, Fluß, Brücke, Kohlenfeuer, u.s.w. alles lebendig, aber — wahnsinnig![5]

In writing this he may have had in mind, for example, the ponderous clock in *Dombey*, which ticked loudly 'How is—my lit-tle friend?', or the race between the kettle, the clock, and the cricket at the beginning of the *Cricket on the Hearth*. He was interested in the technique, but not very satisfied with the result.

The language he praises for a special quality:

> Eine Hauptsache, womit Dickens sich wie Shakespeare von z. B.

[1] p. 81.   [2] Op. cit., p. 28.   [3] *Epische Studien*, p. 95.
[4] p. 67.   [5] p. 81, on *Little Dorrit*.

Goethe und Schiller unterscheidet, ist, daß seine Figuren nie wie ein Buch sprechen dürfen. Es ist wunderbar, die reiche Variation der Mittel zu sehen, durch welche es den beiden Engländern [Dickens and Scott] gelingt, den Dialog vom Buchartigen zu emanzipieren.[1]

This praise must be modified, however, by an opposite criticism of the language in *Hard Times*:

Eine schwache Seite von Dickens ist die Schilderung des Volkes. Nie sprechen die Leute aus dem Volke ihre eigne Sprache oder denken ihre eignen Gedanken, immer nur in einer der Volkssprache angenäherten konventionellen Weise die Gedanken des Autors über das Volk.... Dies fällt sehr unangenehm auf....[2]

It is important to remember that this criticism is applied to *Hard Times* and should not be widely generalized. It is certainly true, to a large extent, of characters like Stephen Blackpool, and, if viewed correctly, only slightly modifies the previous praise. But the second criticism links with a much more serious one of the whole polemic nature of so many of Dickens' books. Ludwig writes: 'Seine Werke sind recht eigentlich Tendenzgeschichten... die offene Absicht erkältet.' These are *unwürdige Künste*:

Abgesehen davon, daß uns seine dargestellten Menschen als solche so lange nicht interessieren können, als sie die Sprachröhre des Dichters sind und die eigne Existenz verlieren. Der Endeindruck ist ein durchaus unharmonischer.... Wie tief steht er in diesem Stücke unter Shakespeare![3]

Finally, it may be noticed that Ludwig agreed with Dickens on most of the larger outlines: the arrangement of a story, and its whole tone—its poetic justice and poetic realism (e.g. p. 64, and p. 75—'Poesie der Wirklichkeit, die nackten Stellen des Lebens überblumend, die an sich poetischen nicht über die Wahrscheinlichkeit hinausgehoben'). And he particularly noticed the general pleasantness of Dickens' work; for example:

Bei Boz handelt sich's immer um die behaglichste Ausmalung; seine Wirkung ist, den Leser mit seiner Behaglichkeit anzustecken. Selbst das Unbehagliche an sich weiß er so behaglich zu schildern.[4]

The interest of this very brief summary is to afford a slight idea of how attentively and deeply Ludwig studied Dickens, chiefly in the years which followed the writing of his own narrative works. It is not possible to discover which were the new elements in his

[1] p. 159.   [2] p. 71.   [3] From pp. 69–72.   [4] p. 66.

criticism of Dickens after 1855; but it can be taken as most likely that his expressed opinions of Dickens after that date were not very dissimilar from his earlier unexpressed valuations. It is consequently of some importance that his narrative work should be studied, and compared (with care, and without too great an insistence on detail) with the *Epische Studien*, to discover what influence, if any, his general appreciation of Dickens had on his stories. The first to make a thorough investigation on these lines was H. Lohre, in 1910,[1] who occasionally, however, appears to lose sight of the essential and rather hampering fact that the *Studien* are of later date than the published works. In the same year Fritz Lüder's Greifswald dissertation[2] on the subject was composed, independently; Lüder examines the question at length, and fortunately with emphasis less on the *Studien* than on the history of Ludwig's technique and the details of that of Dickens; in fact, his is the opposite method from that employed by Lohre. Recently (1929), the Frankfurt thesis of Johanna Betz, *Otto Ludwigs Verhältnis zu den Engländern*, has, in so far as it concerns Dickens, found very nearly a true balance between the two methods.

Lohre concentrated on the *Heiteretei* and *Zwischen Himmel und Erde*, the two famous works in which the influence of Dickens on style and technique can occasionally be seen quite clearly. He did not consider the smaller narrative works, though R. Müller had given a few pointers to them in his Tübingen thesis of 1904–5,[3] and still more in the two editions of his full work, published under the name of Müller-Ems and the title *Otto Ludwigs Erzählungskunst* at Berlin in 1905 and at Halle in 1909. Müller wrote, for example, that in *Aus dem Regen in die Traufe* all the characters are caricatured. It was left to Lüder to continue this point and show its significance in his consideration of the minor works.

Lüder finds traces of Dickens' influence as early as 1846, in the tale *Das Märchen vom toten Kinde*, where the human figures are characterized rather in Dickens' manner; that is to say, with emphasis on external details and peculiarities of manner and gesture; the best example is Doctor Fuselius, who plays on his walking-stick as if it were a flageolet. Again, in the fragment *Es*

---

[1] *Otto Ludwig und Charles Dickens* (cit.).
[2] *Die epischen Werke Otto Ludwigs und ihr Verhältnis zu Charles Dickens* (cit.).
[3] *Otto Ludwigs Erzählungskunst*.

hat noch keinen Begriff, written after 1847, the central figure is a child, as in so many of Dickens' stories; Liesle asks naïve and serious questions, of the sort Paul Dombey might have pondered on—'Was schickt sich denn eigentlich, Base Annemarth?' — 'Was recht ist.' — 'Und was ist denn recht?' The characterization of the parents is again in Dickens' manner, with much repetition of the same motive; the mother's characteristic gesture is to wrap her hands in her apron and sit with her chin on her knees.

All the investigators agreed that *Die Heiteretei* (1854) gives clear examples of Dickens' influence; Müller-Ems had suggested that it could be seen even in the plan of the story, in the manner in which the different threads of the narrative were interwoven. This Lüder very properly rejects as unnecessary, suggesting instead that the slight contrast between rich and poor in the story is rather more in Dickens' manner; though an insistence on social differences was never Ludwig's theme.

It is in the characterization, especially of the secondary figures, that the influence of Dickens is most clearly visible. Here the well-known methods of humorous comparison, characteristic gesture, and constantly recurring phrase are used. The 'Morzenschmiedin', for example, is compared, at her introduction, to a Schwarzwald clock, and this comparison is continued throughout the tale. The watchmaker Zerrer (a picturesque and descriptive name) has apparently learned to talk from his clocks, and 'aus seinem Knarren und Schnarren ist kaum klug zu werden'. The best example of this Dickensian method is given by the 'Valtinessin'; she repeats time and again the characteristic phrase 'Und obschon mein Vater selig ein Weber ist gewest . . .', just as Mrs. Micawber perpetually speaks of the days when she lived with her dear papa and mama; her characteristic and significant gestures are a settling of her bonnet on one side of her head, and an annihilating sideways flourish of the hand to mark disapproval; very much the gesture, later, of Mr. Podsnap.

The technique of supplying each character with a particular gesture or expression runs through the whole tale, and even the two main characters are not (as Lohre supposes) quite free from it; whenever he is beginning to be angry, the 'Holdersfritz' clutches at his coat-collar, and the 'Heiteretei' herself uses the recurrent phrase 'Und so ist's, und nu ist's fertig!' It should be noticed, however, that there is a double reason for the use of this latter method; it not only characterizes a figure and provides an easy method of recognizing him, but it is especially well employed here to depict peasants, to whom the use of a few recurrent phrases is natural. Moreover, the use of humorous repetitions was an original method of Ludwig—it appears already in the *Hausgesinde* —and Dickens' influence can have been no more than a stimulant. Equally, the judgement on Ludwig's use of dialect must remain subjective; Dickens certainly introduced it into his books (the Wellers, Mr. Peggotty), but it is natural also to the characters of the *Heiteretei*. Dickens' influence was again probably secondary in the case of the personal reflections and short discursions which Ludwig introduces into his story; but it was of larger importance in the expression of the strange and the wonderful elements of the tale—the animation of nature, for example, in the case of the elder-tree which watches over the fortune of the Heiteretei; and in the humorous and much-emphasized comparisons. The whole tone of the humour, with its very faint irony, is much reminiscent of Dickens, and Müller-Ems showed how close, in this respect, was Ludwig's outlook to that of Dickens, when he wrote of *Die Heiteretei*:

Der satirische Zug, der in den ersten Novellen Ludwigs hervortrat, ist fast ganz verschwunden. An dessen Stelle ist der Humor getreten. Ludwig lacht nicht mehr über seine Personen, er lächelt höchstens über sie und es ist ein wohlwollendes Lächeln. Es ist die Art, wie Scott und Dickens Welt und Menschen sehen.[1]

As has been mentioned, Müller-Ems had pointed out Dickens' influence on the characters of *Aus dem Regen in die Traufe*; but Lüder was the first to carry out a full examination. This of all Ludwig's stories is the most clearly based on Dickens' methods, and in it Lüder rightly sees the highest point of Dickens' influence. Indeed, he goes so far as to say that the tale almost gives the impression of a conscious imitation of Dickens, both in the motive and in the characterization. Here, again, are the humorous repetitions, the stereotyped phrases, the recurrent gestures and comparisons; Ludwig has carried them too far, and allowed Dickens' methods to distort the proper use of his own powers.

But *Zwischen Himmel und Erde*, written in 1855, is very different. Here Ludwig allowed his own genius full play; the external humour of *Die Heiteretei*, which hardly suited his outlook, has

[1] Op. cit., Berlin, 1905, p. 54.

given way to deep examination of the minds of his characters; and with it there consequently disappears the free use of those humorous methods, modelled in Dickens' manner, which were so clearly seen in the two earlier stories. Some influence from Dickens can still be traced, but here it is only of secondary importance.

It can be seen, for example, in some mannerisms of characterization: recurrent expressions (here used without humorous effect) such as that of old Nettenmair: 'Es hat nichts zu sagen!'—typical gesture; outward appearance. As in Dickens, a comparison or description once made is frequently continued through the tale; thus Apollonius is perpetually called the 'Federchensucher' ('eine Charakterbezeichnung, die zur Formel erstarrt', says Lüder),[1] and his blue coat is equally often brought to the reader's attention. In the language used there are also traces of Dickens'. methods; Ludwig fixes the intonation of a sentence by the free use of dashes and brackets. Double questions, of opposed sense, conditional questions, occasionally slightly artificial metaphors, are also reminiscent of Dickens; and Adolf Bartels, early in the century, had blamed Dickens' influence for the direct questions, the personal exclamations and reflections to be found so frequently in the story:

die sogenannte Zwischenreflexion, die in die Erzählung eingeschobene, sie unterbrechende selbständige Reflexion, meist eine moralische Ausführung des Dichters, so gleich zu Anfang die über die Heimat und dann noch manche . . . .[2]

Lohre, too, has seen a possible influence of Dickens (probably one among many) in the careful realism of the story; especially in the descriptions of the trade of the Nettenmairs.[3] Ludwig later expressed wonder at the careful technical studies carried out by the English authors before they began to write;[4] of the introduction of such descriptive passages he writes: 'Nur so kann [der Autor] unsern Glauben wecken und erhalten und die Mittelglieder zwischen den Effektszenen hinlänglich beleben und interessant machen.' It is to the latter end that these passages are used in *Zwischen Himmel und Erde*. Lüder disagreed with the suggestion that Dickens was influential in this matter;[5] the final judgement

---

[1] Op. cit., p. 128.
[2] Introduction to his edition of Ludwig's works, Leipzig, n.d. [1900], vol. i, p. lv.
[3] Op. cit., pp. 40–1.
[4] *Epische Studien*, pp. 60 and 65.
[5] Op. cit., p. 156, footnote.

must remain personal, but it is not too much to say that Dickens had at least a stimulating influence. In considering the realism of the story, it is interesting to notice that Müller-Ems parallels the description of the storm in Ludwig's tale with that in *The Chimes*;[1] there are certain likenesses, most noticeable in the manner in which the wind is described. This point also interested Lohre, who refers to the storm in *Copperfield*.[2]

In examining Ludwig's use of the supernatural element, it is always difficult, and frequently impossible, to distinguish between possible connexions with Tieck, Hoffmann, and Dickens. It was certainly an element of Dickens' work which interested Ludwig, as the *Studien* were later to demonstrate. The prophetic, significant dreams in this story are of interest, but it is not possible to decide whether they are natural to Ludwig or if a German or an English influence must be considered; and Lüder has said what must be the last word on this subject:

> In *Zwischen Himmel und Erde* kann man nur soviel feststellen, daß Träume häufig vorkommen, die Art ihrer Verwendung — nicht der Charakter der Ausführung—deutet auf Dickens.[3]

Very much the same must be said of the psychological examination of the characters. There is no doubt that this was in essence the result of a long development of a natural interest of Ludwig; Dickens, however, may have accelerated his use of it, and just possibly have shown him new methods. The deep analysis of the motives of an action, the careful study of the apparently disconnected thoughts which pass through the minds of the characters in states of strong emotion, 'das Kommen und Gehen der Bilder, die aus dumpfem Unterbewußtsein wie Blasen aus schwärzlicher Flut aufsteigen und zergehen',[4] is proper to both writers. Examples from Ludwig are the descriptions of the state of mind of Apollonius and of Fritz, especially of the latter as the idea of the murder of his brother first germinates in his mind; and from Dickens of the emotions of Ralph Nickleby before his suicide, of Fagin at his trial, and of Carker before his death—a detail of his genius which Julian Schmidt, especially, had noticed in 1852 and which he was to examine fully in 1870. An essential difference is that, while Dickens gives just so much psychological examination

---

[1] *The Chimes*, p. 1. R. Müller-Ems, op. cit., pp. 63–4, and in J. Betz, op. cit., pp. 95–6.   [2] *Copperfield*, chapter 55. H. Lohre, op. cit., p. 41.
[3] Op. cit., p. 133.   [4] H. Lohre, op. cit., p. 43.

as is necessary to the development of the story, with Ludwig it becomes a main interest; in its use he was in advance of his time, but it cannot, unfortunately, be said that *Zwischen Himmel und Erde* is for that reason a better story, as such. Indeed, it can very well be said that it contains too much psychological examination for proper balance. Viewed as a whole, however, the story is an advance, in depth and in content (though not artistically) on *Die Heiteretei*; it showed Ludwig at work almost completely independently, and Dickens' influence can only be seen in a few stylistic mannerisms, probably maintained since they allowed the psychological character-study to be carried out with rather more directness.

It is clear, then, that Dicken's influence is most apparent in Ludwig's methods of characterization, more especially those humorous or purely comical methods employed in *Die Heiteretei* and in *Aus dem Regen in die Traufe*. It may also be traced at times in the manner in which the correct atmosphere is created for the relating of an event—sometimes, for example, by reflecting the temper of the characters by the animation of the objects around them; also, to a slight extent, in the visual nature, not only of the characterization but of the narrative itself. It is of interest to compare these conclusions with the summary of Ludwig's criticism of Dickens given above: many of these points, particularly the characterization and in less degree the creation of atmosphere, were details of Dickens' work of which, within a few years, Ludwig was to write long and usually appreciative studies.

But the danger of carrying a search for Dickens' influence too far must once more be emphasized. In almost all these matters it can be shown that the detail of technique in question was not something entirely new to Ludwig, and so it can seldom, if ever, be declared that the Englishman introduced him to fresh methods. Many of the likenesses noticed above are necessary, implicit in the nature of the two men; a few can very well be explained by reference to common literary ancestors—the sentimental novelists of the eighteenth century, for example, whose influence on the narrative methods of the German was of long duration. Ludwig's personal talent, especially for realistic description of simple circumstances, must also never be underestimated. A fair final judgement is probably that Dickens stimulated Ludwig's use of certain technical methods; some more than others, since the dramatic talent of the German made him rather more susceptible, for example, to influences from those details of Dickens' manner which caused him to write in the *Studien*: 'Die Bozischen Romane sind wahrhafte Schauspielerschulen'.[1] To Dickens also Ludwig probably owed a wider (but not deeper) appreciation of the details of everyday life, and their clear portrayal in his later work. Whether the later intensive study of Dickens might have been of value to Ludwig is quite a different question; it has been shown that the great example of the Englishman at one period definitely checked the natural development of Ludwig's own powers, as it was within a few years to be an actual hindrance to Raabe's eventual consciousness of his own genius.

[1] *Epische Studien*, pp. 66–7.

IV
WILHELM RAABE

RAABE has been called 'the German Dickens'; the unsatisfactory nature of the title is clear when it is known that he had to share it with such widely different writers as F. W. Hackländer and Fritz Reuter. Suggested comparisons between his work and that of Dickens were a commonplace in books on Raabe in the early years of the present century, but no attempt at a full summary of Dickens' influence on Raabe was published until 1915, when J. T. Geissendoerfer devoted a few pages of his thesis[1] to the subject. Almost all his details, however, were provided by the fruitful book of H. Junge: *Wilhelm Raabe: Studien über Form und Inhalt seiner Werke*,[2] which was published in 1910. It was not until 1921 that the definitive study was produced, under the title *Raabe und Dickens*, by the German authority on Raabe, Professor W. Fehse, in collaboration with Professor E. Doernenburg of the University of Pennsylvania, whose dissertation on the subject, prepared in 1908, had remained unpublished. To this detailed and penetrating book, of which the following pages give a brief summary, there is little to be added except a discussion of a few further points of detail, of slight importance, which may show a certain influence of Dickens.

There is very little direct evidence for Raabe's reading of Dickens. It is known from H. A. Krüger's book *Der Junge Raabe*[3] that Dickens' works were special favourites of Raabe's mother, and it seems likely that she may have transferred something of this appreciation to her son, who first became acquainted with them during his years as a student in Berlin (1854–6). If Krüger is to be believed—and he could speak with the authority of personal acquaintance—Raabe rated Dickens lower than Thackeray, despite the much greater popularity of the former in Germany at that time. This, however, was not to prevent a rather deeper study

[1] *Dickens' Einfluß auf Ungern-Sternberg, Heßlein, Stolle, Raabe und Ebner-Eschenbach* in *Americana-Germanica*, vol. xix, 1915, pp. 16–24. I have a note of a book by A. Schirmer; *Raabe und Dickens*, described as being in preparation in 1912, but there seems to be no further news of this: it was apparently not published.
[2] *Schriften der Literarhistorischen Gesellschaft, Bonn*, no. 9; Dortmund, 1910.
[3] Leipzig, 1911, pp. 34–5.

of Dickens which Raabe seems to have undertaken in the early sixties, though almost the only direct evidence of this is an entry in his diary mentioning the reading of *Pickwick* and *Copperfield* in July 1863. These two books together with the *Christmas Carol*, *Master Humphrey's Clock*, *Oliver Twist*, *Dombey*, *Chuzzlewit*, and *Nickleby* were among the books Raabe possessed in his later years, the last four having been acquired in 1878, 1880, 1889, and 1899 respectively.[1] These dates have little special importance, and certainly cannot be taken as indicating that Raabe then read the books in question for the first time; there are traces, for example, of *Chuzzlewit*, indeed an actual mention of it, in *Die Leute aus dem Walde*, written nearly thirty years before 1889.

It seems at least likely that Raabe read Dickens' books in the original. The standard of Raabe's knowledge of English is difficult to judge, but the many English quotations in his books make it appear probable that he had a good command of it, as of other foreign languages. H. A. Krüger gives definite information:

> Mit der Lektüre verband der junge Raabe energisch ein Sprachstudium. So las er nicht nur Thackeray, Goldsmith, und Dickens, sondern auch später Seneca, Spinoza, und manche Lateinchronik im Urtext.[2]

This assertion, however, as it regards Dickens, seems tacitly to be taken as of doubtful authority by Doernenburg and Fehse;[3] there can, consequently, be no complete reliance on his having read Dickens originally in English, so that conclusions regarding a possible influence of his methods on Raabe's use of language will be difficult to draw, since Dickens inevitably loses in translation, in which form Raabe may have studied him. The same uncertainty arises in the question of how many of Dickens' books Raabe read; it is at least definite, however, that he read all the most important, especially *Copperfield*, and likely that he read most of the others.

Apart from a notice of the 'Meister Boz' in the *Chronik der Sperlingsgasse*, the only occasion on which Raabe mentioned Dickens by name was in the story *Deutscher Adel* (1877), which is set in the winter of 1870. In the first chapter Achtermann meditates on the events of the war in France and on the recent deaths of Dumas and Dickens. At the end of the story, in the twentieth

[1] E. Doernenburg and W. Fehse, op. cit., p. 5.
[2] H. A. Krüger, op. cit., p. 35.
[3] Op. cit., p. 56.

chapter, which tells of the death of Ferrari, 'Pulvererfinder', there is a rather more explicit notice:

> Natalie Ferrari hatte sich mit einem Schrei über die ausgestreckte Leiche ihres Vaters geworfen. 'Down at last!' murmelte der Übersetzer [Wedehop]. Das war das letzte Wort eines Mannes, der durch seine Phantasie Vieles und Großes auf dieser Erde ausgerichtet hat. Charles Dickens rief es, als er vom Schlage getroffen zusammenbrach.

That can probably be taken as a section, at least, of Raabe's final opinion of Dickens. It is the only personally expressed opinion available, but there can be little doubt of its finality; by the time he wrote *Abu Telfan*, ten years before, Raabe had discovered himself and his own position relative to other authors. The brief mention in *Deutscher Adel* may be an intended recognition of this fact for the particular case of Dickens; with it, but for one exception, all clear relationship to Dickens vanishes from Raabe's work.

In the books Raabe called the 'Kinderbücher', however, that is those prior to *Abu Telfan*, there are a few fairly definite traces of themes from Dickens.[1] Raabe's first book, the *Chronik der Sperlingsgasse*, has an actual reference to the *Christmas Carol* under the date 24 December:

> Welch ein Gang war das! Die Geister, die den alten Scrooge des Meisters Boz über die Weihnachtswelt führten, hätten mich nicht besser leiten können, als Herr Ulrich Strobel.

Since Raabe himself draws this slight comparison, it is interesting to carry it a little further. The description of the Christmas walk of Wachholder and Strobel is carried out in a manner very reminiscent of that of Dickens, and the way in which the small boy Alfred is brought home to the Sperlingsgasse—on Strobel's shoulder—is just the way Bob Cratchit brings Tiny Tim home from church in the *Carol*. The little spirits of Elise's dream, related under 21 March, who take her, invisible, to a tour of the insides of the neighbouring houses, also have a savour of Dickens' elves and fairies as seen in the *Cricket on the Hearth*, both in the text and in John Leech's illustrations; the same motive, perhaps mingled with reminiscences of E. T. A. Hoffmann, was to come up once more in 1857 in the tale *Weihnachtsgeister*. Also under 21 March

---

[1] The examination of these traces is based very largely on the evidence suggested by E. Doernenburg and W. Fehse, op. cit., pp. 9–24, with some new material, and a few additions from H. Junge (op. cit.) and S. Fliess, *Wilhelm Raabe, une Étude*, Grenoble, 1912, pp. 190–206.

Raabe (in the person of Wachholder) mentions the story of a man who after great misfortunes wished to lose his memory, had his wish granted, and found his second state far more terrible than the first; that is the theme of another of Dickens' Christmas stories, *The Haunted Man* (1848). H. Junge has also pointed out[1] that the motive of the ring which proves the relationship of Gustav and Elise, and which is eventually put safely out of the way by being thrown into the river, is also to be found in *Oliver Twist*; but there is no reason to insist on this parallel.

Raabe's second tale, *Ein Frühling* (1857), contains definite traces of the influence of *Nicholas Nickleby*. This is apparent in the description of Madame Mecker's dressmaking establishment, which can be compared with that of Mrs. Mantalini; and the overseers of both, Fräulein Laura Sauer and Miss Knag, are similar, each being represented as a jealous old maid. The 'social pathos' of *Ein Frühling* doubtless also owes its origin to that of *Nickleby*; the bad conditions of work for the unfortunate girls employed by the dressmakers are emphasized in each case. As an extension of this, both books attack that form of charity to the poor which is merely a cover for curiosity; Dickens shows how it can degenerate into a search for the romantic, picturesque, and probably unworthy object, Raabe compares it to the 'Caritas der Gassen', which is the result of sympathy and fellow-feeling.

Die Leute aus dem Walde (1862) mentions *Chuzzlewit* in chapter 7 as an authoritative description of America. In this the two authorities see:

... eine Art versteckter Quellenangabe, wie sie Raabe auch sonst häufig in seinen Werken durch seine wissenschaftliche Ehrlichkeit abgenötigt wurde,

and they add that Raabe might also have mentioned *American Notes*, which were probably also a source of much of his detail.[2] Two of the minor characters of *Die Leute aus dem Walde*, Aurora Pogge and Julius Schminkert, are drawn in Dickens' best humorous manner, with rather exaggerated comedy of speech; Aurora, moreover, keeps a slightly ridiculous diary in the way Dora did in *Copperfield*, has, perhaps, something of the relations to Herr Mäuseler that Mrs. Bardell had to Mr. Pickwick, and supports vague and pointless foreign missions of the sort Dickens ridiculed

---

[1] Op. cit., p. 89.   [2] E. Doernenburg and W. Fehse, op. cit., pp. 14–15.

in *Pickwick*[1] and condemned in *Bleak House*; her diary reads, for example:

> 10. April. Beschlossen für die Mission unter die schwarzen Indianer drei Paar wollene Socken zu stricken.

Julius Schminkert has something of the free-and-easy manners of Dick Swiveller in the *Old Curiosity Shop*; the same book may have suggested the meeting of Fritz Wolf with the 'Puppentheaterdirektor' Joseph Leppel and his wife Julie, who combine the arts of Codlin and Short and their cronies, 'Grinder's lot' and Jerry, by exhibiting a marionette show, stiltwalking, and a performing dog.[2]

The life of Hans Unwirrsch, the hero of Raabe's next book, the famous *Hungerpastor* (1863), follows the same stages as that of David Copperfield, from a narrow and not very joyful childhood, through doubts and difficulties to eventual peace in a well-assorted marriage. In the middle of his work on this story Raabe re-read *Copperfield*, so that it is justifiable to search for further influence from this tale on Raabe's book. The early chapters of the *Hungerpastor* tell of the school for poor children in Neustadt and of its teacher Karl Silberlöffel; the colours in which this description is carried out are clearly reminiscent of those used by Dickens in drawing Salem House and the poor usher Mr. Mell, with something of those used for Dotheboys Hall in *Nickleby*. Hans, who like David is soon fatherless, gets on badly there; at his second school he is happier, though (and in this he is unlike David) his poverty causes loneliness. Moses Freudenstein, the young Jew whose acquaintance he makes at this stage, is occasionally reminiscent, in his relations with Hans, of Steerforth in *Copperfield*. Further, it is known that the original plan of the *Hungerpastor* envisaged a much more tragic ending to the story; it is possible that Raabe's re-reading of *Copperfield* in July 1863 caused him to abandon this scheme, especially as he also changed the original setting of the story to arrange his scene by the Baltic and so allow for the masterly description of the storm and shipwreck, clearly influenced by the same description in chapter 55 of *Copperfield*. The story of Kleophea, whose fate is here finally decided, has gained something from the story of Steerforth and Emily; and it should be noticed that this was probably not the first time Raabe used this motive from *Copperfield*, for the story of Röschen Wolke in the tale *Wer*

---

[1] Chapter 27.   [2] *Die Leute aus dem Walde*, chapter 18.
[2] Raabe, chapter 10; Dickens, chapters 16–18.

kann es wenden? of 1859 is probably based on Emily. Röschen also leaves a true but low-born friend to run away (also to Italy) with a rich young man of a higher social class.

Raabe's next tale, *Drei Federn* (1865), also shows the continued influence of *Copperfield* in one of its themes. H. Junge writes:

Pinnemann hat ganz auffallende Ähnlichkeit mit Uriah Heep in Dickens' *David Copperfield*, sowohl in seinem Charakter, wie in der Art und in dem Beruf, in welchem er diesen betätigt. Uriah Heep steht zu Wickfield in fast genau demselben Verhältnis wie Pinnemann zu Hahnenberg.[1]

Just as Heep works his way into Wickfield's confidence and eventually becomes the virtual director of his affairs, so Pinnemann gains more power over Hahnenberg until at length, by the fourth chapter, the situation is: 'Pinnemann ist der Herr geworden und August Hahnenberg der Diener.' The relations between Hahnenberg and his godson August Sonntag are, further, approximately those which existed between Martin Chuzzlewit and his uncle.

Of the mature works, *Abu Telfan* and *Der Schüdderump* show trifling parallels with some of Dickens' material, but these are of minor importance. Horacker, however, in the book of the same name written in 1875, is described in very much the same way as Jo in *Bleak House*.[2] *Fabian und Sebastian*, written in 1880, shows certain connexions with *Dombey and Son*; Sebastian Pelzmann's cold attitude to his niece Konstanze is much like Dombey's to Florence, and something of Carker's story has gone to make up that of Sebastian. The copy of *Dombey* in Raabe's library bore 1880 as its date of acquisition.

It is clear, then, that what Raabe took from Dickens was not complete characters—which would have been an impossibility for Raabe's manner of creation—and not very often finished situations, but rather purely geometrical schemes of relationship between two or more characters; he then worked out the details of the figures and the narrower details of their interplay himself. It is also clear that the material influence of Dickens was almost entirely confined to the 'Kinderbücher'; and that it was, all told, not very large.

Materially, indeed, the two writers differ, frequently very considerably, and there is full justification for the remark that, as regards the material handled, *das Trennende überwiegt bei weitem*.[3]

[1] H. Junge, op. cit., p. 111.   [2] See *Horacker*, chapter 7.
[3] E. Doernenburg and W. Fehse, op. cit., p. 24.

It is agreed that a few of the wider outlines run parallel; thus S. Fliess writes:

> Les deux romanciers ne sont à leur aise que dans la description d'une étroite intimité. Ils trouvent des détails charmants, des accents émus pour nous dire le charme de la vie peu mouvementée, dans ces milieux étroits et pittoresques dont les plaisirs et les chagrins sont tout intimes. Ils ne se lassent pas de nous décrire les impressions quotidiennes, les aventures ordinaires qui sont le fond de notre existence...[1]

Neither Dickens nor Raabe manifests much desire to portray other classes than this one he knows best; if the nobility appears, as it occasionally does, it is seen satirically for the most part. But Dickens' attitude to that lower middle class he portrays is full of a deeply-rooted sense of justice and injustice; where he finds the latter, he displays its results with a rhetorical pathos which demands reform. This was not Raabe's way; he certainly had sympathy, but he was well aware that a book with a moral mission is often a failure aesthetically. Where 'social pathos' does appear in his work (*Ein Frühling, Der Hungerpastor, Horacker*), it is almost beyond doubt the result of Dickens' influence; the three books mentioned as examples are all noticeably influenced in other ways by Dickens. The two writers touch in the excellence of their animation of nature, but in that quality only; for while Dickens allows the tone of natural phenomena to accompany and illustrate changes in personal feeling, Raabe uses his powers in this matter in a prophetic, a foreboding sense, to prepare his characters, as well as his readers, for what is to follow. In the historical novel, a genre of which Raabe was especially fond, he showed a far better feeling for the historical scene than Dickens, in whose work the historical background is usually nothing more than an external framework. There is also a difference in the place of the action in the books of the two authors; Raabe was by no means bound to one spot, as Dickens was largely to London—a restriction which admittedly produced excellent results in his work. Dickens' astonishing visual powers are a point of further difference. In Dickens' case, the unequalled visual strength of his memory allowed him to produce some wonderful pictures, but was too great to allow him time for depth or room for the psychological development of his characters. Raabe balanced his use of detail better, and minute descriptions in

---

[1] S. Fliess, op. cit., p. 199.

Dickens' manner are seldom to be found in his mature works, while his characters, drawn from all classes and types and realistically described as were those of Dickens, are less set, more complete; even the purely comic characters of his earlier books. These, however, do show the influence of Dickens' methods of characterization: stereotyped expressions and phrases; peculiarities of speech; the use of significant names, and possibly the misformation of learned and foreign words. *Die Leute aus dem Walde*, as was seen, and also *Christoph Pechlin* give examples of this.[1]

There are a few further points in the style of Raabe's earlier works which may show an influence of Dickens. Discursive and humorous or satirical chapter-headings, of the type Dickens favoured, can occasionally be found in Raabe; for example, in *Die Leute aus dem Walde*. H. Junge suggested[2] that Raabe may have remembered the example of Dickens in inserting short tales into his novels, a device employed in *Pickwick* and *Nickleby* among other books. It is important, however, to remember that in content and effect the inserted tales are quite different; those of Dickens serve generally for contrast with the larger story, those of Raabe for emphasis of its tone. For this reason H. Richter[3] does not accept Junge's suggestion. Junge also proposed the example of Dickens for the digressions made by Raabe personally on various phrases in his books, such as those on 'Unser Herr!' and 'Sein eigner Herr sein!' in the *Hungerpastor*.[4] The repetition of long titles and of names, the piling of adjectives, the use of rhetorical exclamations and invocations, to be found in Raabe's earlier books, may also perhaps be attributed to Dickens. There are also some early parallels in general form; the 'Kinderbücher' show those romantic touches, the wide range of story, the crowd of characters, associated with Dickens as well as Scott.

All these points of style and composition occur in Raabe's early work, but they were methods which Raabe soon surpassed. In composition particularly his mature books excel those of Dickens;

---

[1] The chapter on 'Humor und Komik' in E. Doernenburg and W. Fehse, op. cit., pp. 41–9, should be read with due regard for the different senses of the words 'Humor' as understood by a German and 'Humour' as understood by an Englishman. Much of Raabe's 'Humor' is not in the least humorous in the general English sense.

[2] Op. cit., p. 29.

[3] *Untersuchungen zum Stil Wilhelm Raabes* (Diss. Greifswald), Stettin, 1935, p. 73, footnote. [4] See H. Junge, op. cit., p. 29.

they are more carefully planned, and all the details contribute to the progress of the main theme, which is worked out completely logically. There lies a major difference from Dickens.

It was because Raabe's inventive powers were not strong that he borrowed, in his earliest attempts, from other writers, and particularly from Dickens. These earliest works did not satisfy him, and he turned later to the 'Erziehungsroman', attempting, as was recently demonstrated,[1] a synthesis of the methods of Goethe and Dickens as seen in *Wilhelm Meister* and *Copperfield*—'Goethes heitere Lebenstiefe und Dickens' buntbewegte Lebensweite zu einer neuen Einheit zu verschmelzen'. *Die Leute aus dem Walde* was the result of this attempt, but this too, he found, was not his natural theme; and with that discovery the way was open for him to find the proper channel for the expression of himself. That he had found by the time he wrote *Abu Telfan*, and from that time his development was unhesitating and steady.

It was only in his early years of hesitation that he allowed himself to be influenced by the great example of Dickens; and he found that example, if anything, misleading, since it drew him away for some time from his proper path and so concealed his own powers from him. His deviation from Dickens' way and the subsequent development of his powers are clearly summarized by S. Fliess:[2]

Raabe s'est vite affranchi de l'influence de son modèle; il le surpasse sous bien des rapports. Car Dickens, observant la vie, prend plaisir au jeu de l'élaboration poétique des mille détails qu'il a vus; il devient un conteur de génie. Raabe, lui, prend conscience de la façon dont il envisage les choses et devient philosophe en observant la vie.

[1] W. Fehse, *Wilhelm Raabe, sein Leben und seine Werke*, Braunschweig, 1937, pp. 188 f.
[2] Op. cit., p. 206.

V

FRITZ REUTER

IT is known from Reuter's letters, as well as from other sources, that he took a certain interest in English literature. He there mentions Walter Scott, as having had the greatest influence on him;[1] the poetry of Robert Burns, as an example of dialect verse;[2] Goldsmith's *Vicar of Wakefield*,[3] and Macaulay's *Frederick the Great*.[4] From other sources it is known that he was acquainted with some plays of Shakespeare[5] and with books of Marryat and Carlyle.[6] His letters also give the information that, for some time at least, he studied English; but his progress does not seem to have been sufficient to enable him to read the *Vicar of Wakefield* in the original, nor, apparently, to judge an English translation of his own *Franzosentid*.[7]

The direct evidence for his acquaintance with Dickens' works in particular, however, is scanty, and nowhere gives us the actual name of a book by Dickens read by Reuter. The first twelve volumes of the Lorck edition of Dickens, however, were in Reuter's library at Eisenach;[8] this included all the books up to *Hard Times*, and it can be assumed, as will be shown, that Reuter had read most if not all of these. His letters do not mention Dickens, but most of his biographers say, chiefly in connexion with his stay at Thalberg, that Dickens was one of his favourite authors.[9] Their source for this was probably Reuter's friend Fritz Peters, who would be able to give reliable information; both A. Wilbrandt and K. T. Gaedertz discussed Reuter with him. The most interesting account is that given by Gaedertz:[10]

Außer der Zeichenkunst besaß Reuter die Gabe des Mimens und

---

[1] *Briefe*, hrsg. O. Weltzien, Leipzig, n.d., 20 Dec. 1862 (p. 472).
[2] Loc. cit., Jan. 1863 (p. 473).   [3] Loc. cit., 19 Oct. 1839 (p. 214).
[4] Loc. cit., 11 April 1867 (p. 685).
[5] See, e.g., *Stromtid*, chapter 10.
[6] H. Geist, *Fritz Reuters literarische Beziehungen zu Charles Dickens*, Diss. Halle, 1913, p. 7.
[7] *Briefe*, 26 Nov. 1834 (p. 84); 19 Oct. 1839 (p. 214); 24 July 1867 (p. 694).
[8] H. Geist, op. cit., p. 5, footnote 1.
[9] e.g. A. Wilbrandt, *Fritz Reuters Leben und Werke* (foreword to Reuter's *Sämmtliche Werke, Volksausgabe*, Wismar, 1877), p. 27; K. T. Gaedertz, *Reuterstudien*, Wismar, 1899, p. 201; A. Römer, *Fritz Reuter in seinem Leben und Schaffen*, Berlin, 1896, p. 57.   [10] Op. cit., p. 201.

Vorlesens. Häufig verschönte er die Winterabende auf Thalberg durch kleine Vorstellungen... Noch genußreicher war sein Vorlesen, zumal von Boz-Dickens und Walter Scott, oder richtiger sein Vortrag, sein Nacherzählen, Stunden lang. 'Oft haben wir sein riesiges Gedächtnis bewundert' sagte mir Peters, 'wenn er wie an der Schnur aus den englischen Romanen, welche er auf der Festung gelesen, alle, sogar die Nebenpersonen, herzunennen wußte.'

There is only this indirect evidence that Reuter read Dickens' books while he was in prison, but various passages in his letters show that he carried on what work he could there, and that he was allowed several newspapers and a good many books.[1] He had greater freedom at Dömitz than elsewhere, and it was probably there that he read at least the *Pickwick Papers*. He was freed in October 1840, by which time the first four of Dickens' books had appeared in German translation: the *Sketches*, *Pickwick*, *Oliver Twist*, and *Nickleby*.

A. Römer, in his book *Fritz Reuter in seinem Leben und Schaffen*,[2] provides the rest of the evidence for Reuter's acquaintance with Dickens' books and his opinion of them. He prints an amusing *Julklappgedicht*, written by Reuter for Fritz Peters, whose present to his wife one Christmas was a set of Dickens' books:

> An meine Maria:
>> Lämming, Lämming, zürne nicht!
>> Endlich dies mein Weibchen kriegt!
>> Dies ist, denk' ich, für mein Weib
>> Wunderschöner Zeitvertreib;
>> Doch hat draußen sie zu tun,
>> Laß' sie diesen Inhalt ruh'n;
>> Doch hat Zeit sie, les' sie trotz
>> Aller Kinderunruh — Boz!

But he also recalls an incident which shows that Reuter was certainly no blind admirer of all that Dickens produced:

> Die Schwächen des Verfassers der *Pickwickier* müssen ihm, bei aller Vorliebe für den geistesverwandten englischen Realisten, doch nicht entgangen sein. Als er mal Frau Peters um ein Buch bat und sie ihm einen Roman von Dickens reichte, wies er ihn zurück, und meinte: Nach Boz frag' ich nicht mehr; gleich aber fügte er hinzu: Na geben Sie mir das Buch nur, Boz ist doch ein guter Schriftsteller!

[1] *Briefe* for 26.11.34, 10.10.38, 5.12.38, 10.2.39.
[2] Berlin, 1896, pp. 57–8.

Reuter, another of those German authors named *der deutsche Boz* (although this was sometimes specialized in his case to *der plattdeutsche Dickens*), was compared with Dickens as early as 1874 by A. Wilbrandt;[1] not many years after this the first suggestions of actual influence of Dickens on Reuter were made. There had never been any doubt of the similarity in outlook and production of the two men; certain passages of Gustav Freytag's *Charakteristik* of Reuter, written on his death in 1874, can so well be applied to Dickens that they read, *mutatis mutandis*, like actual extracts from an appreciation of Dickens by, say, Julian Schmidt. The following are the outstanding examples:

> Freilich war er einer von den Glücklichen, bei denen der Leser gern die Kunst über dem strotzenden Reichtum der Naturkraft vergißt. Fast zahllos sind die Charaktere aus dem Volke, die er dargestellt, und jeder mit einer Fülle von originalen Zügen ausgestattet, ganz unbegrenzt erscheint sein Reichtum an ernsten und komischen Situationen. Ihm war die schönste Gottesgabe verliehen, der Humor. Ein echt deutscher Humor, in welchem über der launigen Darstellung menschlicher Beschränkung und Verkehrtheit überall die herzliche Liebe zu den Menschen fühlbar wird....
>
> ... Den kleineren Kreisen des Volkslebens ... hat dieser Dichter die Familie, das Hauswesen, die Arbeit verklärt wie kein anderer. Hunderttausende haben durch ihn das Bewußtsein erhalten, wie tüchtig und brav ihre Existenz ist, wie viel Wärme, Liebe und Poesie auch in ihrem mühevollen Leben zu Tage kommt. Sie alle sind durch ihn freier, reicher und glücklicher geworden.[2]

Freytag did not point out the parallel with Dickens, as he might well have done if he had remembered Julian Schmidt's appreciation of *Pickwick*, for example, which showed, it will be recalled, for Schmidt:

> ... handgreiflich vor Augen, ... wie viel Freude, Schönheit und Idealismus in dem ganz gewöhnlichen Leben zu finden sei.[3]

or his own of the same book, where he described:

> ... die schöne Wirkung ..., welche das Buch auf Männer und Frauen ausübte.... Hunderttausenden gab das Buch frohe Stunden, gehobene Stimmung....[4]

---

[1] Op. cit., 1877, p. 76; this essay was first published in 1874.
[2] G. Freytag, *Gesammelte Aufsätze*, Leipzig, 1888, vol. ii, pp. 208–9.
[3] J. Schmidt, *Boz (Dickens), eine Charakteristik*, Leipzig, 1852, p. 24.
[4] G. Freytag, op. cit., vol. ii, p. 241.

But the long passage quoted will in any case serve as a justification of the following suggestions of direct and indirect influence of Dickens on Reuter.

The matter has been very thoroughly studied by H. Geist in his doctorate thesis *Fritz Reuters literarische Beziehungen zu Charles Dickens*, published at Halle in 1913; with the exception of some of the foregoing remarks, there is little to add to the results of his investigation, on which the following pages are very largely based, though they have been supplemented on occasion by various incidental remarks from H. A. Eckholt's *Untersuchungen über die Romantechnik Fritz Reuters*, a Münster dissertation of 1912 which Geist does not appear to have known.

A proper appreciation of the likeness in outlook of the two men will show in how many ways Reuter agreed with Dickens' general views, and consequently how sympathetic he must have found most of Dickens' books; which, in turn, will be further justification for the suggestion that they influenced his work.

Dickens confined his attention almost entirely to the middle and lower classes, with the admitted object of bettering the conditions of the ignorant and poor. His pictures of the aristocracy are failures, and the few members of this class to appear in his books come off as badly as most of the kings in his *Child's History of England*. He also frequently criticized the government of the country. These characteristics of his work were specially agreeable to Reuter. He, too, had more sympathy for the middle and lower classes, and he had reason to disagree with the government of his country. Most of his characters are inhabitants of country towns, owners of small properties, village parsons, country labourers; and these he supports (the best example is naturally *Kein Hüsung*) against the upper class. He expressly denies any 'distinguished' (*vornehm*) qualities to his work, and compares his poems to healthy young street-urchins.[1]

The fact that both writers were realists in description did not prevent them from being idealists in the general plan of their books; idealists, because they show life as they think it should be, not as it is. In their books, almost without exception, the good wins in the end and the bad characters get their deserts. In Dickens' books this system of poetic justice is frequently carried to

[1] In the foreword to the first edition of his *Läuschen un Rimels* (1853).

extremes; it often spoils his work artistically, but it does ensure the necessary happy ending. There is no doubt that Reuter agreed entirely with this method, which he naturally introduced into his own novels; but it would certainly be wrong to insist, as H. Geist does,[1] that he imitated Dickens in doing so. An insistence on poetic justice was so much in the spirit of the age that a following of its principles was almost automatic in such writers. It is also very unlikely that both were forced by public taste to use this method; certainly the public tried to influence both writers—in Dickens' case, for instance, to prevent him from 'killing' Smike, Paul Dombey, Little Nell; but these were only particular cases, and in general, so far from there being any question of external compulsion, both writers were in agreement with the ideas of their public. In studying this point of relationship it is interesting to see how both agreed with each other and with contemporary public taste in showing evil as evil, and in refusing to give it an attractive colour; the books of both men were known for the fact that they could be put without danger into the hands of 'the young person'. One may compare, for example, the well-known passage in the preface to *Pickwick*, where Dickens expresses the hope that there is neither expression nor scene in the book which might hurt the feelings or bring a blush to the face even of the most sensitive reader, and the following letter of Reuter:

... un hir min Hand, dat ick meindag' nich so 'n ungesunnes Tüg as dat Gutzkowsche un Suesche oder gar so 'ne verleiwten Zoterien schriwen will, de Sei Ehren lütten Schäne un Itze nich in de Hand gewen känen.[2]

A further similarity can be found in the religious views of the two men; Reuter whole-heartedly agreed with Dickens in denouncing fanaticism and dogma, and in demanding simple and effective Christianity.

The influence of Dickens can be seen beyond much doubt both in Reuter's technique and material. It has also been suggested that Dickens had some influence on Reuter's use of dialect in his books; this is less certain and less important, though Dickens was certainly an example, even if not a model, for Reuter in this respect. When Klaus Groth attacked Reuter, in 1858,[3] for mixing High and Low German in his *Läuschen un Rimels*, Reuter replied with a pamphlet

[1] Op. cit., p. 37. [2] *Briefe*, 21 July 1864 (p. 558).
[3] *Briefe über Hochdeutsch und Plattdeutsch*, Kiel, 1858, p. 160.

entitled *Abweisung der Ungerechten Angriffe und Unwahren Behauptungen, welche Dr. Klaus Groth . . . gegen mich gerichtet hat*, in which there is this interesting sentence:

> Wenn ich mich dieserhalb [i.e. against this particular criticism by Groth] zu verteidigen brauchte, so könnte ich mich auf Shakespeare (Dr. Cajus: Evans: *Lustige Weiber* u.s.w.), auf Walter Scott, auf Dickens, auf Lessing (*Minna von Barnhelm*), Goethe (*Götz*), Schiller (Capuzinerpredigt) berufen. . . .[1]

This reference to Dickens is one of the very few made by Reuter in his published works. It is of interest to see that as many English authors are quoted as there are German.

It is in Reuter's technique of characterization that Dickens' influence can be most clearly seen. In his books, as in those of Dickens, the characters, who are mostly either very good or very bad, are completely described to the reader at their first appearance, and before they begin to take part in the action of the story. Both authors make use of descriptive names, which give a general impression of the character from the start: Brass, Barnacle, Podsnap, Murdstone ('Murderer, or a name like it', says David's aunt), for example, in Dickens, and in Reuter the merchant Kurz, Nüßler (*nüßlich = lässig*), and Bräsig himself, whose name summons up the impression of a man with a fresh red face.[2] A description of the character's expression and clothing is next given, and these external traits usually correspond with the temper and disposition of the character; in this case the method is simply to make a good character look pleasing, a bad character repulsive. There is occasionally a comparison to an animal; thus Carker in *Dombey and Son* is compared to a cat, the notary Slus'uhr in Reuter's *Stromtid* to a grey rat.

It is in this book that Reuter's use of introductory characterization is most apparent. H. A. Eckholt shows that Reuter developed this point of technique through his successive books; not complete in the *Franzosentid*, it is at its best in the *Stromtid*, where he gave himself:

> . . . die größte Mühe, auf irgend eine Art das Auftreten charakteristisch zu gestalten; jede neue Person sollte sogleich das individuelle Gepräge zeigen, das ihr dann auch die ganze Erzählung hindurch anhaftet.[3]

[1] *Abweisung*, &c., Berlin, 1858, pp. 22–3. The question of Dickens' influence on Reuter's use of dialect is examined by H. Geist, op. cit., pp. 8–14.
[2] H. Geist, op. cit., pp. 18–19.   [3] H. A. Eckholt, op. cit., pp. 71, 76.

The characterization is continued by various methods, three of which should be noticed as common to Dickens and Reuter. The surroundings of the characters are usually shown as being in conformity with the characters themselves, homely and cheerful, rich and uncomfortable, or dirty and evil. A more common method is to give a character a peculiar gesture or action, and to continue to call attention to it. Both authors make frequent use of this; for Reuter it was:

. . . ein wesentliches Mittel, den Dialog anschaulicher, lebendiger, dramatischer zu gestalten. . . . Wir hören seine Personen nicht nur reden, wir sehen sie auch geradezu leibhaft vor Augen durch ihre Gesten, ihren Gesichtsausdruck. . . . Die Personen bewegen sich je nach ihrem Charakter, Temperament, Stand u.s.w., verschieden.[1]

It will be remembered that Otto Ludwig noticed and praised this very point in Dickens' technique. The third method is that of characterization by speech, most frequently used by both authors; the most obvious parallel is in the use of dialect, though it is dangerous to insist on this point, as Low German was in any case a natural medium for Reuter's characters. Of less importance is the mispronunciation of foreign or learned words by uneducated characters, a method of both Reuter and Dickens for comic effect.[2] Of characterization by speech H. A. Eckholt says:[3]

Sie ist für Reuter ein ganz hervorragendes technisches Mittel zur Charakterisierung . . . Wenn er eine humorvolle Person zeichnen will, hebt er sie dadurch charakteristisch hervor, daß er sie mit typischen Redensarten ausstattet oder ihr überhaupt ein Lieblingsthema zuweist, auf das sie bei allen passenden und unpassenden Gelegenheiten zurückkommt.

This was also a point of Dickens' technique described and praised in much the same words, as was shown in a preceding chapter, by Otto Ludwig.

Several of these parallels are probably no more than coincidences; some can be explained as being part of the common stock of literary methods, or by reference once more to common literary ancestors, such as Walter Scott, from whom both Dickens and Reuter learnt much; but the cumulative effect of the evidence is strongly for the conclusion that Dickens was Reuter's model for much of his technical machinery.

[1] H. A. Eckholt, op. cit., pp. 92–3.
[2] From the *Stromtid* for example; Stickstoff > Stinkstoff: Phönix > Ponix = Pony, &c. [3] Op. cit., p. 77.

H. Geist studied the question of Dickens' material influence on Reuter in great detail in Section VI of his thesis. The *Allgemeine Deutsche Biographie*[1] had declared as early as 1889:

Die geistige Verwandtschaft mit dem Liebling des reiferen Mannes, mit Boz, zeigt die *Stromtid* am deutlichsten,

and it is clear from Geist's research that the *Pickwick Papers* had a quite noticeable influence on this book. Particularly noteworthy is the influence of Mr. Pickwick himself on the formation of the character of Zacharias Bräsig. Geist shows the development of this character, mentioning possible traces as early as 1846, and more obvious ones in the comedy *Onkel Jakob und Onkel Jochen* (1856); he then follows the character via the *Unterhaltungsblatt* and the *Abenteuer des Entspekter Bräsig* to the *Stromtid*. An interesting paragraph incidental to the comedy *Onkel Jakob und Onkel Jochen* points out that Onkel Jochen, already quite a Pickwickian character, has a servant named Samuel, with whom his relations are exactly those of Pickwick with Sam Weller, and whom he eventually helps to marry the housekeeper Marianne, as Pickwick helped Sam to marry the servant Mary.[2]

The most interesting parallels are to be found in the *Stromtid* itself, in which Bräsig, like Mr. Pickwick in Dickens' book, plays an essential part in holding together the different themes of the story. H. Geist[3] mentions nine similar situations in the two books, some more striking than others; a few examples may be given.

In the sixth chapter of the *Pickwick Papers* Dickens tells how Pickwick played cards with Mr. Wardle's mother, Mr. Miller, and a 'fat gentleman'. Mistakes during the game were taken as personal insults by the 'fat gentleman', and it was only after some time that he offered Mr. Pickwick snuff 'with the air of a man who had made up his mind to a Christian forgiveness of injuries sustained'. The occasion on which Bräsig, Hawermann, Kurz, and the Rektor play a game of Boston together recalls the scene in *Pickwick* closely, and Kurz acts in much the same way as the fat gentleman; the Rektor, who is not a good player, makes a mistake: ' "Lieber Schwager", säd de Rekter, "ich komme auch noch".—"Äwer tau späd", säd Kurz, un namm de Korten wedder up mit en deipen Süfzer, as hadd de Rekter em nichtswürdig behandelt, hei wull 't äwer as Christ dragen.'[4]

[1] Vol. xxviii, p. 325.
[2] H. Geist, op. cit., p. 26.
[3] Op. cit., pp. 27-30.
[4] *Stromtid*, chapter 22.

The marriage of Mr. Wardle's daughter Bella can be compared in several respects to the account of Mining's marriage to Rudolf.[1] Pickwick in one, Bräsig in the other, give the bride away, and in both cases a humorous description tells how they join in the dancing despite their age.

R. M. Meyer, in an article entitled *Zu Reuters 'Stromtid'; zwei Quellennachweise*,[2] had already discussed a possible parallel between Chapter 18 of the *Stromtid* and Chapter 39 of *Pickwick*. In one, Bräsig climbs a tree to watch Lining meet Gottlieb and Mining meet Rudolf: in the other, Mr. Pickwick climbs a garden wall and shelters under a tree for a moment to speak to Arabella about Mr. Winkle. The parallel is not strong, for there are many essential differences in the situations; and Geist rightly says of this:

Wenn man mit Meyer hier an einer Übernahme Dickensscher Motive durch Reuter festhalten will, so würde gerade diese Stelle deutlich beweisen, wie frei Reuters Phantasie die aus seiner früheren Lektüre stammenden Reminiszenzen verarbeitete und wie seine dichterische Schaffenskraft sie seinen besonderen Zielen anpaßte.[3]

And this is his conclusion on all the parallels he discusses.

A few other possible influences on the matter of Reuter's books may be added. The tale *Woans ick tau 'ne Fru kamm* describes a man who falls asleep on Christmas eve, sees ghosts and spirits in a dream, learns better ways from them, and awakens a changed character. The parallel with Scrooge in the *Christmas Carol*, Trotty Veck in the *Chimes*, or possibly with Gabriel Grub in Chapter 29 of *Pickwick* should be noticed. There are further possible parallels between Simon Tappertit of *Barnaby Rudge* and Fritz Triddelfitz in the *Stromtid*. Finally, Dickens' *Hard Times* should be mentioned as having most probably been of deciding influence on the formation of *Kein Hüsung*, the verse epic which Reuter considered his best production, which was published three years after *Hard Times*, and which, like that book, deals with an aspect of the injustice of the employer to the labourer.[4]

It is not of great value to insist on these parallels. Reuter found rich material for his stories in his own life, in the lives of friends and acquaintances, and in the traditions and gossip of his own

---

[1] *Pickwick*, chapter 28. *Stromtid*, chapter 41.
[2] *Jahrbuch des Vereins für Niederdeutsche Sprachforschung*, vol. xxii (1896), pp. 131–2.   [3] Op. cit., p. 30.   [4] H. Geist, op. cit., pp. 30–5.

province, and it is not of much importance that he did occasionally borrow, consciously or not, from memories of his reading. It was, as has been shown, in matters of technique that Reuter was most indebted to Dickens; and this is easy to understand. For Reuter only came to the novel comparatively late in life, when he had still to learn the technicalities of the genre; and, given the strong affinities in temper and outlook between the two men, it was natural that he should turn to Dickens' books, which he enjoyed and which showed masterly powers of characterization, to learn what he could from their composition.

VI
FRIEDRICH SPIELHAGEN

OF all the authors considered in this section Spielhagen was the best acquainted with the English language and one of the most widely and carefully read students of English literature. In his long searching for the right kind of occupation, he had studied the language, for example, during his years at Bonn; he refers to this once or twice in his autobiography,[1] telling how he used to search out English students to help him with his pronunciation. All these, he says,[2] had some comical peculiarity: 'Sie machten mir in ihrer Schrullenhaftigkeit den Eindruck, als seien sie geraden Weges aus den *Pickwickiern* oder sonst einem Dickens'schen Roman ins wirkliche Leben getreten.'

His English was, indeed, so good that in 1854 it helped him to a schoolmaster's post in Leipzig; and he says, with pardonable pride, 'Als die (erste) Lektion beendet war, gratulierte mir der Direktor zu dem fließenden Englisch, das ich für einen Deutschen mit anerkennenswerter Korrektheit gesprochen habe.'[3] The first works he ever published were translations from English—four books in all (for example, 1857: Emerson's *English Traits*); his first German work, *Klara Vere*, was influenced by Tennyson's *Lady Clara Vere de Vere* (via Freiligrath, admittedly), and the action took place, in the first version, in England. His command of the language was so good that at this time he undertook to translate a collection of German folk-songs into English; the translations were published by an American firm in 1855. Metre, style, and sense were all followed closely.

He was widely read in English literature; Shakespeare, Fielding, Smollett, Sterne, Goldsmith, Scott, Byron, Thackeray, Bulwer-Lytton, George Eliot, he knew well, and there are innumerable references in his critical works to most of them, together with a special essay on Thackeray, whose work he always thoroughly enjoyed. Dickens he knew from a very early time; he and Goldsmith were the first authors he read in the original English. With such an excellent knowledge of the language he of course continued to read Dickens in English; all the references to Dickens'

---
[1] *Finder und Erfinder: Erinnerungen*, Leipzig, 1890; 2 vols.
[2] Op. cit., vol. i, p. 335.   [3] Op. cit., vol. ii, p. 264.

books in, for example, Spielhagen's *Beiträge zur Theorie und Technik des Romans*[1] are to the Tauchnitz English editions. During the winter term 1850–1 at Berlin, his deep interest in the nature and place of humour caused him to read widely, not only German authors such as Jean Paul and Thümmel, but Fielding and Thackeray, and to re-read those books of Dickens which he already knew, with extreme care and a growing enjoyment.

An example of this enjoyment can be found in his account of the pleasure with which he read *David Copperfield*, which at that time had just completed publication:

> Ich war bei meinen englischen Studien ein eifriger Leser und enthusiastischer Bewunderer von Dickens geworden. Eben war sein wundervoller *Copperfield* erschienen, den ich verschlang.
>
> Als er [Bernhard Schallehn, a close friend] zu Weihnachten auf vierzehn Tage nach Haus reiste, saß ich Tag und Nacht, um ihn bei seiner Rückkehr mit einem mächtigen Stück Übersetzung des *Copperfield* überraschen zu können, da er kein Englisch verstand, eine gedruckte Übertragung noch nicht erschienen war, und er doch auch das köstliche Buch, soweit in meinen Kräften lag, genießen sollte.[2]

He rated English authors higher than the French, of whom, among the moderns, he only really appreciated George Sand; and he writes: 'Selbst die köstliche *Consuelo*, für die ich doch wahrhaftig redlich geschwärmt habe, würde ich hingeben, wenn ich *Copperfield* dafür behalte.'[3] Later, however, when he had 'discovered' Cervantes, he was to place *Don Quixote* even higher than *Copperfield*, both for humour and for narrative skill.[4]

During his six years at Leipzig (1854–60) Spielhagen contributed several articles to Gustav Kühne's periodical *Europa: Chronik der gebildeten Welt*, most of which are reprinted in one form or another in his various collections. His autobiography gives the information that one essay was on Dickens, which was, however, not reprinted, as he afterwards found it unsatisfactory.[5] A search in the copies of *Europa* for the years 1854–60 revealed comparatively little on Dickens, and only one article concerning him which is definitely by Spielhagen; this is entitled *Dickens und Thackeray*, and appeared in the issue for 7 May 1859. It only contains a certain amount which cannot be found in the published works, and if this is, indeed,

[1] Pub. Leipzig, 1883.
[2] *Finder und Erfinder*, vol. i, pp. 377, 383.
[3] Op. cit., vol. ii, p. 158.
[4] Op. cit., vol. ii, p. 283.
[5] Op. cit., vol. ii, p. 330.

the article referred to, there seems to be little reason for the refusal to have it reprinted. Parts of it were to reappear in 1867 in a lecture given by Spielhagen on Thackeray, printed in his *Vermischte Schriften*.[1] These two essays, together with references in the *Beiträge* and in *Finder und Erfinder*, are the sources of our evidence for Spielhagen's general estimation of Dickens and particular valuation of Dickens' books.

Spielhagen was always interested in the nature of humour, and had given much time to a study of it. His essay *Der Humor*, written in 1858 and published in the *Vermischte Schriften* in 1872,[2] gives a general idea of his conclusions; but his views were frequently altered as he grew older. The *Europa* essay is chiefly a contribution to the study of the nature of humour and its difference from satire, examined in the works of Dickens and Thackeray; and the general literary valuations of Dickens are in consequence largely incidental and usually in comparison with Thackeray.

Spielhagen compares the personality of the two authors, and sums up his comparison with the words:

[Thackeray] fordert durch seine mannhaften Eigenschaften, seinen Haß gegen alles Kleinliche, Unwürdige, Niedrige, unsere Hochachtung; den Andern [Dickens] achten wir nicht weniger, aber wir lieben ihn mehr.[3]

He shows that the real field of both writers is the everyday life of their time, praises their remarkable powers of observation, and points out what a fruitful ground they have for the use of these powers in the great town of London. As to the results of this use, Spielhagen maintains 'daß Thackeray gerade wegen seiner allzu daguerreotypartigen Genauigkeit in der Prosa stecken bleibt, und Dickens, weil er den Mut hat, die Häßlichkeit bis zum Extrem zu treiben, wahrhaft poetisch wirkt'.[4]

The long discussion of the difference between humour and satire concludes: 'so scheint uns der Beruf Dickens' zum Humor ebenso ausgesprochen, wie der Thackeray's zur Satire'.[5] This was an opinion still held by Spielhagen in 1867, when he repeated it in the lecture on Thackeray, and presumably still in 1872, when the lecture was printed.[6] It is to illustrate this that he examines Dickens' work in columns 648-50 of the *Europa* essay. The basis

---
[1] Leipzig, 1872, pp. 221–58.
[2] pp. 153–72.
[3] Col. 642.   [4] Col. 644.   [5] Col. 648.
[6] In *Vermischte Schriften* (cit.), p. 256.

of this study is the view that 'Der Humor versöhnt und will versöhnen'; and Spielhagen reaches a conclusion which was to be also that of Taine: 'Dickens' sämtliche Schriften sind nur eine lange Paraphrase des Testaments des Johannes: Kinderchen, liebet euch unter einander. — Wenn Dickens den Menschen definieren sollte, so würde er ihn ein Geschöpf nennen, welches lieben kann und soll.' That is why he does not classify according to culture or social standing, 'sondern nach dem Mehr oder Weniger von Liebe, das in den Menschen mächtig ist'; and that is why he champions the simple, the witless, the oppressed against all injustice, showing that although these are poor in many things, they are often rich in charity.

In diesem Doppelscheine, dieser wechselnden Beleuchtung, die bald die dürftige Hülle, bald den inneren Reichtum hervortreten läßt, liegt zum großen Teil das Geheimnis des Zaubers, mit dem uns Dickens für Personen zu interessieren weiß, die auf der untersten Stufe gesellschaftlicher und geistiger Kultur stehen, ja selbst für Blödsinnige, wenn er will.

Spielhagen shows the reconciling power of Dickens' theme in the portrayal of eccentrics, hypocrites—even criminals, for here as elsewhere 'er muß mit uns hineinspringen in den finsteren Schlund, muß uns zeigen, daß der Becher der Liebe selbst dort nicht verloren ist'.

A few new points were added to his valuation of Dickens in the 1867 lecture on Thackeray, where he maintains that Dickens 'viel mehr durch die Phantasie auf die Phantasie, das heißt künstlerisch wirkt',[1] and that the thread of his tales is more closely spun than that of Thackeray's, because he does not need to be discursively satirical. But both Dickens and Thackeray fall short of a possible ideal, because they find it distasteful to occupy themselves with the 'Sphären des philosophischen, künstlerischen, politischen Denkens'. This 'Scheu vor dem Geiste und seinen Taten' robs their work of many of the most interesting and important themes. It is, says Spielhagen, a defect shared by almost the whole of contemporary English literature.

In his *Beiträge zur Theorie und Technik des Romans*, published in 1883, Spielhagen also speaks of Dickens' astonishing powers of observation, which are applied not only to men but to their daily surroundings, an essential extension; Dickens possesses not only

[1] p. 256.

this 'Conditio sine qua non des epischen Poeten in höchstem Maße', but also 'mit dieser Grundbedingung in analogem Grade das, was ihn selbstverständlich erst zum Poeten macht: Phantasie'.[1] Elsewhere Spielhagen remarks that 'selbst Thackeray, ja — ich wage es zu sagen — selbst Dickens — sie haften, mit der Geistes- und Gemütstiefe dieser unserer Dichter [Freytag, Auerbach] verglichen, an der Oberfläche des Lebens, haben einen banausischen Anstrich';[2] he nevertheless feels Dickens, with Goethe and Goldsmith, to be the 'Epiker von Gottes Gnaden'.[3]

Finally, it should be noticed that an incidental comparison in his autobiography places the characters of *Copperfield* and those of *Wilhelm Meister* side by side—these works are chosen as being typical of their authors in their methods of characterization—and shows that Dickens' strongly individual characters and the typical characters of Goethe can be equally true and lifelike.[4]

With the exception of *Copperfield*, few of Dickens' books receive much particular criticism. The *Pickwick Papers* and *Copperfield* are the most frequently mentioned, and it will be shown that there are traces of these two, especially of the latter, in Spielhagen's own works. In all, nine of Dickens' books are mentioned in various essays and articles. The *Sketches by Boz* are noted as the first signs of Dickens' genius,[5] and among these first *novellistische Skizzen* are counted the *Pickwick Papers*. Elsewhere Spielhagen asks 'Wer vergißt jemals... Pickwick und Sam Weller?', and mentions the *Pickwick Papers* as characteristic of Dickens' genius.[6] *Oliver Twist* and *Nickleby* are quoted in connexion with *Copperfield* as examples of how the various heroes of a novelist frequently resemble one another—to prove that even the greatest novelists frequently portray their own character in that of their central figures, with more or less truth, but with largely temporal differences.[7] *Barnaby Rudge* is mentioned as an example of Dickens' skill in drawing the London scene;[8] the death of Carker in *Dombey and Son* to show how the mechanical age gives the novelist a wide selection of quite new effects which, with skill, he may use in his books;[9] and the

[1] p. 227.   [2] p. 262.   [3] p. 235.
[4] *Finder und Erfinder*, vol. ii, p. 221.   [5] *Beiträge*, 1883, p. 227.
[6] *Vermischte Schriften*, 1872, pp. 252, 230.
[7] *Beiträge*, p. 187.   [8] *Vermischte Schriften*, p. 224.
[9] *Neue Beiträge zur Theorie und Technik der Epik und Dramatik*, Leipzig, 1898, p. 49.

Europa essay speaks of the *Abgrund von Scheußlichem* in *Bleak House* and *Hard Times*.[1]

But of all Dickens' books *Copperfield* occupied Spielhagen most; it has already been shown with what enthusiasm he greeted it on its appearance in Germany. He perpetually refers to it, especially in his essay on the 'Ich-Roman', as an example of what a book should be, as the highest achievement of the contemporary novel. It fitted his theory of the 'Ich-Roman' exactly, and since he read it in the years when his theory was evolving, it is possible that it influenced the development of his valuation of this class of novel.

His rather peculiar theory was that true genius is also truthful, and consequently must (and in certain cases can do nothing else but) draw itself in its heroes. To do this properly, and so to create a good book, certain conditions must be fulfilled. In changing the naïve 'I' into a reflected 'he' the author must aim at ideality and totality; he must know when to go beyond the limits of his own bounded self, and how to include characteristics which will make his central figure no longer particular, but general. The onesidedness which makes the great man, who is a proper subject for biography (or even autobiography), of its nature makes him unfitted to be the hero of a novel. If this extension can be successfully carried out, the author will find he has much greater freedom to introduce his personal views and opinions as the views of the central figure himself, without destroying the illusion or disturbing the balance of the story; but he must be careful to keep proper proportion in such freedom.

The extension of the hero's fortunes beyond the *vielleicht beklemmende Enge* of those of the author is a difficult matter; and Spielhagen writes:

Das vermag keiner, der nicht, wie der Verfasser des *Copperfield*, auf der Höhe seiner Kunst steht und im stande ist, ganze Kapitel aus einer angefangenen Autobiographie wörtlich in den Roman herüberzunehmen, ohne daß selbst der kritische Leser die Naht merkt, wo das Gefundene an das Erfundene geheftet ist.[2]

The autobiographical details in *Copperfield* are again noticed in the *Beiträge* in the essay on the 'Ich-Roman',[3] where some pages later the book is given very high praise:

Mit *David Copperfield* habe ich den besten Ich-Roman genannt, den ich kenne; der mir als ein möglichst vollkommenes Beispiel der Species

---

[1] Col. 650. [2] *Finder und Erfinder*, vol. ii, p. 395. [3] pp. 205, 207.

bei diesen theoretischen Erörterungen immer vorgeschwebt hat, und zu dessen Zustandekommen wahrlich die günstigsten Sterne kulminieren mußten.[1]

Spielhagen shows how exactly the book fits his theory of the 'Ich-Roman'; it is, he concludes, 'zugleich die wundervollste praktische Bestätigung unserer Theorie vom Roman im allgemeinen und vom Ich-Roman im besonderen'; and he quotes a long passage for special praise. The highest praise, however, is to be found at the conclusion of the essay, where he refers to the book to prove that the method of the 'Ich-Roman', in the hands of a true narrative writer, can make possible a novel:

in welchem der Dichter der einzig legitimen (objektiven) Darstellungsweise nicht das mindeste vergab und doch durch die angewandte Modification derselben seinen Standpunkt zu einer ästhetischen Höhe freiester humoristischer Weltübersicht steigern konnte, die das moderne epische Ideal zu verwirklichen scheint, wie die homerischen Gedichte das klassische verwirklichten: — *Copperfield*.[2]

This study of his valuation of Dickens' work shows that it is, strictly, only at the point of the 'Ich-Roman' that the two writers meet; in other matters they are often far apart. A few details of Spielhagen's technique can be paralleled from Dickens, but there can seldom be any question of direct influence here. M. Geller, for example, speaks of the *anschaulich lebendige Naturbeseelung* to be found at times in Spielhagen's work,[3] and gives the excellent example of his description of the tree on the opposite Rhine bank from his rooms in Bonn.[4] J. Dresch also mentions this point:

En général les paysages, assez nombreux dans les *Natures Problématiques*, sont habilement amenés par l'action même du roman et colorés par les sentiments des personnages.[5]

This was a well-known detail of Dickens' own technique, and, indeed, H. Mielke had already compared Spielhagen to Dickens in this matter,[6] though Julian Schmidt had declared in 1870 that in this case 'mit Dickens . . . kann Spielhagen an Virtuosität, dies Wort in seinem guten wie im schlimmen Sinn gemeint, nicht

---
[1] pp. 226–7.   [2] p. 240.
[3] *Spielhagens Theorie und Praxis des Romans*, Diss. Bonn, 1917 (pub. complete in *Bonner Forschungen*, Neue Folge, Bd. 10), p. 81.
[4] *Finder und Erfinder*, vol. i, p. 342.
[5] *Le Roman Social en Allemagne, 1850–1900*, Paris, 1913, p. 208.
[6] *Der Deutsche Roman*; ed. of 1890, p. 118.

wetteifern'.[1] The Harts also mention occasional examples of 'realistische Kleinmalerei ebenso wie ... nüchterne Beobachtung des alltäglichen' in his works,[2] which again places him close to Dickens—as E. de Morsier did six years later in his discussion of *Was will das werden?* Spielhagen here produced some excellent descriptions of the back-streets of Hamburg, and de Morsier writes:

Sur ces égouts du monde civilisé, Spielhagen a écrit là quelques pages, qui, pour la vérité poignante de l'observation et l'intensité de l'émotion contenue sont parmi les plus belles qu'on puisse citer. Cela égale Dickens....[3]

The most likely influences of Dickens on his technique have been dealt with by M. M. Skinner.[4] In *Hammer und Amboß*, a work which, it will be shown, displays evident traces of Dickens' influence in other ways, Spielhagen may very probably have followed Dickens in his methods of characterization—by peculiarities of speech, manner, or appearance; and Skinner adds: 'Another element in Dickens' technique in *Copperfield* is the conjuring up before his mind of a picture of a certain scene, event or person as it was in the past. Spielhagen develops this device and uses it in a more artistic and effective manner.' Skinner has overlooked the significant fact that it is this very element in the technique of *Copperfield* which Spielhagen singles out for long quotation and special praise in the essay on the 'Ich-Roman'.[5]

In general content, too, the two writers are mostly far apart. Both champion the cause of the badly treated and inarticulate masses, but in very different ways and for different ends; both disagree with the privileged position of the nobility, but with varying force and for different reasons. There was also little to connect their personalities, though L. Ziemssen compares Spielhagen to Dickens in that both felt quite free to portray their friends and acquaintances in their works:

Beiden gegenüber ist — und wenn recht verstanden, nicht mit Unrecht — jenes an Kestner gerichtete Wort: 'Sauf le respect pour votre ami, mais il est dangereux d'avoir un auteur pour ami' wiederholt gel-

---

[1] *Neue Bilder*, &c., Leipzig, 1873, p. 189.
[2] H. and J. Hart, *Kritische Waffengänge*, Leipzig, 1884, Heft 6: *F. Spielhagen und der deutsche Roman der Gegenwart*, p. 7.
[3] *Romanciers Allemands Contemporains*, Paris, 1890, p. 107.
[4] 'The Indebtedness of Spielhagen to Dickens', *Journal of Eng. and Germ. Philology*, 1910, pp. 499-505.   [5] *Beiträge*, &c. (cit.), pp. 228-30.

tend gemacht. Beide haben es, um ihrer großen Zwecke willen, leicht getragen.[1]

But for this minor point, the two men were personally so different, and went about their work in such completely different ways, that it is clear that any search for direct influence of Dickens on Spielhagen would produce comparatively little result.

Once or twice, however, clear reminiscences of Dickensian themes and situations can be found in books by Spielhagen. Geller, for example, discussing the character of Primula in *Problematische Naturen*, compares her[2] with Mrs. Leo Hunter in Chapter 15 of the *Pickwick Papers*. The parallel is close, and Primula may even be a conscious part-copy of the Dickens character; especially her poems 'Auf einen toten Maulwurf', 'An ihren Haushahn', 'An einen Maikäfer, der auf dem Rücken lag' are fairly clearly imitated from the style of Mrs. Hunter's 'Ode to an Expiring Frog'. It is interesting to notice that in Geller's opinion this is 'Wohl das einzige vollgelungene Beispiel von Charakterkomik in Spielhagens Romanen'.

The most obvious parallel is that between the fortunes of Georg Hartwig, the hero of *Hammer und Amboß*, and of David Copperfield. Evidence for the way in which Dickens' lifelike characters became fixed in his mind is given by Spielhagen himself in the *Europa* essay, where he writes of the extraordinary powers of observation possessed by the English writers, and adds:

Daher haben auch ihre Gestalten eine Wahrheit, daß wir mit ihnen verkehren können wie mit Menschen von Fleisch und Blut, daher kommt es, daß wir uns nach Jahren an diesen oder jenen Dickensschen Charakter erinnern, wie an einen alten Universitätsbekannten.[3]

It was noticed above that Spielhagen, like Dickens, was quite ready to use living models for his characters. As Dickens' figures were so real and lively to him, it is not surprising to meet some of them again in his books; least of all in the case of the characters of *Copperfield*, the book of all Dickens' books that Spielhagen knew best and enjoyed most, and of which he had even translated a large section.

Julian Schmidt was the first to demonstrate the parallel between *Copperfield* and *Hammer und Amboß*, as early as November 1870, the year following the publication of the first part of Spielhagen's

[1] *Friedrich Spielhagen* (*Deutsche Bücherei*, Nr. 26), Breslau, n.d. [1883], p. 15.
[2] M. Geller, op. cit., p. 123.   [3] Col. 644.

book. As David marries twice, first Dora, then after Dora's death the much more compatible Agnes, so Georg marries Hermine, then Paula. Schmidt says:

Dem Dichter scheint das Beispiel *Copperfield's* vorgeschwebt zu haben; die Parallele zwischen Georg, Hermine und Paula mit Copperfield, Dora und Agnes ist augenscheinlich.[1]

In 1884 the Hart brothers also discussed it in the sixth part of their outspoken *Kritische Waffengänge*.[2] They outline David's story, and point the parallel: *Hammer und Amboß*

... beruht nicht nur der Anregung, nicht nur der Form nach auf dem *David Copperfield* Dickens'. Eins der Hauptmomente dieses Romans, die zweimalige Vermählung des Helden, ist direkt in den Spielhagenschen Roman übergegangen und in gleicher Weise ausgeführt. ... Bei Spielhagen ist die Entwicklung genau dieselbe; Hermine hat Ähnlichkeit mit Dora, Paula aber ist geradezu eine Kopie von Agnes.

Moreover, the German book is also in autobiographical form, though Spielhagen does not handle it very well, and Georg has not the modesty of David.

In 1910 the point was again taken up by Skinner in the *Journal of English and Germanic Philology*.[3] Here several interesting points were added, including a parallel between Emily, David's ill-fated child-love, and Konstanze, Georg's first love; both tire of life at home, and both elope with a young man of higher social class. A second parallel is between Amalie Duff and Julia Mills; Skinner says:

Each is a confidante of the spoiled little girl, Hermine or Dora; each favours the suit of the hero, Georg or David; each is sentimental and has a decided inclination for highly extravagant and poetic phrase and quotation to characterise situations that arise in the love affairs of her precious ward.[4]

Skinner also points out possible influences in stylistic devices, and in Spielhagen's 'depreciation of the lawyer and the legal profession', an attitude very frequently found in Dickens' work. To these points it may also be added that the graphic description of the storm in *Copperfield*[5]—a description which so many German authors admired—may very probably have influenced Spielhagen to treat such a subject in *Hammer und Amboß*, and to produce a

[1] J. Schmidt, *Neue Bilder* (cit.), p. 223.
[2] pp. 54 f.   [3] pp. 499–505.   [4] p. 501.   [5] Chapter 55.

description of which Schmidt says: 'Die ganze Gewalt seiner Naturschilderung konzentriert sich in dem Bilde vom Sturm'.[1]

At the conclusion of his article Skinner demonstrated satisfactorily that Spielhagen did take the storm in *Copperfield* as a model for such a description in one of his later books—*Noblesse Oblige* of 1888.[2] In Dickens' book a ship is wrecked in a great storm at Yarmouth; there is one man left on board, and Ham swims out with a rope to save him. Both are killed, and David finds that the man for whom his friend has lost his life is Steerforth, the seducer of Emily. The shipwreck scene in *Noblesse Oblige*, taking 'much the same place in the economy of the novel', follows Dickens' model in some respects very closely. The prelude to the storm is the same in each case; setting and sequence of events are parallel. In Spielhagen's story it is Hypolit who goes out in a boat with a rescue party, despite Minna's efforts to hold him back, to save the sole survivor on the wrecked ship; the man is Theodor Billow, the one man, of course (just as in Dickens), to whom the rescuer has most reason to wish ill. The ship is smashed by the great waves, and the mast falls on Hypolit in the boat; he dies when he is eventually brought ashore.

These are the essential resemblances. Skinner adds in a footnote: 'There are, as might be expected, many divergencies, incident on a difference of general plot as well as of locality.' This restriction must be emphasized for all these probably quite unconscious borrowings; *Problematische Naturen, Hammer und Amboß, Noblesse Oblige*, are Spielhagen's own stories, and unless one is to criticize as severely as did Heinrich and Julius Hart, it is no reflection on Spielhagen's peculiar powers that in them he incorporated details or themes from Dickens. It is worth remembering that he wrote in the preface to his autobiography:

Dies ist mir sicher: der Poet, nenne er sich einen Idealisten oder Realisten oder Naturalisten oder wie immer, muß — er mag wollen, oder nicht — Finder und Erfinder sein.

Spielhagen was writing of actually observed models from life, but his remark applies with equal force to the use of literary models.

[1] *Neue Bilder*, p. 191.   [2] Book 3, chapters 19–20.

VII

GUSTAV FRENSSEN

IT has frequently been hinted that there is some connexion between Dickens' work and that of Gustav Frenssen; indeed, as soon as the latter's famous novel *Jörn Uhl* appeared in 1901, it was pointed out that there was a quite noticeable influence on it of Dickens' *Copperfield*. Frenssen has now published three volumes of extracts from his diary: *Grübeleien*, Berlin, 1920;[1] *Möwen und Mäuse*, Berlin, 1928; and *Vorland*, Berlin, 1937—which cover the years 1890–1935, and make it possible to decide fairly exactly, from a study of the relevant extracts, what his attitude to Dickens was, and how useful he found the example of Dickens' work.

His criticism of Dickens, spread through these three volumes, is less concerned with particular books than with his general artistic personality. An important passage among the extracts for 1890–5[2] affords Dickens, by clear implication, a valuation which is, for Frenssen, a high one. Frenssen reports that he had written to a friend: 'daß der Ruf eines Dickens und eines Freytag mir begehrenswerter erschiene, als der eines Kleist, Ludwig oder Hebbel'. The friend then supposed that Frenssen would be glad to be valued as were Keller and Storm: but these Frenssen rejects too, in the sense that, for all five, one must say: 'Ihre Kunst ist teils seltsam, teils steht sie nicht mitten im Volk. . . . Alle diese Di   er sind Dichter genug, aber sie sind nicht breite, einfache, völkische Persönlichkeiten genug.' The implication is clearly that Frenssen feels Dickens and Freytag possess these qualities, or at least are not far short of them.

Breadth, calm, and simplicity are the qualities in Dickens' work most frequently praised in the three volumes of *Grübeleien*; breadth and calm in parallel with Raabe, Keller, and Ebner-Eschenbach,[3] simplicity in parallel with Keller and Tolstoy.[4] Frenssen says further:

Die Größe und Breite von Dickens' Erfolgen beruht, abgesehen von seiner großen, suggestiven Kunst, darauf, daß die Gemüter seiner

---

[1] Quotations are from the new revised edition of the *Grübeleien*, Berlin, 1934; from the other books as above. They form a continuous series, and will be referred to as vol. i, ii, and iii respectively.
[2] Vol. i, pp. 96–8.   [3] Vol. i, p. 180.   [4] Vol. ii, p. 62.

Figuren einfach sind und also auch die Bewegungen dieser Gemüter. Dadurch wurde er den vielen deutlich und wert[1],

and he compares him, in this sense, with Homer, Shakespeare, and some parts of Goethe. In the same way Frenssen criticizes Raabe[2] for his often confusing habit of quotation and anecdote—for adding *köstliche Seltsamkeiten* to his stories—and refers to Dickens and to Balzac, who had not this habit: 'sie gingen nicht abseits, wurden nicht aufgehalten, blieben immer auf ihrem Weg, und schritten so weiter; und die Leser konnten alles mitmachen.'

Dickens is once more paralleled with Tolstoy, and this time also with Ibsen, Fontane, and Storm, in a discussion of the fact that these were all writers 'die sich erst im bürgerlichen und geschäftlichen Leben und seinen weltanschaulichen und ethischen Fragen umtrieben und erst nach und durch diese Erfahrungen zur künstlerischen Darstellung kamen'.[3] These are perhaps not the pure, the 'Nur- und Ganz-Künstlern'. Elsewhere[4] Frenssen points out that Dickens was the mouthpiece of the third estate, and in this connexion speaks of the forcefulness of his artistic imagination.

The calm, breadth, simplicity, experience, and forceful imagination behind Dickens' books were, then, the qualities which Frenssen found most noteworthy. He found some points to criticize; especially strongly the false attitude to matters of sex,[5] though in more recent years he modified his earlier judgements, saying that such idealization in these matters as is shown in Dickens and Keller is merely *bedenklich, eine schwere Sache*.[6] A re-reading of Dickens in the early years of the new century also gave him the impression that the English and the German spirit were not so similar as, for example, George Meredith would have him believe, and he writes that in Dickens 'es ist, als wenn gewisse Weiten und Güten des germanischen Gemüts nicht mehr vorhanden sind'.[7] Later, however, Frenssen added a little to his appreciation of the Germanic nature of Dickens' work. In a discussion of Balzac he confesses to a feeling that the French writer's work is rather hollow, and says: 'Ich versteh' nicht, wie ein germanischer Kritiker ihn mit Dickens in einem Atem nennen kann.'[8] A few pages farther he remarks: 'Die Germanen kommen aus Sonnenlosigkeit und Nebel,

---

[1] Vol. ii, p. 284. [2] Vol. iii, p. 115. [3] Vol. ii, p. 72.
[4] Vol. i, p. 114. [5] Vol. i, p. 62; vol. ii, p. 34.
[6] Vol. ii, p. 255. [7] Vol. i, p. 236. [8] Vol. iii, p. 103.

wohnen dort meistens noch, und glauben daher an das Licht'; and includes Dickens in a list of typical representatives of this Germanic mentality.[1]

There are very few direct criticisms of separate novels by Dickens, though *Copperfield* is very frequently mentioned in passing, and several times in particular. It is once included in a short list of examples of the fact that 'Zu einer erstklassigen Erzählung gehört eine ganze Reihe schönster Unmöglichkeiten';[2] and once more[3] in a list of the few great works of art in the class of narrative literature. The only other book mentioned by name is the *Pickwick Papers*:

Es gibt große Begabungen, die wundervolle Werke mit dämonischer Kraft hinstellen; ich denke mir, daß Shakespeare am *Sommernachtstraum*, Schiller an den *Räubern*, Dickens an den *Pickwickiern* nur eine kurze, stürmische Zeit gearbeitet haben.[4]

On Dickens' work in general Frenssen makes two more interesting remarks. Mentioning the fact that Dickens lived in and with his characters, he says: 'Diese Art schadet zuweilen der Form. Das übervolle Herz zerbricht die Form. Aber es gilt auch in den Künsten zuerst das Herz, das Feuer, dann die Form.'[5] And finally, in a discussion of the necessary merits of a great author, he writes:

... die Sprache macht es nicht. Es kommt darauf an, ob einer ein geborner Erzähler ist, oder nicht ... Balzac ist trotz seiner Nachlässigkeiten in der Sprache, und Homer, Cervantes, Dickens, Flaubert sind auch in Übersetzungen allergrößte Erzähler. Das Spintisieren in Worten, das patente und aparte Wortsuchen, dies Seltsamkeitenformen hilft alles nicht, wenn das Herz dürr ist, der Strom der Phantasie dünn, der Zug der Gestalten blaß. ...[6]

This is once more, by clear implication, full praise of Dickens.

There is also in these three volumes rich evidence for the influence Dickens' work had on Frenssen's literary development. His attitude to Dickens as an example changes; in the early extracts he commonly feels that Dickens' methods are right, but that he himself has not the talent to work by them; later he declares more than once that he will produce great work in the way that Dickens did; more recently he draws comparisons between Dickens' work and his own.

The early lack of confidence in his powers can be judged from

[1] Vol. iii, pp. 115–16.   [2] Vol. ii, p. 149.   [3] Vol. iii, p. 190.
[4] Vol. iii, pp. 214–15.   [5] Vol. iii, p. 116.   [6] Vol. ii, p. 280.

two paragraphs[1] in his meditations of the period 1895–1900. The first, having discussed the lack of writers in Germany who were of 'einfacher, schlichter, breitgesunder Seele', rather in the way that Dickens and Freytag were, concludes: 'Ich selbst bin wohl einfach genug dazu, aber nicht breitschulterig genug.' The second extract considers Dickens as the mouthpiece of the 'third estate', emphasizes the necessity of such a writer for the sake of the 'fourth estate', who would help Germany to some sort of internal unity, and concludes: 'Mir selbst fehlt zu diesem großen Werk die Gewalttätigkeit, ja Brutalität der künstlerischen Phantasie, die Dickens hatte.' Two further extracts from a later 'Lebensbericht' substantiate this material. He speaks of his early dissatisfaction with Storm, Keller and Raabe, whose work was not fitted for the ordinary people; it was 'zu zart ... oder ... zu gelehrt oder zu vornehm'.

Dem großen, einfachen Volk aber wollte ich dienen.... Eher schon hätte mir Dickens ein brauchbarer Wegweiser und Lehrer sein können; und ich habe später auch von ihm gelernt. Ich kannte ihn ein wenig; aber ich sah noch nicht, wo von ihm ein Weg ... in deutsche Verhältnisse hinüberginge. ... [2] In meinem ersten Buch habe ich Gartenlaubengeschichten nachgeahmt, danach haben Goethe, Keller und Raabe Einfluß auf meine Arbeiten gehabt, später Dickens. Es wäre vielleicht richtiger gewesen, wenn ich von Anfang an mein Feuer an Dickens entzündet hätte, denn er hat die Gabe und den Willen, den ich auch habe — der die Quintessenz meines ganzen Schriftstellertums ist — das ganze Volk zu einem Stand vereint zu sehen. Ich war aber zu lange unklar in dieser Erkenntnis; ich wußte nicht, was es mit meinem Talent auf sich hatte.[3]

In the last extract one can see how close he eventually considered his own work to be to that of Dickens. The change from the early uncertainty was not long in coming; he is very soon able to write with some confidence: 'ich will — je älter und sicherer ich werde — ... viel kräftiger zugreifen, so in der Art, wie Dickens es tut. Ich weiß nun, daß ich Kraft habe.'[4] Looking back on this period after some years, he says that the material for his very early work came from rather unworthy sources; but when he knew something of his own powers, he turned to '*Stromtid, David Copperfield, Hungerpastor, Frau Sorge* und anderen, und hoffte, gleichwertiges hervorzubringen.'[5] And he can write: 'Ich habe in den letzten vier

[1] Vol. i, pp. 98, 114 [2] Vol. ii, p. 240. [3] Vol. ii, pp. 33–4.
[4] Vol. i, p. 119. [5] Vol. i, p. 174.

Jahren doch wohl viel gelernt von Dickens, Raabe, der Ebner-Eschenbach, von Keller. Nicht im einzelnen, sondern indem die Ruhe und Breite ihrer Persönlichkeiten mir unbewußt geholfen haben. . . .'[1] Elsewhere he writes of a discussion on Dickens' value to England, which was decided to lie in his showing the ordinary people its own worth and so teaching it confidence and reliance in itself as a unity.[2] Frenssen adds: 'Das ist, was auch ich tue, unbewußt, von meiner Natur getrieben . . .'; and this is supported later, when he declares himself a German from the middle and mass of the people, as Homer was from the Greek and Dickens from the English: 'und ich erzähle, wie jene getan, dem ganzen Volk seine eigenen Wunder.'[3] Still later, he says: 'Wie lange, und was ich auch immer gearbeitet habe, habe ich immer für ein besseres Deutschland gearbeitet, so gut ich es verstand. Wie Dickens zu seiner Zeit in seinem Volk.'[4]

There are a few further parallels between himself and Dickens given elsewhere. He is simple, as Dickens was;[5] he belongs to those *nicht Nur- und Ganz-Künstlern* who have had experience of the world for an appreciable time before they produced their artistic creations: Dickens is an example.[6] He writes: 'Wie verwandt sind meine Bemühungen mit den Erzählungen von Dickens' (and others).[7] He lives in and with his characters, just as Dickens did.[8] Finally, Dickens is included in a list of eleven men who were 'ferne und gute Geister' to Frenssen for over thirty years; he says of them 'sie sind mir Begleiter, Führer und Wegweiser zu wertvollen, hohen Erkenntnissen gewesen'.[9]

It is evident that the example of Dickens' work influenced Frenssen to some noticeable extent in the formation and direction of his own life's work. But it is important to realize that (as Frenssen points out frequently) there are natural affinities in the outlook of the two writers; so that it can be taken as a probability that Frenssen would eventually have struck the same path for himself without the example of Dickens, which was apparently more in the nature of an accelerating than a fundamentally changing influence.

A remarkable feature of the Memoirs is the frequency with which *David Copperfield* is mentioned; except for a reference to

[1] Vol. i, p. 180.
[2] Vol. i, p. 136.
[3] Vol. ii, p. 90.
[4] Vol. ii, p. 203.
[5] Vol. ii, p. 62.
[6] Vol. ii, p. 72.
[7] Vol. ii, p. 156.
[8] Vol. iii, p. 116.
[9] Vol. ii, p. 236.

the *Pickwick Papers* at the end of the last volume, *Copperfield* is the only book by Dickens which Frenssen quotes by name. His opinion of it has been mentioned above: 'a story of the first class', 'one of the few great works of narrative literature'. Since Dickens appears so largely in the three volumes of *Grübeleien*, and since *Copperfield* is the one of all Dickens' books which most interested Frenssen, and received his praise, it is not surprising that there is to report a certain influence of this work of Dickens on two of Frenssen's books: *Jörn Uhl* and *Otto Babendiek*. Frenssen himself was never pleased to hear comments on his supposed literary dependence; he writes, for example, with sarcasm:

Ich höre, daß man in gewissen hohen Kreisen urteilt, ich hätte Kipling viel abgelauscht. Natürlich. Wie kann ein Deutscher etwas aus sich leisten? Es muß doch vom Ausland kommen. Was ist gut, groß, echt, imponierend? Das Englische!...[1]

There are, however, reminiscences of several styles in his work,[2] and he himself leaves a small loophole for this criticism when he remarks later:

... Freilich kann man einen bestimmten Stil nachahmen. Wenn ich drei Stunden Goethe oder Storm gelesen habe, kann ich, wenn ich mir den Spaß machen will, eine Zeitlang genau in diesem Stil schreiben. Selbstverständlich kann ich das. Denn es ist eben mein Metier, mich in die Haut anderer Leute hineinzuversetzen.[3]

But he asks why any writer should consciously borrow the style of another, when he already possesses his own.

There is no doubt that Frenssen has a style of his own. But in the case of the influence of *Copperfield* on his work, it is less an influence of style (though there is a slight one to be traced) than of composition which is to be noticed. The two extracts above have been quoted to show that Frenssen was susceptible to influences from other authors, and, in this case, what apparently happened was that he read and studied *Copperfield* so long and deeply that the details of the framework and composition of the story became firmly imprinted on his mind, so that he used them as the foundation both for *Jörn Uhl* and *Otto Babendiek*.

Soon after the appearance of *Jörn Uhl*, the Polish-French critic

[1] Vol. i, p. 173.
[2] For a recital of those authors who have been said to have influenced him, see H. Keiter and T. Kellen, *Der Roman*, Essen, 4te Auflage, 1912, pp. 222–4.
[3] Vol. ii, pp. 144–5.

T. de Wyzewa reviewed it in a French periodical,[1] and devoted a considerable amount of his article to a discussion of its relationship to *David Copperfield*. He gives a short account of the story, and shows that the plans of the two books are closely related. Jörn Uhl will stand for David; Wieten Klook, the old servant who looks after him after his mother's death, for Peggotty; Lena Tarn, Jörn's first wife, for Dora (possibly, though there is no deep resemblance); and Lisbeth Junker, the childhood friend, whom Jörn marries after Lena's death, for Agnes. Elsbe, Jörn's sister, seduced and abandoned by Harro Heinsen, takes the place of Emily; and Thieß Thiessen, her uncle, who spends so many years searching for her, stands for Mr. Peggotty.

De Wyzewa, however, defends the enormous success of Frenssen's book as perfectly legitimate. There can be no doubt that the plan of the story owes much to *Copperfield*; but, as he finds it usual in Germany, Dickens' influence has affected the plan alone. He writes:

... M. Frenssen, s'étant proposé de nous décrire les mœurs et les sentiments d'un coin de l'Allemagne qu'il connaît à merveille, a simplement demandé à Dickens de lui fournir un cadre assez large et assez solide pour que la peinture qu'il voulait nous offrir pût y tenir bien à l'aise. *David Copperfield* n'a été vraiment pour lui qu'un cadre, l'enveloppe extérieure de son œuvre personnelle.[2]

He emphasizes that Dickens supplied only the framework, which Frenssen used with excellent effect to display his own very real originality as a poet and a painter. 'Ce sont bien des caractères allemands, c'est la vie allemande dans ce qu'elle a de plus intime et de plus profond, que M. Gustav Frenssen s'est constamment efforcé de nous représenter.'[2] Dickens showed us very little of the inner development of his David: Frenssen, benefiting from fifty years of further evolution in novelistic treatment, works with greater freedom for the discussion of personal subjects and individual progress, and shows us the development of his Jörn Uhl, especially in religious and moral matters, with great detail and clarity.

Several details can be added to de Wyzewa's general comparison. The best parallels of those he draws are Elsbe=Emily and Lisbeth =Agnes, especially the latter. Elsbe, like Emily, is unsettled and

---
[1] *Revue des deux Mondes*, 15 Sept. 1902, pp. 457–68.
[2] Loc. cit., p. 460.

unhappy at home: as a result of the dismissal of Fiete Krey (who may here stand for Ham in *David Copperfield*) she runs away with Harro Heinsen. There is here a deviation from Dickens, for Ham is not sent away from Emily; but the final account of Elsbe's homecoming is strongly reminiscent of *Copperfield*. Lisbeth, the childhood friend, and the wife who eventually helps Jörn Uhl to the realization of his dreams, is very close to Agnes; her confession of love to Jörn sbould be compared with that of Agnes to David. Some dissimilarities in plan should be remembered; there is no parallel in *Jörn Uhl* to the early love of David for Emily, because Elsbe is Jörn's sister. Harro Heinsen cannot be said to be a Steerforth as in *Copperfield*, for he has no relations with Jörn like those of Steerforth with David. And Jörn Uhl only makes his fortune spiritually, not materially and spiritually as David does.

The most Dickensian figure in the whole book is that of Thieß Thiessen, whose character would have been thoroughly in place in any of Dickens' books. He has his own pronounced peculiarities, like any Dickensian character: all his experiments end in comic failure (like the episode of the boat early in the book); he is much too ready to fall asleep; he dreams of travel and exploration, he studies books and maps of foreign countries, and yet until he goes to Hamburg to look for Elsbe, he has hardly been out of his native region, and once in Hamburg can hardly stay there for homesickness. The comparison between him and his house,[1] if translated into English, would almost certainly be taken for an extract from Dickens:

> Das Haus, in dem Thieß Thiessen fast sein ganzes Leben zugebracht hatte, und der Kopf, den Thieß Thiessen auf den Schultern trug, hatten eine unzweifelhafte Ähnlichkeit miteinander. Unaufgeklärt blieb allerdings für alle Zeiten, wer sich nach dem anderen gerichtet hatte, ob Thieß' Kopf im Laufe der vielen Jahre dem geliebten alten Hause ähnlich geworden war, oder ob das Haus sich etwas nach Thieß gerichtet hatte.
> Das Haus Thieß Thiessens war lang und schmal; das hohe, dunkle, Strohdach hing über die kleinen, blinkernden Fenster tief herab; vorne war ein kleiner, waghalsiger Giebel. Der Kopf Thieß Thiessens war sehr lang und schmal, und das lange, dunkle Haar hing tief über Ohren und Stirn hinab bis an die blanken, blinkerndern Augen; seine Nase war klein und wenn nicht waghalsig, doch kühn; eine feine geschwun-

[1] *Jörn Uhl*, chapter 4.

gene Nase in einem kleinen, verwitterten, vertrockneten und verknitterten Webergesicht.

Elsbe sagte es oft zu ihm: 'Du hast gerade so'n Kopf wie dein Haus'.

'Kann wohl nicht anders sein', sagte er dann. 'Wir sind nun schon über vierzig Jahre bei einander, das Haus und ich, und immer allein'.

The more recent semi-autobiographical *Otto Babendiek*, published in 1926, also shows affinities with *Copperfield*, which were worked out by H. W. Church in an article in the *Germanic Review* of 1936.[1] Church devotes a few pages to a short summary of Frenssen's attitude to Dickens (but without reference to *Jörn Uhl*), then presents the full parallel between the two books; he also makes occasional references to *Great Expectations*, *Barnaby Rudge*, and the *Pickwick Papers* for further comparisons. It is clear from his research that still more of the characters of *Copperfield* can be found in *Babendiek* than in *Jörn Uhl*; the similarities in design are, indeed, surprisingly strong.

Both stories are told in the first person, and both begin before the central figure is born. The events before and at the birth of Otto Babendiek are reminiscent of the parallel scenes in *Copperfield*; and in both books some pages are devoted to a recital of the earliest recollections of the hero, where Otto asks: 'What is the first thing I remember?' and David: 'What else do I remember?' David reads about crocodiles to Peggotty; Otto about the South Seas to Engel Tiedje. The fathers of both boys die early in the story, the mothers a little later; both boys fall into the hands of cruel guardians and cruel schoolmasters.

At Creakle's school David meets Steerforth, a boy much spoilt by a widowed mother; Otto at his school makes the acquaintance of Fritz Hellebek, who is of much the same nature and upbringing as Steerforth, and whose airs at school are exactly those of Steerforth. In *Copperfield*, Steerforth breaks up the Peggotty family; in *Babendiek*, Hellebek disgraces the family of Otto's benefactress 'Tante Lene' by a false charge of theft. Both these characters play the part of distinguished but evil genius of the hero, and both come to a bad end. Steerforth is drowned, Hellebek is killed in the world war.

Meanwhile Otto, like David, has fled from his cruel superiors to the home of a kind and slightly eccentric woman; 'Tante Lene', who here takes the place of Betsey Trotwood as the benefactress of

[1] Vol. xi, Jan. 1936, pp. 40–9.

the hero. She outfaces his cruel guardians and takes care of his education. In Tante Lene's house there is in the person of Uncle Neel a parallel with Mr. Dick in *Copperfield*. From this point in *Babendiek*, only the larger outlines correspond—Gesa, Otto's first wife, takes the place of Dora, especially in her pleasure-loving nature and lack of attention to even the simpler duties of her home; Eva, his second wife, corresponds to Agnes, more especially in the personal description Frenssen gives of her; and, finally, Otto, like David, eventually finds that his real work in life is to be a writer.

Several of the secondary characters present even closer parallels; the most obvious are perhaps Paul Sööth, Dutti Kohl, Mamsell Boehmke, and Fräulein Lina. Paul Sööth, a friend of Otto since his unhappy schooldays, is almost exactly David's Traddles, even to his stiff and rebellious hair; when he is married he still supports large numbers of poor relations, just as Traddles does. The oily Dutti Kohl takes the place of Uriah Heep; his machinations cause the loss of the fortune of Otto's relatives, but he, like Heep, ends in prison. Mamsell Boehmke, whom Otto knows when he is a boy, and who eventually marries Engel Tiedje, has points of resemblance to Peggotty, David's nurse; she is little and fat, and has shiny plump cheeks, like Peggotty (whose cheeks are hard and red, like apples). One of her favourite ornaments is a velvet model of the Lüneburg town hall, which stands in the middle of her sewing-table; Peggotty treasures a work-box 'with a view of St. Paul's Cathedral (with a pink dome) painted on the lid' Both these architectural fancies appear more than once in the respective stories. Finally, Fräulein Lina, Gesa's friend, is a clear reminiscence of Miss Julia Mills, Dora's high-minded and romantic companion.

Some points of style may perhaps also be traced back to Dickens, although with much less certainty; among these are the use of expressive names, and the trick of characterizing different individuals in the story by their use of peculiar actions or expressions, frequently repeated.

But in spite of these many similarities, it must be emphasized that de Wyzewa's opinion of *Jörn Uhl*—that Dickens supplied only the framework—holds good also for *Babendiek*. At most a few extra details and minor characters, besides those necessary for the main plan, have been borrowed from *Copperfield*. The fundamental difference is in the nature of the characters themselves; although they are placed and contrasted in very much the same way as those of *Copperfield*, they are essentially German, and in particular North German individuals. Church can say fairly that *Babendiek* 'attains quite a Dickensian flavour', but the book is none the less a German creation, and because of that fact, perhaps even because of both those facts, Frenssen's expectation[1] that it will be even more popular than was *Jörn Uhl* is quite likely to be realized.

[1] *Vorland*, Berlin, 1937, pp. 205–6.

VIII
MINOR INFLUENCES
ALEXANDER VON UNGERN-STERNBERG

A TEMPORARY influence of Dickens on Ungern-Sternberg's work can be traced in the latter's novel *Diane* of 1842. This book came as something of a surprise, for Ungern-Sternberg had written nothing of its type before, and it was, indeed, a novel of a sort then practically unknown in German literature. The periodical *Europa*, reviewing the book in 1843, said of it:

Seine Haupteigentümlichkeit aber ist die, daß es in unserer Zeit, in den Jahren 183? bis 184? spielt, daß es seine Handlungen nach Berlin, Ostpreußen, Rom, kurz nach lauter wirklichen, reellen Schauplätzen verlegt, daß ferner lauter eben so reelle und wirkliche Personen, als da sind: Leutnants, Referendare, Advokaten, Kriminalräte, Minister, Schauspielerinnen u. s. w. auftreten, daß schließlich die ganze moderne Wirklichkeit sich vor unseren erstaunten Augen, die so etwas noch gar nicht gewöhnt sind, in überraschend treuer Anschaulichkeit entwickelt. Es war das ein kühnes Unterfangen von Herrn v. Sternberg und fast unerhört in deutschen Gauen....[1]

Ungern-Sternberg himself attributes this change in his work to the influence of English novelists, and especially of Dickens. In his memoirs, where he writes fully and still appreciatively of *Diane* after fourteen years, he says that the book not only marks a great advance in his own literary activity, but also, since it handles modern, everyday life and people, shows a considerable expansion of the scope of his production. He adds:

Ich hatte mich mit dieser Arbeit völlig losgesagt von dem Märchen- und Toilettenroman des achtzehnten Jahrhunderts: es wäre mir nicht mehr möglich gewesen, eine *Galathee* oder einen *Fortunat* zu schreiben. Die Engländer, besonders Boz-Dickens, mit dem ich mich zu befreunden anfing, hatten mich unmerklich in diese Bahn gelenkt. Dann trieb auch die Zeit dahin, und zwang Jeden — wenn er es auch nicht wahr haben wollte — sich mit Realitäten zu beschäftigen.[2]

To the influence of Dickens, it should be noticed, that of Balzac and of Bulwer-Lytton should probably be added.[3]

[1] *Europa* (Stuttgart), 1843, vol. i, pp. 581–2.
[2] A. von Ungern-Sternberg, *Erinnerungsblätter* (6 vols., Berlin, 1855–60), Teil 2 (1856), p. 133.
[3] E. Weil, 'Alexander von Sternberg'. *Germanische Studien*, Heft 130, Berlin, 1932, pp. 130–1.

Further influence of Dickens on *Diane* was noticed by H. Mielke, who sums it up in the following sentence:

Der Haß gegen die Juristen, der in einer stark aufgetragenen Figur eines Advokaten kraß hervorbricht, gegen das Geld und seine Macht, die Eigenart, wie Typen der Adelsklassen und der unteren Bürgerschichten in humoristisch-satirische Beleuchtung gestellt werden, deuten auf Dickens' Einfluß.[1]

These points were also noticed by J. T. Geissendoerfer, who briefly studied Ungern-Sternberg's indebtedness to Dickens in a thesis published in 1915.[2] The figure of the lawyer, Barnabas Lobmeyer, perhaps owes some of its colour to Dickens' Sampson Brass in the *Old Curiosity Shop*, he suggests; and he draws a few further parallels between Dickens' characters and those of *Diane*, among which may be noticed that between Miss La Creevy (in *Nickleby*) and Annette Zobel. He sees further probable influences of Dickens in the way in which the local colour of Berlin is introduced; in the long descriptive chapter-headings; in the large number of characters, and in the casual insufficiency of the motive for their appearance. It should be noticed, however, that though Sternberg, like Dickens, declares that his characters are drawn entirely from life,[3] he has not Dickens' skill in handling especially the minor characters, which in *Diane* are not drawn with sufficient clarity to become individuals.

Apart from these details, however, the book has sound literary merits; both the manner and the matter are interesting, and the appearance of such a type of novel at so early a date is significant. It was popular; Sternberg says:

Im Publikum fand das Bild des modernen Berliner Lebens — es war das erste damals, jetzt gibt es deren unzählige — großen Beifall.[4]

MARIE VON EBNER-ESCHENBACH

By including her name in the list of German writers on whom he proposed to study the influence of Dickens, J. T. Geissendoerfer gave a title to his thesis[5] which is misleading as far as Ebner-Eschenbach is concerned; for in her case he has not even succeeded

---
[1] H. Mielke, *Der deutsche Roman*, 7th ed. (cont. by H. J. Homann), Dresden, 1920, p. 100.
[2] *Dickens' Einfluß auf Ungern-Sternberg, Heßlein, Stolle, Raabe und Ebner-Eschenbach*, Americana-Germanica, vol. xix, 1915, pp. 1–5.
[3] *Erinnerungsblätter* (cit.), Teil 2, p. 131. Sternberg here refers to the characters of *Diane*. [4] Ibid., p. 132.
[5] *Dickens' Einfluß auf . . . Ebner-Eschenbach*, &c. (cit.), 1915.

MINOR INFLUENCES

in showing that there exists any influence of Dickens for him to analyse.

He deals with Ebner-Eschenbach on pp. 24–7 of his book. Without insisting on any influence from Dickens, he points out that there is a certain similarity in theme between *Oliver Twist* and *Das Gemeindekind* (1887); both stories deal with the life of a boy brought up by the parish authorities. But with that, as Geissendoerfer himself says, the similarity ceases. The treatment of the material is totally different, as one would expect from the essential differences between the temperaments of the two writers: 'die Schilderung der Episoden in Oliver Twist's Leben ist immer äußerst temperamentvoll und packend; bei Ebner-Eschenbach ist alles sachlich, objektiv, temperamentlos'—and he goes to the length of quoting two full extracts (of which one describes the chase and capture of Pavel after he had killed the peacock to get feathers for Vinska, the other the chase and capture of Oliver after the theft of Mr. Brownlow's handkerchief) for the sole purpose of demonstrating this difference in treatment. It is significant that both extracts describe the chase of a fugitive; but if Geissendoerfer only intended to demonstrate difference, and not dependence, it was certainly unnecessary to go to such lengths, if indeed it was necessary to touch the matter at all. In any case, he has not succeeded in showing any influence of Dickens in the terms of the title of his thesis beyond an extremely doubtful one on the general theme of *Das Gemeindekind*.

A comparison of the two writers is not very fruitful for our purpose, though a study of their ideas and methods, based largely on *Oliver Twist* and *Das Gemeindekind*, does show a few points of contact. Both are keenly interested in the lower classes, and both have a warm sympathy for their condition. Both are idealists in their belief that man can rise above circumstance, and both are, to a large extent, realists in their descriptive passages. Here the general similarities cease, and a further examination of them reveals dissimilarities in particular details; for it could not be expected that the widely and carefully educated aristocrat, with her caustic wit and essential balance, and the benefit of a further fifty years development in literary and social theories, should agree with Dickens in anything but the most general outlines. For Dickens, the lower classes of society meant largely those living in towns, while

Ebner-Eschenbach's interest was to a large extent in the peasants of her native land. Warm sympathy for their condition in her case 'never degenerated into mere lachrymose sentimentality',[1] and while it is forcefully apparent in Dickens, with her it is never urged too strongly forward. The belief that man could rise above circumstance depended largely in Dickens on his firm belief in the essential goodness of man, which would show itself eventually in spite of bad education and chances (Oliver; Dickens himself?) while Ebner-Eschenbach emphasized the importance of education as a power for the good. Realism with her did not allow an idealization of the peasants and workers she drew, although it frequently did in Dickens' case; she was more realistic, perhaps because she was more tolerant, and she never descended to caricature.

These points must be borne in mind in any discussion of a possible influence of Dickens on Ebner-Eschenbach. There were some parts of his work which she would have disliked, and many which she certainly would not have copied; but in one or two respects their temper and disposition were generally the same, and it is in these things, as detailed above, that the path was open for a slight deciding influence from Dickens.

Only one investigator has successfully shown an influence in detail of Dickens on her work: Dr. R. Fürst[2] in 1902. His article on *Literarische Verwandschaften*, in which he gives what he calls 'bescheidene Beiträge zu dem nicht reizlosen Kapitel des geistigen Wechselverkehrs', discusses briefly the reminiscences of *Nickleby* which are apparent in the short story *Rittmeister Brand* of 1896. The similarities, which are so strong as to be obviously unconscious recollections of Dickens' book, are between the story of the dressmaker 'Madame Amélie Vernon' and her husband Eduard Weiß, and that of the Mantalinis in *Nickleby*. The businesses are the same in both stories, even to the hours of work. In both the manageress has married a man younger than herself, whom she loves deeply, but who is a complete philanderer. Both Eduard Weiß and Mr. Mantalini dress with extreme elegance, and they even look alike, especially as to beard and moustache, to which special attention is called in each case.[3] Both are vain, lazy, and

---

[1] E. M. O'Connor, *Marie Ebner*, London, 1928, p. 58.
[2] *Die Zeit* (Vienna), 1902, 27 Dec. (= vol. xxxiii, no. 430).
[3] See, e.g., *Nickleby*, chapter 10, and *Rittmeister Brand*, ed. Paetel, Berlin, 1896, p. 95.

cowardly; both immediately overcome all opposition from their wives by gross flattery ('wenn er sagte "Mein Herz, mein geliebtes" war sie verloren und hatte keinen Willen mehr als den seinen'), and neither Frau Vernon-Weiß nor Mrs. Mantalini is ever free from trouble with them. 'Das schließliche Schicksal des Ehepaars ist wieder ein Verwandtes; nach einem unheilbar scheinenden Bruch läßt sich die Frau von dem Mann nochmals betören.'[1] There are of course differences; Herr Weiß does not threaten suicide at every hour like Mr. Mantalini, nor is Mantalini so great a schemer as Weiß; at the end of *Nickleby* Mrs. Mantalini pays for her weakness with ruin, while in the German story the Vernon-Weiß business is simply removed to Paris.

Fürst's conclusion should be noticed; he writes:

Man muß sich die Freude an der schönen 'Erziehungsnovelle', besonders an dem tieferfaßten Charakter des Helden [Rittmeister Brand] keineswegs durch die Erkenntnis verkümmern lassen, daß eine freilich nicht unwichtige Episode nicht als Eigenbau gelten kann'.

[1] R. Fürst, loc. cit., col. 3.

PART III
THE AFTER-FAME OF DICKENS IN GERMANY

LATER CRITICISM AND POPULARITY, 1870–1937

THIS section is in part an attempt at a history of German criticism of Dickens since his death in 1870, and in part an examination of more general evidence of his fame in Germany since that date.

The scope of the critical bibliography requires some explanation. All the books and essays (except those few specially marked as unobtainable) given in the list appended to this section have been studied, but only the more important are mentioned in the text; short notices of no value, repetitions of earlier work, and chapters in literary histories are not considered. The term 'German' is given a linguistic rather than a geographical scope, and is held to include a few Swiss and Austrian essays. Attention is concentrated on books, dissertations, and articles in literary periodicals, but references to a few newspaper articles and some reviews of Dickens' work in general literary histories are included in the book-list for comparison. The large number of books and essays which demanded a mention made it impossible to give more than a brief summary of each, but it is hoped that this will nevertheless serve to draw attention to the large amount of excellent work produced on Dickens in Germany, much of which is not sufficiently known and appreciated in England. Considerable interest, too, lies in discovering the general trend of German appreciation of Dickens during the period studied; such a summary is a yardstick by which other things than purely literary values can be measured.

I
1870–1900

FOR the first thirty years after Dickens' death German critics were mostly occupied in studying his books in relation to his life. For this, of course, John Forster's great biography of Dickens was their stand-by; it was completed in 1873 and was immediately published in Germany both in English (by B. Tauchnitz, 1872–4) and in a German translation by F. Althaus (1872–3–5). Six German books and essays, based largely or wholly on Forster's biography, deserve notice; they appeared between 1873 and 1894.

K. Hillebrand was in England at the time of its publication; his *Briefe aus England*, dated in the summer and autumn of 1873, and published in collected form in 1876,[1] deal to a large extent with Dickens and with Forster's biography. A page in the fourteenth letter sums up Dickens' nature and concludes that he suited his generation, class, and period perfectly; letters XV to XIX are entirely concerned with Dickens, and form together a complete short 'Charakteristik', evoked by the feeling that Forster's book 'ist eben kein Buch, am wenigsten eine Biographie, sondern eine annalistische Brief- und Notizensammlung'. It is, Hillebrand feels, full of interesting and authentic material, but it should be called simply 'Beiträge zu einer Lebensbeschreibung Dickens'.' His commentary on it grew into a neat characterization of Dickens in fifty pages.

'Der Gesamteindruck, der dem Leser bleibt, ist . . . der einer kolossalen Lebenskraft', he writes; and he gives a short history of Dickens' early life, his success, the rush of first works; there was 'dieselbe Fülle und Gesundheit im Genuß', but 'bei alledem war sein Gemüt ein tiefes und ein weiches'. Dickens showed 'Humanität im schönsten Sinne des Wortes — Entrüstung gegen Unrecht und Härte'; and he may be compared, in this sense, with Mazzini. Hillebrand notes several faults in his works, in style and composition, but does not insist on them. 'Wir wollen hier nur von dem Menschen sprechen, soweit er im Schriftsteller zu Tage tritt.' This he does well, discussing Dickens' attitude to religion, for example, and to social questions, the poor, the aristocracy, foreign

[1] *Zeiten, Völker und Menschen*, vol. iii, Berlin, 1876.

countries. He shows the importance of Dickens' reliance on healthy common sense, and also of his conception of the author's duty—'er sah im Romanschreiben ein Apostolat'. The last letters recount Dickens' nervously restless existence after about 1855; he accounts for this partly by Dickens' desire to gain more money, but adds: 'Die Familienverhältnisse und die dunkle Empfindung der abnehmenden schöpferischen Kraft kamen als Zweites und Drittes hinzu.' He calls Dickens' last years 'einen allmählichen Selbstmord'.

Equally based on Forster is W. Dilthey's essay *Charles Dickens und das Genie des erzählenden Dichters* (1877).[1] It is less a literary than a psychological study, examining the sources and the nature of the poetic imagination; Dilthey is consequently more interested in Dickens' early experiences and observations, and so draws heavily on Forster, then the only source. There is a certain amount of discussion of Dickens' books—*Pickwick*, *Nickleby*, *Barnaby Rudge*—but the writer says: 'Es ist nicht meine Absicht, die Geschichte der einzelnen Werke von Dickens darzustellen; nur um das handelt es sich, was geeignet sein kann, ein Licht auf die Natur und das Genie des erzählenden Dichters zu werfen.' The essay has an unfinished air; a note announced a second article, but nothing further appeared.

Julian Schmidt added to his already detailed work on Dickens with a short article in his *Portraits aus dem Neunzehnten Jahrhundert*, published in 1873.[2] This also is directly inspired by Forster's biography, a study of which gave Schmidt information on several points he had suggested in earlier articles, most of them correctly: autobiographical details in *Copperfield*, for example, and points in the composition of *Dombey*. He discusses Dickens' powers of observation and imagination, his politics, his literary connexions; and has some blame for the unpleasant story of Dickens' separation from his wife, where his actions were in part 'ungenerous and ungentlemanly'; in the nervous rush of his last years there is 'etwas Ungestümes, Hastiges, Friedloses, was den Idealen seiner Dichtung widerspricht'. But Schmidt ends his article with a quotation of Carlyle's praise, and declares that, with Dickens' qualities, these few defects were perhaps to be expected.

[1] *Westermanns Monatshefte*, Feb. 1877 (vol. xli). There are further incidental remarks on Dickens in Dilthey's *Dichterische Einbildungskraft und Wahnsinn* (Leipzig, 1886) and in *Das Erlebnis und die Dichtung* (Leipzig, 1906).
[2] (Berlin) pp. 261–81.

H. A. Taine's work on Dickens[1] was discussed by Rudolf Boxberger in an article *Charakterzeichnung bei Dickens* (1882).[2] A long introduction details the work of the nineteenth-century humorists and critically compares Forster's praise with Taine's antagonism; Dickens' characters are discussed in groups under the heads Hypocrisy: Selfishness: Pride. The essay relies largely on Forster and Taine, but apparently owes nothing to Julian Schmidt; the criticism of characters is well done, and the work is useful in spite of its shortness.

The first German thesis on Dickens: *Autobiographisches in 'David Copperfield'* was published in 1891 by G. R. Bluhm,[3] a student rather older than most, and one whose work is consequently of a higher standard than is generally expected of doctorate theses. The interest of *Copperfield* is, he thinks:

keineswegs das Autobiographische an sich, sondern vielmehr die Fülle des aus dem eigenen Leben Gegriffenen, die Treue einzelner Teile und die kunstvolle Aneinanderreihung der autobiographischen Tatsachen sowie die geschickt durchgeführte Verwebung des Wirklichen und des Erdichteten, wodurch der Roman einer vollständigen Autobiographie gleichzukommen scheint.

He recounts the story in sections, and compares it with Forster and later sources of knowledge of Dickens' life; and so shows 'wie weit Dichtung und Wahrheit in *Copperfield* sich decken oder auseinandergehen'.

Ein Lebensbild von Charles Dickens (1894),[4] by P. Branscheid, born from a feeling of dissatisfaction with Forster's too strictly chronological study, uses the more recently published *Letters* of Dickens[5] as a supplement, and attempts:

auf der Grundlage der genannten Briefsammlung ein übersichtlich zusammengestelltes knappes Lebensbild zu entwerfen, durch welches wir Dickens in seiner äußeren Umgebung, im Familienkreise, in seiner Lebensarbeit, seinen Grundsätzen und seiner Stellung zu Staat und Kirche kennen lernen.

That was too much to attempt in seventeen pages; it is serious work, but no more than a sketch of the subject. There are long sections of the letters included in German translation.

---

[1] *Histoire de la Littérature Anglaise*, Paris, 1864, vol. iv. (German translation, 3 vols., 1878-80).
[2] *Prog. der Höheren Bürgerschule zu Havelberg*, Ostern, 1882.
[3] Diss. Leipzig, pub. Reichenbach i. V.   [4] *Prog. Schleusingen.*
[5] Published 1880-2, and simultaneously by Tauchnitz.

LATER CRITICISM AND POPULARITY, 1870–1900 145

Two other references may be given here, one to an article by R. Wülker: 'Zur Jugendgeschichte von Dickens',[1] which corrects or substantiates Forster and R. Langton[2] in their accounts of Dickens' life in 1823–4, the second to P. Heichen's supplementary volume to his translation of Dickens: *Charles Dickens, sein Leben und seine Werke* (1898).[3] The biographical section, 250 pages long, was intended as a useful supplement to the already existing work on Dickens in German, and is based almost entirely on Forster, F. T. Marzials,[4] A. W. Ward[5] and the *Letters*. The rest of the book is a kind of reader's companion for German lovers of Dickens' works, and contains particular and general criticisms drawn from the existing authorities.

All these were based on or influenced by Forster's biography. There was also some good independent research published during this period; the first article under this head is *Die Dialektsprache bei Charles Dickens* (1888) by W. Franz.[6] He only treats London (the Cockneyisms of the Wellers are the chief examples), but he has used all the relevant books and produced a long and comprehensive study of dialect peculiarities in pronunciation and grammar, with etymological discussion and examples. The conclusion is that Dickens knew what he was doing, and that the dialect in his books is far from being invention.

A very interesting essay on *Dickens Beziehungen zu Carlyle* appeared in 1895 in a school programme at Hagen. As a useful and independent piece of research, it deserved a wider publication and better printing. The author, A. Banning, recounts the first meeting and subsequent slowly developing friendship of the two men; shows Carlyle's interest in the Chartist movement, and gives evidence of Dickens' careful study of Carlyle. He then demonstrates the influence of Carlyle on the *Christmas Carol*, the *Chimes*, and especially *Hard Times*, which is dedicated to Carlyle. There are comprehensive references, and the main argument is clear, though some of the less important, purely biographical detail might well have been cut. It is an interesting introduction to an

---

[1] *Archiv f. d. Studium d. n. Sprachen*, vol. c, 1898, pp. 287–92.
[2] *The Childhood and Youth of Charles Dickens*, Manchester, 1883; 2nd ed., London, 1891.
[3] Naumburg, 1898; 723 pp.
[4] *The Life of Charles Dickens*, Great Writers series, 1887.
[5] *Charles Dickens*, English Men of Letters series, London, 1882.
[6] *Englische Studien*, vol. xii, pp. 197–244.

important subject; marked 'Part I', but a second part did not appear.

The second German thesis on Dickens appeared in the same year: *Studien über die Anfänge von Dickens*, by S. Benignus, a Strassburg dissertation which is again a good piece of research by a rather older student. This was the first of a long series of detailed books, theses, and essays which attempted to trace Dickens' literary predecessors, a series which culminated in 1910 in the two volumes of *Englische Romankunst*, by W. Dibelius. The apologia of Benignus for such a study applies to all the following work of this type; he maintains:

... daß es bei Dickens nicht bloß auf seine tatsächliche Umgebung und Lebensbeobachtung ankam, sondern auch stark auf ein ästhetisches Können, auf eine literarische Technik, der, wie allen künstlerischen Errungenschaften, eine große Tradition vorausgehen mußte; ... indem man sie näher untersucht, wird Dickens zwar als ein minder unabhängiger Schriftsteller erscheinen, aber als ein größerer Künstler.[1]

His is a clear, decided, and very widely documented work, which studies only the *Sketches*, but those thoroughly. Part I treats the different editions of the book; Part II studies the sources, with reference to the *Spectator*, the *Idler*, Fielding, Smollett, Goldsmith, Crabbe, Lamb, Thomas Moore, and Mary Mitford; and there is an interesting list of the books Dickens must have known when he wrote the *Sketches*. Part III discusses Dickens' connexions with contemporary social and political movements, as demonstrated in the book. The thesis owes much, as Benignus acknowledges, to the teaching of Alois Brandl, who was professor at Strassburg (where Benignus was a student) from 1892 to 1895. His well-known theories of literary appreciation, which laid stress in part on the study of an author's place in the development of his country's literature, and of the quantity of his indebtedness and the quality of his originality, had marked effects on the criticism of Dickens in Germany. The studies undertaken by Benignus were the first-fruits of this method, and the work continued on these lines, inspired in almost every case by Professor Brandl (from Berlin after 1895), until it reached its peak in the productions of

---

[1] It is clearly pointless to dismiss the whole important question, as does the compiler of a recent English *Dickens Dictionary*, by saying that it 'appears to amount to a charge of plagiarism against Dickens, and nothing else'.

LATER CRITICISM AND POPULARITY, 1870–1900

W. Dibelius, whose great study of Dickens, published in 1916, is dedicated to Brandl.[1]

The next two theses, both presented to the University of Leipzig in 1899, belong to the same class; the authors follow Benignus and were doubtless influenced to some extent by his thesis. A. Winter discusses *Joseph Addison als Humorist in seinem Einfluß auf Dickens' Jugendwerke*; as he says:

> Mag eine Dichternatur noch so ursprünglich sein, ihre erste Betätigung ist nicht denkbar ohne irgendwelche Schulung und Anregung; ... wenn Dickens nun schöpferisch tätig war, dann wird seine lebhafte Phantasie alle ihr gegenwärtigen Eindrücke, ob sie nun der Lektüre oder dem wirklichen Leben entnommen waren, in sich verkörpert und zu vollen und ganzen Gestalten vereinigt haben...

He discusses Dickens' knowledge of the *Spectator* and the *Tatler*, and their influence on the characters and situations in the *Sketches*, *Pickwick*, and *Master Humphrey's Clock*; and finds a general agreement in the methods used to produce humour. His work is good, though he has to push his points hard; he shows definite influences in method and atmosphere, but few direct borrowings. The second thesis; *Dickens in seinen Beziehungen zu den Humoristen Fielding und Smollett*, by F. W. Wilson, owes a certain amount, in form and introduction, to Winter, as both do to Benignus; here again there is, of course, no attempt to belittle Dickens' production, but a clear and readable attempt to show how his mind worked in certain particulars. Wilson analyses Dickens' acquaintance with Fielding and Smollett, and, concentrating mostly on the earlier works (especially *Pickwick*), the general relations in the drawing of characters, the building of situations, the composition, style, diction, and humoristic methods.

The most important work on Dickens in this period, however, was produced by A. Ball and P. Aronstein. The first-named published a series of three articles in 1885 under the title *Dickens und seine Hauptwerke*,[2] which represent the first serious attempt made

---

[1] An excellent example of this method of study, carried out by Brandl himself, is given by his article 'Zur Vorgeschichte der Weird Sisters in "Macbeth"' (1921), reprinted in *Forschungen und Charakteristiken von Alois Brandl ... zum 80. Geburtstag* (Berlin, Leipzig, 1936). Brandl was professor in Prague, 1884; in Göttingen, 1888; in Strassburg, 1892; and in Berlin from 1895. His recent autobiography *Zwischen Inn und Themse* (Berlin, 1936) mentions that he gave lectures on Dickens as early as the time of his professorship in Göttingen.

[2] *Archiv f. d. Studium d. n. Sprachen*, vols. lxxiii, lxxiv; 1885.

in Germany at a full-length discussion of the man and his work; and, with his wide knowledge of European and classical literature, the author produced a work of importance, which analyses Dickens and his books with penetration and perspective. The first section discusses the different types of literature, epic and dramatic, in various forms from pathos to humour and satire (tragedy—comedy—tendentious comedy) with an interesting table, and fits Dickens' work into its place in European literature. The second studies Dickens' characters, and shorter sections follow under the heads: Erotik in Dickens; Naturschilderung; Tendenz; Stil (Phantasie); Architektonik der Werke. The second and third articles are devoted to a very thorough discussion of eight books (*Pickwick, Oliver Twist, Nickleby, Chuzzlewit, Dombey, Copperfield, Bleak House, Hard Times*) and explain clearly all the reasons for appreciation or dislike. The general plot is first considered, then, in detail, each main character, then the interplay and contrast of figures and the construction of the book. Ball likes the character-construction in *Oliver Twist*, feels *Nickleby* to show promise, finds *Chuzzlewit* fit for a better class of reader than that of the earlier books, *Dombey* very good (though some opportunities are lost), and *Copperfield* a little distasteful (more the character of David than the style of the book). *Bleak House* he considers to be on the right lines, but to fail eventually; and *Hard Times*, he thinks, shows failing powers. His conclusion tables good and bad points in Dickens' work and expresses the hope that the younger German writers, avoiding these mistakes, will follow in the *gesunden Bahnen des großen Meisters*.

P. Aronstein's 'Charles Dickens' Weltanschauung', which appeared in 1896,[1] is an excellent, original, and influential essay, clearly divided, well documented from Forster's biography, the *Letters*, the *Speeches*[2] and Dickens' books and illustrated from contemporary criticisms and from F. G. Kitton's *Dickensiana*.[3] There are three major sections:

1. Dickens religiöse Ansichten.
   Das Dogma: Praktisches Christentum: Verhältnis zum Katholizismus: Die Juden.
2. Dickens politische Anschauungen.
   Dickens als politischer Lehrer: Dickens praktischer Anteil am politischen Leben.

[1] *Anglia*, vol. xviii, 1896.
[2] R. H. Shepherd, *The Speeches of Charles Dickens, 1841–1870*, London, 1884.
[3] London, 1886.

3. Dickens als Sozialpolitiker.
Dickens als Volksfreund: Dickens und die herrschende Nationalökonomie: Die Erziehung des Volkes: Die Armenpflege: Allerhand Philanthropen.

Aronstein's conclusion is that Dickens, without much education and without a philosophical system, found his way well, in all important matters, through the confusion of theories in the second third of his century.

Aronstein's second article, 'Dickens und Carlyle', published in the same year and the same periodical, reaches quite independently much the same conclusions as A. Banning's essay, discussed above, which had appeared in 1895. Aronstein adds that there are further traces of Carlyle's influence to be found in the *Tale of Two Cities*, the *Child's History of England*, *Little Dorrit*, and *Our Mutual Friend*, and also in those chapters of *Copperfield*, *Bleak House*, and *Edwin Drood* which are directed against unworthy philanthropy. A third article by Aronstein, 'Die sozialen und politischen Strömungen in England im zweiten Drittel unseres Jahrhunderts in Dichtung und Roman', appeared from 1896 to 1898[1] and contains, in the section which discusses the novel, a sociological and literary discussion of *Hard Times*. The conclusion of this is that Dickens was, in spite of prejudice, correct in his definition of cause and cure of social unrest in England at the time.

So the turn of the century was reached. In thirty years from Dickens' death much interesting work had been produced, and some that was of real importance. The study of Dickens' literary forerunners had already been undertaken by S. Benignus, followed by A. Winter and F. W. Wilson; R. Boxberger, and several others, had commenced analysis of the methods Dickens used to produce his characters and to depict their interplay; and, generally, by careful studies of Dickens' life the way had been prepared for a deeper analysis of his works. These, together with the study of Dickens' influence on German writers[2] were to be the main currents in German work on Dickens in the early twentieth century.

[1] *Archiv f. d. Studium d. n. Sprachen*; *Hard Times* is discussed in vol. c, pp. 46–52.
[2] Books, theses, and articles on this subject are not examined here, as they are thoroughly discussed in the appropriate chapters of Part II.

II
1900–1916

A FEATURE of this period is the discovery by German students of Dickens as a subject for doctorate theses. The nineteenth century had produced four such theses; in the first fifteen years of the twentieth century twenty were published, wholly or largely concerned with Dickens, of which fourteen appeared between 1907 and 1912. They were of very varied standard; only the more important and interesting are examined here.

W. Frieser's thesis; *Die Schulen bei Dickens, auf ihre geschichtliche Wahrheit geprüft*, a Leipzig dissertation of 1909, is sufficiently characterized by its subtitle *Ein Beitrag zur Geschichte der Erizehung in England*. It is a long, carefully ordered and documented account of English schools in the nineteenth century, more a history of education than a literary study. Dotheboys Hall, of course, takes a prominent place, and Frieser's conclusion is that Dickens' account is largely true, certainly not exaggerated, and in many respects moderate.

K. Grünewald's study, *Die Verwendung der Mundart in den Romanen von Dickens, Thackeray, Eliot und Kingsley*, presented to the University of Giessen in 1914, is purely philological, but has an interesting conclusion; he finds that these authors make a far better use of dialect in their novels than did the writers of the eighteenth century, and adds that this is especially the case for Dickens and Eliot, both of whom handle dialect with great certainty and exactness.

Considerable interest was shown during this period in the composition of Dickens' characters and in the study of their place in his novels. The three theses mentioned below are the best examples of the results of this interest.

Über die Technik der Charakterisierung in den Jugendwerken von Charles Dickens, a Halle dissertation of 1912 by R. Jügler, is a sound piece of research, of the right length, well divided and well supported. He deals with Dickens' four earliest books and examines the various methods of characterization used in them, especially the indirect method Dickens handled so well. The development of Dickens' technique through the four books is neatly

LATER CRITICISM AND POPULARITY, 1900–1916

summarised. The thesis shows that in this respect the *Sketches* are a mixture of much that is good and much that is certainly bad; *Pickwick*, the best of the four, shows great development, to which *Nickleby* adds a few new points. Jügler finds that *Oliver Twist* is not up to the standard of either *Pickwick* or *Nickleby*, as the characterization there is frequently primitive; perhaps because the book was written too quickly, and because Dickens was more interested in the matter than the manner of the tale.

Something was added to Jügler's results by E. Edelmann's thesis of 1915: *Die Charakterzeichnung in den Romanen von Dickens*, a Giessen dissertation, which makes a thorough investigation of direct and indirect characterization in Dickens' novels. Edelmann defines three main periods in the development of this point of Dickens' technique: *Pickwick* to *Nickleby*, the *Old Curiosity Shop* to *Bleak House*, and the latest books; the second of these is, in his opinion, the period of the greatest balance and perfection. Methods of characterization, he points out, had already reached a high standard in the earlier English novels; and so

Dickens' Bedeutung liegt vor allem in der Ausgestaltung einiger Methoden, die vor ihm nur geringe Geltung besaßen, der Geste, der körperlichen Schilderung, der Wiederholung und des typischen ersten Auftretens.

These are all methods of indirect characterization, so that Dickens considerably enriched the science of this important technique.

W. Johannpeter's *Handlungs-, Charakter- und Situationskontrast in den Jugendwerken von Charles Dickens*, a thesis presented to the University of Halle and published in 1914, represents a further development of the interest in Dickens' characters. In this thesis, which studies Dickens' books from the *Sketches* to *Nickleby*, each book is considered separately, and there are simple graphs to demonstrate the contrasting of the characters. The conclusion praises *Nickleby* for better balance in contrast than is to be found in the earlier books; *Pickwick* was almost entirely comedy, *Oliver Twist* almost entirely the opposite, but in *Nickleby* 'kommen Tragik und Komik zu gleichem Rechte, so daß das ausgelöste Kontrastempfinden ein gleichmäßigeres ist'. There is a short reference to Dickens' use of contrast in his later books; in the *Old Curiosity Shop*, whose plan of contrasted figures closely resembles that of *Oliver Twist*, in *Copperfield*, and in *Dombey*—where Johannpeter finds *die höchste Vollendung*.

The greatest interest was shown, however, in the study of Dickens' literary predecessors, inspired by Professor Brandl and commenced in 1895 by S. Benignus. A few theses which study this subject may be mentioned. In 1908 A. Berndt examined the *Entstehungsgeschichte der 'Pickwick Papers'* in a dissertation for the doctorate of Greifswald. After a short account of the external origins of the book (the publishers' proposals, Seymour's history), he studies with great thoroughness the more intimate sources, the composition, the choice of and sources for characters and events, and gives an interesting, though at times slightly confusing, examination of the literary forerunners of *Pickwick*, including the *Spectator*, Goldsmith, Crabbe, Lamb, Fielding, Smollett, and Washington Irving; a special chapter discusses Dickens' debt to Pierce Egan. His thesis, which makes a good attempt to show how Dickens fits into his period, is interesting and well written.

Der Dickenssche Roman 'Hard Times', seine Entstehung und seine Tendenzen, by W. Stumpf,[1] considers, for the evolution of the book, partly the direct history (the strike at Preston, Dickens' friendship with Carlyle), and partly the literary history, for which Dickens' models in eighteenth-century and contemporary novels are examined; the thesis concludes with a study of the social and educational programme of the book. Stumpf's work is well written and abundantly supported from a wide acquaintance with English literature.

A third thesis inspired by Professor Brandl's teaching was F. Fiedler's *Entstehungsgeschichte von Charles Dickens' 'Oliver Twist'*[2]. There are four sections, of which the most interesting deals with the inner evolution of the book, discussing characters, scenes, and events by the well-known method of comparing Dickens with his predecessors. The material is good, but not always well handled, and some of the 'models' suggested are very far-fetched. Another section deals with the workhouse, and, where this is directly concerned with Dickens and his work, it is good; but no less than twenty-five pages, just under one-quarter of the whole, are devoted to a complete history of the institution, which is far outside the scope of the thesis. The same must be said of the last section, which turns without warning to a study of the technique of the story. The work as it is is good but unbalanced; a third of its matter could with advantage be pruned out. Its

---

[1] Diss. Greifswald, pub. Freienwalde a./O., 1910.   [2] Diss. Halle, 1912.

LATER CRITICISM AND POPULARITY, 1900–1916

author, however, was to make a certain position for himself in German work by a series of useful articles which he began to publish in 1919.

Two independent studies of the ideas and sources behind Dickens' books may find a place here. The first was an article of some importance and certain interest, entitled *Dickens und Malthus*, published in 1910 by B. Fehr.[1] Fehr says the *Christmas Carol* is by no means so innocent a Christmas story as it appears to be; he attempts to show how it is directed in part against the teachings of the Malthusian school. This was, he says, the first time Dickens had ever directed his satire against an actual theory; in this he owed much to Carlyle's teaching. Fehr discusses Carlyle's attitude to Malthus, and gives a history of Malthus' ideas in England; they were a subject of much interest in the thirties and forties, just at the time Dickens was producing his Christmas stories. He shows the stern results of Malthus' theories especially in the treatment of the destitute, and demonstrates Dickens' satire of these ideas in the *Christmas Carol*. Unfortunately Dickens himself had no sound solution of the problem to put forward; his Christian socialism is too vague to be satisfactory.

The second study is by C. Böttger: *Dickens' historischer Roman 'A Tale of Two Cities' und seine Quellen*.[2] Böttger shows that Dickens used for this book, beside Carlyle's *French Revolution*, L. S. Mercier's *Tableau de Paris*, published at Amsterdam in 1782-8. Chapter V of Böttger's thesis, which compares the novel and its sources, is of special interest. Frequent parallel passages show close reference by Dickens to his sources, especially for numbers (of e.g. crowds, servants); most particularly to Carlyle's book, which he knew very well. A further chapter shows interesting parallels between the situation of some characters in the *Tale of Two Cities* and that of certain characters in *Barnaby Rudge*. This is a sound average thesis, which succeeds in what it attempts, but might have attempted more.

It is refreshing to turn from consideration of these secondary studies to the first work of Wilhelm Dibelius, later to become the German authority on Dickens. He had studied under Brandl and was for a time Privat-Dozent under him in Berlin; as was mentioned above, it was his service to continue and to complete the study of

---

[1] *Germanisch-Romanische Monatsschrift*, 1910, pp. 542–55.
[2] Diss. Königsberg, 1913.

Dickens' work by those methods inspired by Professor Brandl and first followed in S. Benignus' thesis in 1895. His interest in Dickens was first aroused in 1903. In that year, having found that the immense number of works on Dickens rather confused than enlightened the student, he began to work on a book 'das die Persönlichkeit und die literarische Leistung des großen Autors in die Literatur- und Kulturgeschichte seines Volkes einreiht'.[1] He published none of his results for seven years, and waited a further six years before producing the final, definitive work.

In 1910 there appeared the two volumes of his *Englische Romankunst: die Technik des englischen Romans im 18. und zu Anfang des 19. Jahrhunderts*. This, as he says in the Foreword, was originally intended as an introductory chapter to the larger work on Dickens; but the subject was so important for a proper understanding of Dickens' position, and yet had been so little studied, that he decided to widen its scope, publish it as an independent book, and so make 'a proper foundation for the real building'.

Unzweifelhaft dankt seine Kunst ihre ersten Anregungen und Richtlinien den großen Erzählern und Humoristen der drei vorhergehenden Generationen, Fielding, Smollett, Goldsmith, Sterne, auch Hook und Marryat, und ist dann schnell selbständig geworden. Das alles ließ sich jedoch nicht anschaulich machen, solange die Kunst der Vorgänger noch nicht untersucht war. . . . So wurde aus einer Skizze von Dickens' Vorgängern eine weitschichtig angelegte Untersuchung über die Erzählungstechnik des 18. Jahrhunderts.

The book is not a history of the English novel. It had to be limited in several ways, and Dibelius says 'meine Aufmerksamkeit ist im letzten Grunde gerichtet auf das Verhältnis der künstlerischen Individualität zur Tradition'. He explains the scope of the work, from Defoe to the immediate predecessors of Dickens, and his introduction is a useful part-summary of the book. He discusses at length the technique of the authors mentioned above, besides Defoe and Richardson, the novel of sensation, the social novel, the woman's novel, and the novel of Walter Scott; and in the last chapter, 'Der englische Roman in der Ära der vier George', produces a useful general summary. In several cases (for example, Hook and Marryat) he relates the author directly to Dickens.

His own summary must find a place here. He attempts to show

[1] W. Dibelius, *Charles Dickens*, Leipzig, Berlin, 1916; preface.

LATER CRITICISM AND POPULARITY, 1900–1916

how, in the English eighteenth-century novel, there are two types side by side:

(a) *The (Defoe-) Fielding type*: 'der alte Abenteuerroman; reichbewegte Handlung, viel subjektiver Vortrag, gut gegliederte Handlung, viel Satire und Milieu, viel Humor.'
(b) *The Richardson-Goldsmith type*: 'der — wohl schließlich auf französischen Vorbildern beruhende — Persönlichkeitsroman; wenig Handlung, dafür eingehende Psychologie, ganz überwiegend objektiver Vortrag, wenig Gliederung der Handlung. Didaxis statt Satire, Pathos und Tragik statt Humor'.

These two types attempt to unify, but without much success for some time. 'Die Synthese tritt ein zunächst in der Erweiterung und Verschmelzung beider Typen zum historischen Roman bei Walter Scott, ohne diesen historischen Hintergrund erst bei Dickens in *Oliver Twist* und bei allen seinen weiteren Romanen.'

This 900-page work is of the first importance for a proper understanding of Dickens' merits. It is authoritative, supported by a vast knowledge of the English novel; detailed, but essentially a unity. Dibelius had really remarkable expository powers, and used them excellently here. Some criticism made a few years later by Professor E. Eckhardt[1] must, however, be noticed at this point; he has two minor objections, both valid, to what he feels is otherwise a *gediegene und hervorragende Arbeit*. The first springs to the mind at once on a consideration of the book; Dibelius is rather too ready to assume a literary connexion between two authors when the second makes use of an event or a motive also to be found in the first writer; although a much simpler explanation, and one probably nearer the truth, would be that both drew their material directly from life. The second objection is one which necessarily arises from the restrictions Dibelius imposed on his work; Eckhardt feels that since the technique alone is studied, a disproportionate view of the various authors is given; Hook and Marryat, because of their strongly developed technique, are given more attention than they deserve, while a really important writer like Defoe loses his due position for the opposite reason.

It is consequently important to keep in mind that *Englische Romankunst* was intended as an introduction to a thorough study

[1] *Germanisch-Romanische Monatsschrift*, 1914, p. 563 f.

of Dickens, and not as a history of the English novel. If it is accepted for what the author intended it to be, the criticisms of Eckhardt lose a little of their importance. To the student concerned chiefly or solely with Dickens, the book is invaluable.

In the same year (1910) Dibelius also produced two articles on the same aspect of Dickens' own work, showing to some extent his connexions with the authors treated in the longer work.

'Das Erstlingswerk von Charles Dickens', an essay of thirty pages,[1] supports the research of Benignus, Wilson, and Winter, and amplifies it considerably; they showed Dickens' relation to the work of Addison, Fielding, Smollett, and Lamb, and to these writers Dibelius adds Pierce Egan, Hook, Leigh Hunt, and Washington Irving. This done, he says:

> Sodann möchte ich nachweisen, daß die ganze Auffassung des Lebens, wie sie Dickens in seinen Erstlingswerken zeigt, sich in der Schule der moralischen Wochenschriften gebildet hat und daneben den Einfluß der Romantik verrät. Drittens läßt sich der Stil seines Erstlingswerkes namentlich in seinen humoristischen Bestandteilen genauer analysieren und zum beträchtlichen Teil durch literarische Einflüsse erklären; aber auch die persönlichen Eigenheiten von Dickens' Wesen treten in diesen ersten seiner Schriften schon deutlich hervor.

The second article, 'Pierce Egan und Dickens',[2] is short but of considerable interest. The relation of Dickens' work to Egan had been touched on by earlier writers,[3] and A. Berndt had devoted a few pages to it in 1908; Dibelius rounds off this work, mentioning that Berndt was partly right, but had overlooked some essential points. He explains that the importance of Egan lies in the fact that he gives a very clear example of the taste of the decade in which Dickens, as a boy, received his first literary impressions; in this light he discusses Egan's work, and shows how important a forerunner of Dickens he was. He points out parallels between Egan's books and *Pickwick*, not only in actual events but also in the whole general character:

> Da haben wir komische Ereignisse als Grundstock des Ganzen, darüber eine dünne Schicht von Pathos und Sentimentalität, und Aben-

---

[1] *Englische Studien*, vol. xliii, 1910.
[2] *Archiv f. d. Studium d. n. Sprachen*, vol. cxxiv, 1910.
[3] See, e.g., P. Fitzgerald, *The History of Pickwick*, 1891, pp. 113, 157; W. L. Cross, *The Development of the English Novel*, New York, 1899; and F. G. Kitton, *The Novels of Charles Dickens*, London, 1897, p. 5 f.

teuer, die nicht mehr in ganz England spielen, sondern das Londoner Leben darstellen wollen. Das letztere Moment hat die *Sketches* entscheidend beeinflußt, die Mischung von Komik, Pathos und Sentimentalität außerdem die *Pickwick Papers*.

So it is clear that in his first two works Dickens followed the taste of the day, which explains his immediate popularity and helps to explain Dickens himself; but he broke away from this style energetically with *Oliver Twist*.

A third article by Dibelius, published in 1911, was entitled 'Zu den Pickwick Papers'.[1] This was also meant to supplement the work of the same four earlier investigators of Dickens' relations to his literary predecessors as shown in the book. Here a definite influence of Combe's *Doctor Syntax* on *Pickwick* is shown, and a few new points of relation to Addison, Steele, Smollett, Fielding, Hook, and Marryat are made. Dibelius concludes that, as was to be expected, Dickens' relations to his forerunners were by no means small:

> In den meisten Fällen ... sind auch nur die Umrisse der Überlieferung von Dickens übernommen worden und die eigentliche Aufgabe ist vollkommen selbständig gelöst. Aber es finden sich doch auch überraschende Übereinstimmungen im Einzelnen.

These three articles are excellent examples of Dibelius' methods and style. All are extremely clear, and though in each there is a wealth of very detailed information, they are never confusing. The last of the three is perhaps the least, for there he is chiefly concerned with very minor points, and Eckhardt's criticisms of *Englische Romankunst* once more come to mind.

Professor Eckhardt's lecture 'Zur Charakteristik von Charles Dickens' was printed in the October and November issues of the *Germanisch-Romanische Monatsschrift* for 1914. Extracts from this have already been given in the consideration of *Englische Romankunst*. Eckhardt felt the time had come to consider Dickens' work in its true perspective, to reach definite conclusions about his originality, his dependence on literary models, his temporary and his lasting merits—'gleichsam eine Bilanz seines Schaffens aufzustellen'. The article is, consequently, not biographical; its chief concern is to summarize the work of Benignus, Wilson, Winter, and Dibelius, to add a few points and to act as a very necessary corrective to their rather too enthusiastic search for

[1] *Anglia*, vol. xxxv, 1911.

literary models. There is a good comparison of Dickens with Thackeray, and a most interesting discussion of Dickens' place in literature half a century after his death. Much of his satire, Eckhardt says, and some of his exaggerated pathos have not stood the test of time; but his lifelike, indirect characterization, his 'Germanic' humour and the poetic realism of his London scenes have proved to be of lasting worth. It is an excellent essay, providing the natural reaction to the type of criticism carried out in *Englische Romankunst*; while studying Dibelius it is important to keep in mind the leitmotiv of this article—'die Wirklichkeit als Romanquelle kommt bei ihm entschieden zu kurz'. Finally, the appreciation of Dickens' real merits is pleasant and generous.

There is a further short article by Dibelius in the *Shakespeare-Jahrbuch* for 1916, entitled *Dickens und Shakespeare*. Dibelius gives a brief summary of the evidence for Dickens' acquaintance with Shakespeare's works, shows points of contact, and attempts to explain some surprising similarities. Dealing first with direct resemblances — probable reminiscences or even borrowings — he continues with a study of the other, often very close, indirect resemblances. These were not matters of pure chance; 'die dichterische Anlage ist die gleiche . . . beide sind Vertreter der gleichen romantischen Auffassung des Lebens'; and Dibelius shows how both Dickens and Shakespeare find pleasure in the extreme and the enormous, how both unite grotesque comedy and dark tragedy, high virtue and blackest vice, realism and mysticism. There were also resemblances in the age in which each lived; the temperature of the literature in the age which produced Dickens had some affinities with that of the period from which Shakespeare sprang. And Dickens probably drew a number of his themes from the melodrama, whose unliterary but very popular traditions go back in part to Elizabethan times.

The great study of Dickens' place and work published by Dibelius in 1916[1] overtopped all other criticisms. There is nothing to equal it in any language; no one else was so well prepared by long and wide study to write the authoritative book on Dickens. As has been shown, it is the result of no less than twelve years work; the 'foundation for the real building' was laid in the exhaustive *Englische Romankunst* of 1910, and since that date

[1] *Charles Dickens*, Leipzig, Berlin, 1916.

LATER CRITICISM AND POPULARITY, 1900–1916

several articles had shown with what care and attention to detail the final work was being produced.

The literary background having been studied, the next duty was to examine the historical background—social, religious, and political; the first chapter of the new book carries out this task with deceptive ease. An immense reading is summarised with balance and proportion, and the tangle of traditions, beliefs, and theories of half a century is straightened into a remarkable clarity. With such a broad basis the new study of Dickens' work could not fail to be authoritative.

The contents are usefully varied. After the historical introduction, Dickens' early life is studied; then his early books, and his first conception of his life's work. There follows a second historical chapter, which provides the background to his Christmas stories and his later semi-political novels of the type of *Hard Times*. Then his later life is reported, and his latest books; there is a general criticism of his complete technique; and a chapter on his influence and his cultural value to his country. It is noteworthy that the sections are fluid; it would have been easy for the writer to divide his work into three parts and to study separately the history, the novels, and the technique, but the method actually adopted not only sustains the interest by variation, but presents at once a more comprehensive and better-supported argument. The thirteen chapters cover 462 pages, and notes, references, index, and full bibliography 62 more.

The book has four main objects, which may be summarized as follows:

1. To assess Dickens' originality and his debt to his predecessors.
2. To show Dickens' position in contemporary culture.
3. To discuss Dickens' personality, as man and as creative writer.
4. To assess Dickens' value:
    (*a*) to English literature,
    (*b*) to English culture.

As might be expected from the methods of Dibelius' early works, as well as from the dedication of this to Alois Brandl, the first of these objects ranks first in importance. A host of obvious or suggested literary reminiscences are traced to account for the plan, the events, and the characters of Dickens' novels; the method is well known and need not be discussed further. But now Dibelius is ready to point out what is really new in Dickens; with such a wide knowledge of earlier authors he can show, with authority, what Dickens brings to English literature that is really fresh. In the main, he details why it is that Dickens is not noteworthy for the composition of his books, and that his real strength is in the characters of his novels; and he shows clearly how 'das eigenste Wesen von Dickens ist die Verbindung von scharfem Realismus und symbolischer Mystik'. On Dickens' position in contemporary culture he is absorbingly interesting; he demonstrates that though Dickens himself produced no new ideas, he was yet in a sense the saviour of English liberalism:

Er ist ein Radikaler von kräftigster Färbung, dem aller politischer Konservatismus ein Greuel ist. Aber die geistigen Ideen der konservativen Strömung hat er zum großen Teil in sich aufgenommen. ... So war dieser Radikale dazu befähigt, die Gedanken der konservativ-romantischen Welt in die liberalen Massen zu werfen.[1]

He is good and fair on Dickens' personality, not at all afraid of passing a really severe judgement wherever that is necessary; and the short section headed 'Dichter und Wahrheit', which discusses Dickens' claim that he only reported reality, is of great interest. The fourth main theme, which is the estimate of Dickens' value to English culture, is of all probably the most useful to English students: in this country attempts to assess Dickens' influence have too frequently been made ridiculous by an uncritical enthusiasm to which Dibelius is not subject. The conclusions he reaches are set out fully in the last chapter of the book, 'Das Lebenswerk von Dickens', especially the seventh section. Dickens originated no single reform, and several reforming movements which he eventually supported were well under way before he wrote a word; the two occasions on which he gave his independent and uninfluenced support to reforms were both distinct failures. 'Zum Führer fehlte ihm alles, die umfassende Bildung, der beherrschende klare Blick, die Fähigkeit, die praktischen Folgerungen allgemeiner Grundsätze zu erkennen, die Mäßigung im Erfolg'.[2] Dickens' real importance lies in his remarkable power as an organizer of public opinion:

Er war für die englischen Reformer ein unschätzbarer Bundesgenosse. Sie kämpften gegen die Machthaber mit Hilfe der öffentlichen

[1] pp. 208–9.   [2] p. 232.

Meinung, und die öffentliche Meinung stand unter Dickens' Einfluß. Nur Dickens war der große Prediger des Fortschrittes, den sie alle hörten, der Mann, der begeisterte, anfeuerte und die Stimmung schuf, daß etwas Großes getan werden mußte.[1]

A list is given of those reforms for which he pleaded successfully with the mass of the people.[2] So also one can say of him: 'Dickens gehört zu den Männern, denen die englische Nation es dankt, daß sie durch die Folgen der neuen Industrialisierung nicht in zwei getrennte Lager auseinandergerissen wurde'.[3]

The criticism of the novels is excellent, but too detailed to be considered fully here. On the comparative worth of the books Dibelius says:

die 'Zwei Städte' [*Tale of Two Cities*] sind Dickens' Meisterleistung auf dem Gebiete des ernsten Romans, wie 'Copperfield' die Höhe seiner idyllischen Kunst, 'Pickwick' das Meisterwerk seines Humors ist.[4] 'Unsterblichkeit' wird eine nüchterne Kritik nur den 'Pickwickiern', dem 'Copperfield', dem 'Weihnachtslied' [*Christmas Carol*], vielleicht dem 'Oliver Twist' und den 'Zwei Städten' zuerkennen können.[5]

Such a brief summary can only give a poor idea of the value of this book. Anything but a 'popular' study, it is only suitable for serious students of Dickens; but to them it is indispensable. Its value in this country lies partly in the fact that it is the work of a foreigner, who is in a position to see details rather more in their true proportion. He is not carried away by the popularity of Dickens, and does not scruple to criticize severely wherever he considers necessary; and as this is carried out with a wide generosity and balanced historical sense, the reproofs carry full weight. He is writing for foreigners, and so spares no pains to make his detailed arguments perfectly plain, starting on no assumed knowledge other than a general acquaintance with Dickens' life and books; thus his exposition of the historical background of Dickens' work is a miracle of clarity.

There is comparatively little on Dickens' life, but that was to be expected. The work is a literary and cultural study, not a biography. More to the point is a slight criticism that the historical background is possibly a little too clearly set out, so that we tend to lose sight of the fact that Dickens himself was almost completely unconscious of its details, and that the inquiry into the influences to which he was subjected must be based to some extent

[1] pp. 231, 232.   [2] p. 457.   [3] p. 438.   [4] p. 333.   [5] p. 455.

on supposition. The chief criticism to be made, however, is once more that against the weakness inherent in this system of tracing literary predecessors; it is doubtless a very important part of the criticism of an author, but it is only a part, and in this case one feels that rather less attention might have been paid to it and rather more given to a personal and subjective appreciation of each novel. There is no doubt where Dibelius' chief interest lies; the later books of Dickens were more carefully prepared than the early ones, and in their construction he was less dependent on literary reminiscences; so Dibelius says: 'für den Literarhistoriker sind die Romane dieser Zeit weniger ergiebig als die früheren',[1] and he appears to lose interest in them; there is very little indeed in his book on *Little Dorrit, Great Expectations, Our Mutual Friend,* or *Edwin Drood.* This is the only sign of lack of balance to be found in the whole work. The culmination of Brandl's system of criticism as applied to Dickens, and very much more besides, it is not only the most important work published on Dickens in Germany, but also the outstanding study of Dickens in any language; a harmonious and scholarly piece of research which no student of Dickens, of English nineteenth-century literature, or of German criticism can afford to pass by.

The publication of this work marks the end of the second period of German studies of Dickens, the shortest of the three but the most productive. The peak years were 1910 and the centenary year 1912; a decrease in interest was already noticeable in the years immediately preceding the war, and it was only to be expected that the hostilities between England and Germany should eventually stop publication entirely. No German work on Dickens is to be reported between the years 1916 and 1919. But the studies of these sixteen years, drawn together and completed in Dibelius' *Charles Dickens*, represented what was very nearly a complete examination of Dickens' life and work.

[1] p. 309.

III

1919–1937

POST-WAR studies of Dickens do not show any special continuity, though the influence of Professor Brandl's teaching, transmitted by W. Dibelius' *Charles Dickens* of 1916, was still apparent in a series of six articles published in literary periodicals betwen 1919 and 1923 by F. Fiedler, whose thesis on *Oliver Twist* was discussed in the preceding chapter.

His first article, 'Dickens' Gebrauch der rythmischen Prosa im Christmas Carol',[1] partly follows W. Dibelius, who had made a few remarks on the subject of Dickens' rythmic prose generally.[2] Fiedler suggests that there may be in this case some influence from Shakespeare, gives several examples, and points out that Dickens had the good taste not to overwork this artistic method, which he used more freely, however, in the *Christmas Carol* than in any earlier book. In 1920 his second article, 'Dickens Belesenheit',[3] appeared. The examination of Dickens' indebtedness to earlier authors had already been carried out with great thoroughness by other students, but this article differs from their work in its sensible object of discovering, not what we must assume Dickens read, but what we can prove he had read by the direct method of examining references or quotations in his works, or by other direct means. Fiedler's results, which are as nearly complete as is necessary or even possible, are briefly as follows: The classical lyric and epic, no special knowledge. English drama, a rich knowledge. English comedy, farce, operetta, melodrama, pantomime, a wide acquaintance. English narrative literature, very well known. Small acquaintance with learned works; many biographies, but no histories, except Carlyle's *French Revolution*. Foreign literature, a meagre and unsystematic acquaintance.

In the same year a third article appeared, entitled 'Dickens und die Posse',[4] in which Fiedler studies Dickens' interest and actual participation in many plays, mostly between the years 1842 and 1857; a second section is devoted to a literary study of comedy in

---

[1] *Archiv. f. d. Studium d. n. Sprachen*, vol. cxxxix, 1919.
[2] Op. cit., 1916, pp. 74, 220, 322, 402–3.
[3] *Archiv f. d. Studium d. n. Sprachen*, vol. cxl, 1920.
[4] *Englische Studien*, vol. liii, 1920.

London during Dickens' youth (1827-30), and a third discusses Dickens as a writer of comedies, comparing his productions with those studied in the second part, and concluding that he brought nothing new to the development of the genre.

In 1921 the *Archiv für das Studium der neueren Sprachen* published Fiedler's fourth article: 'Das Weihnachtsfest in England vor und bei Dickens';[1] as far as this concerns Dickens, it refers chiefly to the *Christmas Carol*, a school edition of which Fiedler published in the same year. The article gives a general history of Christmas in England from the earliest times to the 19th century and an account of Dickens' services towards the preservation of the festivities, followed by a general history of Christmas as described in English literature from the earliest traces by way of Washington Irving, Leigh Hunt, and Mary Mitford to the *Christmas Carol*; the conclusion shows Dickens' position in the history of the literature of Christmas.

The same periodical published Fiedler's fifth article in 1922: 'Wie Dickens das "Christmas Carol" feilte'.[2] Here he uses the full material provided by F. G. Kitton's facsimile of Dickens' manuscript[3] and the first proof as it was reproduced in 1843 in the Tauchnitz edition. Alterations in the manuscript and in the proofs are considered, both those of sense and those of style, and the conclusion reached is that all the alterations 'erfolgten fast ausschließlich in dem Streben nach Kürze, Klarheit, Anschaulichkeit und gewählter Rhetorik'. Fritz Fiedler's sixth and last article was published in the same periodical[4] and is concerned with the same book; the title is 'Die Vorgeschichte der Hauptgestalten in Dickens "Christmas Carol"' (1923). The main figures are Scrooge and the four ghosts. The history of the different types of miser in English literature from Anglo-Saxon times, which Fiedler considers necessary for an understanding of Scrooge, is given in far too much detail, and is of very doubtful value in any case, but a few reminiscences from earlier authors are shown to have passed in this case, as in that of the ghosts, into the *Christmas Carol*; Fiedler emphasizes, however, that Dickens greatly improved on his sources.

One of the most important studies of Dickens in this period was

---

[1] Vol. cxli, 1921.   [2] Vol. cxliv, 1922.
[3] *A Christmas Carol . . . facsimile reproduction*, London, 1890.
[4] Vol. cxlvi, 1923.

Stefan Zweig's essay in *Drei Meister: Balzac, Dickens, Dostoiewski*.[1] This opens with a mention of Dickens' great popularity, and shows how this is explained by the fact that Dickens fitted the taste of his age and country exactly. The English tradition, with which Dickens was in such perfect agreement, is discussed, and it is made clear that, though Dickens had more than great powers, he allowed himself to be bound by the restrictions and taboos of his age, and so produced 'nur ein Außerordentliches, und nicht das Gewaltige, zu dem ihn sein Genie prädestinierte'. So we find in his works, Zweig says, the full expression of the comfortable middle-class ideals of his time; so we see that he, like his heroes, is modest in his demands from life. 'Seine große und unvergeßliche Tat war darum eigentlich nur: die Romantik der Bourgeoisie zu entdecken, die Poesie des Prosaischen'. Zweig studies Dickens as a genius of visual imagination, praises the fullness and variety of his work, and shows that he had two unconscious manners of escape from the fetters of tradition; one was the portrayal of children ('hier überwindet er das Englische, das Irdische, hier ist Dickens ohne Einschränkung groß und unvergleichlich'), the other was the use of his incomparable humour, with its faint ironic undertone. Dickens' value to the world, Zweig says, lies in the fact that 'er hat einen Augenblick der Stille in der Welt zum Gedicht gefügt'; and for that he will not be forgotten.

The essay is short, but typical of its author. He says in another book, *Der Kampf mit dem Dämon*: 'Ich suche keine Formeln des Geistigen, ich gestalte Formen des Geistes'; and he has done that here in Dickens' case. His essay is purely personal, and makes no attempt to be a literary history; it is a psychological and historical sketch of great penetration. The preface of *Drei Meister* prepares us for this: there Zweig says that the unwritten subtitle of the book is *Psychologie des Romanciers*.

A few doctorate theses on Dickens published during this period may be noticed. H. Heuer's *Romaneske Elemente im Realismus von Charles Dickens*, a Marburg dissertation, appeared in 1927. This excellent study points out that in spite of a large number of romantic traits in Dickens, he must nevertheless be considered chiefly as a realist 'insofern als er die ganze lebenserfüllte Mannigfaltigkeit des Stadtlebens und Bürgertums zum Gegenstand seiner Kunst macht, und eine Beobachtungsgabe, die mit untrüglicher

[1] Leipzig, 1920. This is the first volume of Zweig's *Baumeister der Welt*.

Sicherheit das Charakteristische der Erscheinungen herausfindet, in den Dienst seiner formenden Schöpfungskraft stellt'. The romantic elements in Dickens' work are discussed in the third section under the heads: contrast as a formative principle; elements of form dependent on the sense of contrast (these include the picturesque, the grotesque, the fabulous); and romantic elements in the portrayal of nature. The work is limited to the study of the novels of Dickens' best period, 1837-50; in these fourteen years his most characteristic books were published, from *Oliver Twist* to *Copperfield*.

A thesis published in 1933 handles a new aspect of Dickens; *Die Formen der Perspektive in Charles Dickens' Romanen: ihr sprachlicher Ausdruck und ihre strukturelle Bedeutung*,[1] by W. Wickardt. The theory, for which W. Dilthey was partly responsible, is introduced by the author as a necessary element of literary criticism; the conception of perspective as a fundamental of visual art has long been familiar, but it has an essential importance for all art, and so in particular should not be overlooked in the discussion of literary work. 'Im Künstler als Prinzip der Veranschaulichung, im Aufnehmenden als das der Anschaulichkeit, bildet die Perspektive in beiden gemeinsam die gleiche spezifische Brücke von der abstrakten zur konkreten Vorstellung.' The application of this principle to the study of Dickens' work is of extreme interest, particularly in the seventh section: 'Die perspektivische Struktur des Dickensschen Stils.' Wickhardt sees a clear and steady development in Dickens' use of this literary method, 'eine Entwicklung, die Dickens nicht nur mit allen Fasern der vor ihm gelegten Tradition verhaftet, sondern gleichzeitig auch als tüchtigen Wegbereiter der nachfahrenden Generation zeigt'.

Die Namengebung bei Dickens, eine Studie über Lautsymbolik[2] by C. Sennewald, published in 1936, is a clear and well-handled study of an aspect of Dickens' work which had never before been exhaustively considered. The first part, on the symbolism of names in thirteen of Dickens' predecessors, is a necessary introduction which is perhaps a little too much developed, as it occupies very nearly one-half of the book; the second section, on Dickens alone, is of great interest. Sennewald shows that in the names of his

---

[1] Diss. Göttingen, unpublished. Available as vol. xxii in the series *Neue Forschung*, Berlin, 1933.
[2] Diss. Berlin, and as vol. cciii in the series *Palaestra*, Leipzig, 1936.

characters Dickens can suggest their occupation, their nature or their general appearance; she discusses the various methods he uses to these ends, and is of great interest on the subject of sound-symbolism. Dickens, she says, uses this method more freely and with greater expressiveness than any of his predecessors, and 'so bestätigt auch die Namengebung Dickens als Meister des Ausdrucks'.

The 125th anniversary of Dickens' birth fell in February 1937, and that date could also be taken as an approximate centenary of the appearance of *Pickwick*, published between April 1836 and October 1837. Various ways were chosen to mark this date: the *Frankfurter Zeitung*[1] printed an article on Dickens by Irene Seligo, which presents him partly as a childhood reminiscence, which makes entertaining reading, partly as the gospeller of confidence and optimism; to demonstrate the confidence he had in himself and his world a neat summary of his life and personality is given. Some reference is made to G. K. Chesterton's well-known study of Dickens, which the Phaidon-Verlag of Vienna had just published in the translation of H. E. Herlitschka.

Almost all the important subjects for research on Dickens had been exhausted in the productive years from 1907 to 1916, and little was left for individual students of his work in the period reviewed in this chapter. Dickens' popularity as a subject for doctorate theses has consequently declined in post-war years; twelve dissertations only are noticed for this period of eighteen years, and of these three are concerned with other authors beside him. Of the eight that were published, however, the best are the more recent ones, those by H. Heuer (1927), W. Wickardt (1933), and C. Sennewald (1936), which is a sign that though the quantity of published work has diminished, its quality has not declined.

The outstanding independent study of this period is Stefan Zweig's essay of 1920. Both of the great books by Dibelius, *Englische Romankunst* (1910) and *Charles Dickens* (1916), appeared in second editions during this period, which is significant of the fact that, at least until very recently, German interest in Dickens was well maintained.

[1] 26 Feb. 1937.

IV

OTHER EVIDENCE

MANY of the writers whose books and essays are discussed in this section or referred to in the appended book-list make incidental or explicit references to Dickens' popularity in Germany. A study of their remarks, compared with their date, makes it apparent that Dickens' popularity with the general reader continued high for many years after his death. Thus M. Weyermann, for example, asked rhetorically in 1885:

Ja, wir fragen nicht nur die englische, sondern auch die deutsche Leserwelt: wer hat nicht mit seinem Sam Weller gelacht, wer nicht mit seinem Copperfield geweint ... ?[1]

A reverse, however, is noticeable towards the end of the century with the spread of the ideas of the Naturalists, so that Heinrich Hart produced a strongly modified appreciation of Dickens in 1895,[2] and in a lecture given in the same year at Weimar, Friedrich Spielhagen had to say:

... Gestalten, wie Copperfield ... voll blühendsten Lebens, als wir jung waren, wie schattenhaft dünken sie den Jünglingen von heute![3]

The lowest point was reached in 1904 with the extremely harsh criticisms of Karl Bleibtreu.[4]

But such criticism only held good for a small class of the reading public. The majority, it seems, still enjoyed Dickens, and E. Engel still thought fit to include a warm appreciation of his books in the sixth edition of his *Geschichte der Englischen Literatur* in 1906.[5] From that date there is no lack of evidence of Dickens' continued popularity in Germany; and in 1914 Professor E. Eckhardt gave an excellent analysis of this popularity:

Was uns in Dickens' Werken als veraltet erscheint, ist verschwindend wenig gegenüber dem bleibend Wertvollen, was er geschaffen hat. ... Wenn auch seine Kunst zeitlich und örtlich begrenzt ist, enthält sie

[1] M. Weyermann, 'Dickens: eine biographische Skizze', foreword to *Fünf Weihnachtsgeschichten von Boz*, Elberfeld, 1885, p. 12.
[2] *Tägliche Rundschau, Unterhaltungsbeilage*, 11–12 June 1895.
[3] F. Spielhagen, *Neue Beiträge zur Theorie und Technik der Epik und Dramatik*, Leipzig, 1898, p. 82.
[4] *Die Vertreter des Jahrhunderts*, Berlin, Leipzig, 1904, pp. 137–42.
[5] Leipzig, 1906, pp. 386–8.

doch genug allgemein menschliche Züge um ihm, wenigstens innerhalb der germanischen Welt, namentlich bei uns in Deutschland auch ein anderes als ein wissenschaftliches, kulturgeschichtliches oder literarhistorisches Interesse, nämlich das Interesse eines ständigen Leserkreises, dauernd zu sichern und zu erhalten[1].

This last remark is supplemented by a reference in the *Dickensian* of April 1915 to a survey, undertaken by a Leipzig society, of what German soldiers read at the front; according to this their readingmatter was half fiction, covering fifty authors, of whom nearly half were foreigners; and Dickens was first in the order of popularity.

Such pointers become fewer after the War. Although Stefan Zweig re-emphasized Dickens' lasting merits in 1920,[2] the most recent opinion appears to be: 'Für die meisten von uns ist Dickens eine Kinderheitserinnerung.'[3] It is worthy of notice, however, that Alfred Rosenberg referred appreciatively to Dickens in *Der Mythus des 20. Jahrhunderts* in 1930,[4] and that Dickens' *Life of Our Lord* was published in Hamburg in 1934, almost as soon as the manuscript was made public in England.

The most convincing evidence, however, is given by details of the publication of Dickens' works in Germany, in the original and in translation, since 1870. Figures of sales, which are a much more reliable guide than figures of publication, are not available in this case; but it may be taken as axiomatic that publications would not be repeated so often and for so long unless the sales were correspondingly good.

A feature of the period is the remarkable use made of Dickens' shorter works, or of adaptations of his novels, for use in schools. It was noticed in an earlier chapter that the *Christmas Carol* was published in a school edition, with a vocabulary, as early as 1847; in the period after 1870 this interest in his books as school texts was strong, and C. G. Kayser's *Bücherlexikon* has long lists of such publications for every five-year period from that date until very recent years. The Christmas stories, especially the *Christmas Carol*, were easily the most popular for this purpose. In 1911–12 there were ten school editions of the *Carol*; *Copperfield* was also frequently used, and appeared in seventeen editions and reprints as

[1] *Germanisch-Romanische Monatsschrift*, 1914, pp. 663, 664.
[2] *Drei Meister: Balzac, Dickens, Dostoiewski*, Leipzig, 1920.
[3] Irene Seligo in the *Frankfurter Zeitung*, 26 Feb. 1937.
[4] München, 1930, pp. 411, 412.

a school text between 1895 and 1926. This aspect of Dickens' work was discussed in 1913 by B. Berner in a special article entitled 'Dickens als Schulschriftsteller';[1] this concludes that, of the shorter books, the *Sketches*, the *Carol*, and the *Cricket on the Hearth* are of great importance for reading in senior classes, while of the novels *Copperfield*, *Nickleby*, *Pickwick*, and the *Tale of Two Cities* are approved, with *Dombey* and the *Old Curiosity Shop* in the second rank.

During the period studied in this section the complete works of Dickens were newly translated more than once, partly as the result of a feeling noticeable soon after 1870 that the existing translations were not of sufficiently high standard. According to P. Heichen,[2] in 1898 the only early translations which were still on the market were those by J. Seybt, which reappeared in the Reclam series from 1875 onwards; C. Kolb (later frequently revised); and O. von Czarnowski, also in revised form. There were many new translators. Frau A. Scheibe was well known early in the period for her translations of the *Pickwick Papers*, *Oliver Twist*, *Copperfield*, *Bleak House*, and *Hard Times*, which were frequently republished by Gesenius, Halle; her 1890 publication of *Pickwick* was based on H. Roberts' early translation. Another well-known translator of the eighties was Helene Lobedan. Paul Heichen's own translation, a great work, was published from 1892 to 1898; a second edition began to appear in 1899. He says in the conclusion to the last volume: 'Das Vorrecht, eine tatsächlich vollständige Ausgabe aller Romane, sowie der bedeutendsten kürzern Erzählungen des großen Briten zu bieten, gehört momentan allein meiner Ausgabe'.[3] His translation was painstaking and thorough. An appreciation in the *Dickensian* for 1908[4] by H. Leffmann says 'Paul Heichen's translations are most carefully done. An examination of the text shows that very rarely is a difficulty ignored or superficially treated.'

The Schirmer edition appeared from 1902, and eventually comprised 34 volumes. Karl Wilding's translation (Berlin, 1906–8) covered 16 of Dickens' books in 30 volumes. The well-known translation by Richard Zoozmann of a selection of Dickens' novels was published in Leipzig in 1909–10, in 16 volumes, and in a small edition of 7 volumes; and the Insel-Verlag selection of 1910–13

---

[1] Prog. Cuxhaven, 1913.
[2] *Charles Dickens: sein Leben und seine Werke*, Naumburg, 1898, p. 718.
[3] Ibid., p. 718.   [4] pp. 262–4, 295–7. Quotation from p. 263.

ran to 12 volumes, with a pocket edition of 6 volumes. Gustav Meyrink's excellent translations were published at Munich from 1909 to 1914, and were planned to cover 20 volumes, of which 16 appeared; of this translation Georg Terramare said in 1912: 'Gustav Meyrink's Übertragungen sind die einzigen Übersetzungen Dickensscher Werke, die nicht im Vergleich zum Original den Eindruck eines Klavierauszuges im Verhältnis zur Partitur machen'.[1]

After the War Karl Wilding's selection was republished in Berlin in 6 volumes (1923); and a thorough revision of C. Kolb's work by P. T. Hoffmann was also produced in Hamburg, 1926–8. The *Works* in 30 volumes were printed in Berlin in 1926 and the following years; and a new illustrated edition in 12 volumes was announced by F. W. Henkel at Leipzig in 1936.

J. T. Geissendoerfer's thesis of 1915,[2] in a 23-page supplement, gives many details of Dickens' works in German translation under the heads complete works; single works; single editions for schools; editions in collections, while the German editions in English are tabulated in a short addition. The list attempts to cover the whole period 1837–1914, but is not quite complete. Anselm Schlösser's comprehensive study, *Die Englische Literatur in Deutschland, 1895–1934*[3] reviews the appearance of Dickens' works in Germany within these limits, in translation and in the original, in great detail, and his results are most interesting. For this period of forty years he has tabulated every German publication of Dickens' books except those designed for use in schools, and he gives some idea of Dickens' enormous popularity by drawing up statistical tables. He is well aware that this method is not finally reliable as a test of popularity; the apparently insuperable difficulty is to know, first, what constitutes the real public, and second, whether the taste of those Germans who bought translations of Dickens in such numbers was really indicative of the taste of their time. His statistics are nevertheless of great interest. Taking as a basis for comparison the total number of books by each author published in translation in Germany, he finds that of the older authors Dickens was apparently by far the most popular: 249 books by him appeared in this period of forty years. He was fol-

[1] *Österreichische Rundschau*, 1 Feb. 1912, p. 227.
[2] *Dickens' Einfluß auf Ungern-Sternberg*, &c.; *Americana-Germanica*, vol. xix.
[3] Jena, 1937, pp. 65 f., 172, 174, 368, &c.

lowed by Marryat with 155, and Scott with 98. Even when modern authors are included, Dickens is still at the head of the table, his closest followers being Oscar Wilde (226), Edgar Wallace (195), and Conan Doyle (175). Schlösser mentions that no fewer than eleven different publishers produced complete editions of the *Works* during the period under review; and that the collected Christmas stories appeared eighteen times.[1]

His examination of the different German editions of each of Dickens' books separately gives the interesting conclusion that *Oliver Twist*, with 35 publications, was apparently the most popular of Dickens' works in the period. The *Christmas Carol* followed, with 25 publications; then, closely, *Copperfield*, with 18, *Pickwick*, with 17, the *Cricket on the Hearth*, with 16, and the *Tale of Two Cities*, with 15. The other books were as follows: *Nickleby*, 11; *Dombey* and *Hard Times*, 10; the *Old Curiosity Shop*, the *Battle of Life*, and *Bleak House*, 9; the *Chimes* and *Little Dorrit*, 8; the *Sketches* and *Chuzzlewit*, 5; the *Haunted Man*, 4, and *Barnaby Rudge*, 3. The rest, including *Great Expectations*, *Our Mutual Friend*, and *Edwin Drood*, appeared once or twice only.

Further details are given of the 249 German editions of Dickens' books according to the years of their publication, and these support the remarks made in the first paragraphs of this chapter on the rise and fall of Dickens' popularity in Germany as seen in the remarks of successive critics. Thus there were 29 publications of Dickens in the five years 1895–9, but only 13 in 1900–4; it will be remembered that 1904 was marked as the lowest point of Dickens' reputation with the critics. The next two five-year periods, however, during which 'there is no lack of evidence of Dickens' continued popularity in Germany', showed 43 and 50 publications. There were only 7 during the War, but in 1920–4 there were 44, and then 51 from 1925 to 1929. Only then is a decline apparent; 12 publications only are noticed for the period 1930–4.

The peak years for the publication or republication of translations of Dickens were, according to further figures, the years 1907–12 and 1927–30. These conclusions bear out in a most welcome way those reached in earlier chapters of this section from an

---

[1] The popularity of these stories during the whole of the period since Dickens' death is remarkable. They appeared in many different translations, and editions of them in English include that of B. Tauchnitz in 1916–18 and that of Rhombus, Vienna, in 1921–4.

OTHER EVIDENCE   173

independent study of German criticism of Dickens. In the summary of Chapter II of this section it was shown that the greatest interest in Dickens was apparent in the years 1910 and 1912; if, however, the interest be measured by the appearance of doctorate theses, it is exactly the years 1907–12 which are outstanding. For the years 1927–30 the supporting evidence from German criticism is less striking, but it was noted in Chapter III that the appearance of W. Dibelius' *Charles Dickens* in a second edition in 1926 was 'significant of the fact that interest was well maintained'.

A few more points of evidence of Dickens' fame in later years, less striking but more picturesque, may be added. In Germany as well as in England his works occasionally received the compliment of dramatization. *Klein Dorrit*, dramatized by Franz von Schönthan, was produced as a three-act comedy in Vienna on 5 October 1905; and it was stated that the play was to be produced at forty theatres simultaneously in Germany, Austria, and Hungary. A year later it had a favourable reception in Berlin. In 1908 O. K. Notovich published an adaptation of *Pickwick* as *Mr. Pickwick und seine Freunde . . . ein Lustspiel*. There also exists an opera entitled *Das Heimchen*, based on the *Cricket on the Hearth*, for which the music was composed by Karl Goldmark; and a suite composed round *Pickwick* by Walter Niemann. The *Dickensian* of 1930[1] describes a performance of this:

At a concert at the Tonhalle, Düsseldorf, the famous pianist Hülser played a suite for the piano called *Pickwick*: *a cycle after Charles Dickens*, composed by Walter Niemann, Opus 93. It had a frank success and was most interesting . . . there were several pieces, each representing a character from the *Pickwick Papers*.

In more recent years broadcasting has also played its part. The *Dickensian* of 1931[2] reports that 'the main scenes of the *Pickwick Papers* were enacted for German listeners by wireless. The humour of Sam Weller and Mr. Jingle happily survived the translation into a foreign tongue.' *The Times* of 1936 also contains a note, dated 30 November, of a German play on *Pickwick*:

In celebration of the Pickwick centenary a play based on the first chapters of the *Pickwick Papers* was broadcast from Berlin last night. The play, which was by Herr Erich Fortner, with incidental music by Herr Hans Priegnitz, took the story down to the happy conclusion of

[1] p. 137.   [2] p. 83.

Mr. Winkle's affair of honour with Dr. Slammer. Further instalments completing the story are to be broadcast at later dates.

That concludes the evidence for the after-fame of Dickens in Germany. The history of German criticism of Dickens since 1870 has shown how wide and many-sided was the interest felt in the study of his works, and how well-balanced and appreciative, in general, were the results of that study. The statistics of the publications of his books, the examination of their many translations and adaptations, and other evidences of his fame, have shown how it was subjected to variations in public taste, but was until very recent years as great as ever.

To attempt a forecast of Dickens' future popularity in Germany would be to try the impossible. The old untranslatable quality of *Gemütlichkeit*, the atmosphere in which Dickens was most appreciated, is at a discount in modern Germany, and for the present, at least, the recent decline in interest seems to continue.

LIST OF GERMAN CRITICAL WORKS ON DICKENS
1870–1937

1870. FREYTAG, G. 'Ein Dank für Charles Dickens.' (*Grenzboten*, ii, pp. 481–4; in his *Ges. Aufsätze*, ii, pp. 239–44.)
1871. SCHMIDT, J. *Bilder aus dem geistigen Leben unserer Zeit.* (Leipzig; Neue Folge, pp. 1–118.)
1872. BEHN-ESCHENBURG, H. 'Charles Dickens.' (*Öffentliche Vorträge gehalten in der Schweiz*, Bd. I, Heft 6.)
1874. SCHERR, J. *Die Englische Literatur.* (Leipzig, 2te Ausg.)
*1876. HILLEBRAND, K. *Zeiten, Völker und Menschen*, Bd. III. (Berlin.)
*1877. DILTHEY, W. 'Charles Dickens und das Genie des erzählenden Dichters.' (*Westermanns Monatshefte*, Februar, Bd. 41, pp. 482–99, 586–602.)
*1878. SCHMIDT, J. *Portraits aus dem neunzehnten Jahrhundert.* (Berlin: pp. 261–81.)
*1882. BOXBERGER, R. *Charakterzeichnung bei Dickens.* (Prog. Havelberg.)
*1885. BALL, A. 'Dickens und seine Hauptwerke.' (*A.S.N.S.*, Bd. 73, pp. 325–70, Bd. 74, pp. 129–80 and pp. 369–446.)
1885. WEYERMANN, M. 'Dickens: eine biographische Skizze.' (Foreword to: *Fünf Weihnachtsgeschichten von Boz*, pub. Elberfeld.)
1887. BLEIBTREU, K. 'Geschichte der englischen Literatur im 19. Jahrhundert.' (Leipzig = Bd. IV, part 2 of his *Geschichte der Weltliteratur*) (pp. 326–30.)
1887. ZOLLINGER, A. 'Charles Dickens, der Humorist.' (*Öffentliche Vorträge geh. in der Schweiz*, Bd. IX, Heft 10. 32 pp.)
*1888. FRANZ, W. 'Die Dialektsprache bei Charles Dickens.' (*Eng. Stud.* Bd. XII, pp. 197–244.)
*1891. BLUHM, G. R. *Autobiographisches in 'David Copperfield.'* (Diss. Leipzig: Reichenbach i. V. 74 pp.)
*1894. BRANSCHEID, P. *Ein Lebensbild von Charles Dickens.* (Prog. Schleusingen, pp. 1–17.)
†1894. GERSCHMANN, H. *Studien über den modernen Roman.* (Festschrift der ... Lehranstalten Königsbergs ...)
*1895. BANNING, A. *Dickens Beziehungen zu Carlyle*; Teil I. (Prog. Hagen i. W. 20 pp.)
*1895. BENIGNUS, S. *Studien über die Anfänge von Dickens.* (Diss. Strassburg. 72 pp.)
1895. HART, H. 'Charles Dickens.' (*Tägliche Rundschau*, 11.–12. Juni; *Unterhaltungsbeilage*.)

* Examined in Part III.   † Not seen by me.

1895. WEBER, L. 'Charles Dickens als sozialer Schriftsteller.' (*Sammlung theolog. und sozialer Reden*, Serie 6, Lief. 3. 18 pp.)
*1896. ARONSTEIN, P. 'Dickensstudien.' (*Anglia*, Bd. 18, pp. 218–62 and 335–59.)
* —— 'Dickens und Carlyle.' (*Anglia*, Bd. 18, pp. 360–70.)
1896. MEYER, R. M. On Dickens and Reuter (*see* General Bibliography).
1896. WÜLKER, R. *Geschichte der englischen Literatur*. (Wien, Leipzig, pp. 563—80.)
*1898. ARONSTEIN, P. 'Die sozialen und politischen Strömungen in England im zweiten Drittel unseres Jahrhunderts in Dichtung und Roman.' (Dickens in part 4; *A.S.N.S.*, Bd. 100, pp. 46–52.)
*1898. HEICHEN, P. *Charles Dickens; sein Leben und seine Werke*. (Naumburg. 723 pp.)
*1898. WÜLKER, R. 'Zur Jugendgeschichte von Dickens.' (*A.S.N.S.*, Bd. 100, pp. 287–92.)
† —— 'Charles Dickens und seine Werke.' (*Hochschulvorträge für Jedermann*, Heft 8. Leipzig.)
*1899. WINTER, A. *Joseph Addison als Humorist in seinem Einfluß auf Dickens' Jugendwerke*. (Diss. Leipzig; Halle. 56 pp.)
*1899. WILSON, F. W. *Dickens in seinen Beziehungen zu den Humoristen Fielding und Smollett*. (Diss. Leipzig. 59 pp.)
1902. FÜRST, R. On Dickens and Ebner-Eschenbach (*see* General Bibliography).
1904. BAGSTER, G. *Charles Dickens, ein Essay*. (Stuttgart; 51 pp.)
1904. BLEIBTREU, K. *Die Vertreter des Jahrhunderts*. (Berlin and Leipzig, pp. 137–42.)
1906. ENGEL, E. *Geschichte der englischen Literatur*. (Leipzig, 6te Aufl., pp. 386–8.)
1907. BAUCH, R. *Studien über Thackerays 'Sketches and Travels in London' und Dickens' 'Sketches'*. (Diss. Leipzig. 74 pp.)
1907. SCHMIDT, T. *Frauengestalten bei Dickens*. (Diss. Halle. 59 pp.)
*1908. BERNDT, A. *Entstehungsgeschichte der 'Pickwick Papers'*. (Diss. Greifswald. 52 pp.)
1908. SCHIEBOLD, W. *Kindergestalten bei Dickens*. (Diss. Halle. 47 pp.)
1908. VÖLK, V. On Dickens and Freytag (*see* General Bibliography).
1909. BOOTH, M. *Charles Dickens und seine Werke in pädagogischer Beleuchtung*. (Diss. Jena: Zürich. 143 pp.)
1909. KELLNER, L. *Die englische Literatur im Zeitalter der Königin Viktoria*. (Leipzig, pp. 27–58.)
*1909. FRIESER, W. *Die Schulen bei Dickens, auf ihre geschichtliche Wahrheit geprüft*. (Diss. Leipzig; Halle a. S. 138 pp.)

* Examined in Part III.   † Not seen by me.

GERMAN CRITICAL WORKS ON DICKENS

1909. LIPPOLDT, K. *Das Gerichtswesen in Dickens' Romanen.* (Diss. Halle. 55 pp.)
1909. NIERTH, H. *Die Weihnachtserzählung in der englischen Literatur.* (Diss. Leipzig, pp. 13–38.)
1909. SCHULZE, F. *Charles Dickens als Schilderer der Londoner Armen- und Verbrecherwelt.* (Diss. Halle. 42 pp.)
*1910. DIBELIUS, W. *Englische Romankunst: Die Technik des eng. Romans im 18. und zu Anfang des 19. Jahrhunderts.* (Berlin; *Palaestra,* vols. 92 and 98.)
*1910. —— 'Das Erstlingswerk von Dickens.' (*Englische Studien,* Bd. 43, pp. 67–99.)
*1910. —— 'Pierce Egan und Dickens.' (*A.S.N.S.,* Bd. 124, pp. 306–17.)
*1910. FEHR, B. 'Dickens und Malthus.' (*Germanisch-Romanische Monatsschrift,* pp. 542–55.)
1910. LOHRE, H. On Dickens and Ludwig (*see* General Bibliography).
1910. LÜDER, F. On Dickens and Ludwig (*see* General Bibliography).
1910. METTGENBERG, W. 'Charles Dickens Briefe über die Todesstrafe.' (*Zeitschrift für die gesamte Strafrechtswissenschaft,* xxx, pp. 532–41.)
*1910. STUMPF, W. *Der Dickenssche Roman 'Hard Times', seine Entstehung und seine Tendenzen.* (Diss. Greifswald: Freienwalde a/O 114 pp.)
1911. ANDRAE, A. 'Zu Dickens' "Household Words".' (*Eng. Studien,* Bd. 43, pp. 293–9.)
*1911. DIBELIUS, W. 'Zu den Pickwick Papers.' (*Anglia,* Bd. 35, pp. 101–10.)
*1912. FIEDLER, F. *Entstehungsgeschichte von Charles Dickens 'Oliver Twist'.* (Diss. Halle. 115 pp.)
1912. FREYMOND, R. On Dickens and Freytag (*see* General Bibliography).
*1912. JÜGLER, R. *Über die Technik der Charakterisierung in den Jugendwerken von Charles Dickens.* (Diss. Halle. 66 pp.)
1912. LÖTSCHERT, H. *Dickens und Thackeray als Humoristen.* (Prog.?- Opladen. 13 pp.)
1912. NOACK, K. 'Charles Dickens und die deutschen Volksbibliotheken.' (*Blätter für Volksbibliotheken und Lesehallen,* Jhg. 13, pp. 50–3.)
1912. RUTARI, A. 'Charles Dickens.' (*Velhagen und Klasings Volksbücher,* 34. Bielefeld, Leipzig.)
1912. TERRAMARE, G. *Gedächtnis und Phantasie: Ein Gedenkblatt zu Dickens hundertstem Geburtstag.* (Österreichische Rundschau, 1. Februar.)

* Examined in Part III.

*1913. BÖTTGER, C. *Charles Dickens' historischer Roman 'A Tale of Two Cities' und seine Quellen.* (Diss. Königsberg. 77 pp.)
1913. GEIST, H. On Dickens and Reuter (*see* General Bibliography).
†1913. BAUMGARTEN, O. 'Charles Dickens.' (*Die Religion in Geschichte und Gegenwart*, Tübingen.)
*1914. ECKHARDT, E. 'Zur Charakteristik von Charles Dickens.' (*German.-Romanische Monatsschrift*, Okt.–Nov., pp. 563–73 and 655–64.)
*1914. GRÜNEWALD, K. *Die Verwendung der Mundart in den Romanen von Dickens, Thackeray, Eliot, und Kingsley.* (Diss. Giessen: Darmstadt. 118 pp.)
*1914. JOHANNPETER, W. *Handlungs-, Charakter- und Situationskontrast in den Jugendwerken von Charles Dickens.* (Diss. Halle. 54 pp.)
*1915. EDELMANN, E. *Die Charakterzeichnung in den Romanen von Dickens.* (Diss. Giessen, Darmstadt. 77 pp.)
1915. MÜLLER, E. *Das subjektive Hervortreten des Dichters im neueren englischen Roman.* (Diss. Giessen: Hamburg. 116 pp. Dickens, pp. 17–58.)
*1916. DIBELIUS, W. 'Dickens und Shakespeare.' (*Shakespeare-Jahrbuch*, Bd. 52, pp. 76–83.)
*1916. —— *Charles Dickens.* (Leipzig, Berlin. 525 pp.)
*1919. FIEDLER, F. 'Dickens' Gebrauch der rythmischen Prosa im Christmas Carol.' (*A.S.N.S.*, Bd. 139, pp. 47–50.)
*1920. —— 'Dickens' Belesenheit.' (*A.S.N.S.*, Bd. 140, pp. 43–71.)
*1920. —— 'Dickens und die Posse.' (*Englische Studien*, Bd. 53, pp. 370–404.)
1920. SCHWEIZER, F. *Die Ausländer in den Romanen von Dickens.* (Diss. Giessen. 41 pp.)
*1920. ZWEIG, S. *Drei Meister: Balzac, Dickens, Dostoievski.* (Vol. I of *Baumeister der Welt*, Leipzig, pp. 52–87.)
1921. KELLNER, L. *Die englische Literatur der neuesten Zeit: von Dickens bis Shaw.* (Continuation of his book of 1909.)
1921. DOERNENBURG, E., and FEHSE, W. On Dickens and Raabe (*see* General Bibliography).
*1921. FIEDLER, F. 'Das Weihnachtsfest in England vor und bei Dickens.' (*A.S.N.S.*, Bd. 141, pp. 59–78.)
1922. DIBELIUS, W. *Englische Romankunst.* (= 2te Aufl.)
*1922. FIEDLER, F. 'Wie Dickens das Christmas Carol feilte.' (*A.S.N.S.*, Bd. 144, pp. 37–53.)
*1923. —— 'Die Vorgeschichte der Hauptgestalten in Dickens' Christmas Carol.' (*A.S.N.S.*, Bd. 146, pp. 60–81.)
†1923. HARTENSTEIN, J. *Dickens' Arbeitsweise auf Grund der Heft-*

* Examined in Part III. † Not seen by me.

Ausgabe von '*Dombey und Sohn*'. (Diss. in typescript, Leipzig. 143 pp.)

†1923. OSTER, E. *Mutter und Kind im englischen Roman von 1760 bis Dickens.* (Diss. in typescript, Bonn.)

†1923. REHFELD, W. *Der Vergleich bei Charles Dickens.* (Diss. in typescript, Greifswald. 38 pp.)

1923. WESTENDORPF, K. *Das Prinzip der Verwendung des Slang bei Dickens.* (Diss. Greifswald. 31 pp.)

1924. GUTERMUTH, E. 'Das Kind im englischen Roman von Richardson bis Dickens.' (Diss. Giessen, unpublished; available in *Giessener Beiträge zur Erforschung der Sprache . . . Englands u. Nordamerikas*, Bd. II, pp. 29–60.)

†1925. THURN, G. *Dickens' Einfluß auf Samuel Warren.* (Diss. in typescript, Erlangen. 46 pp.)

1926. DIBELIUS, W. *Charles Dickens.* (= 2te Aufl.)

1927. FEHSE, W. On Dickens and Freytag (*see* General Bibliography).

*1927. HEUER, H. *Romaneske Elemente im Realismus von Charles Dickens.* (Diss. Marburg. 87 pp.)

1931. ULRICH, A. *Studien zu Dickens' Roman 'Barnaby Rudge'.* (Diss. Jena: Zella-Mehlis. 90 pp.)

1933. RATH, J. *Die Personenbeschreibung der humoristischen Charaktere in der erzählenden (englischen) Literatur von Addison bis Dickens.* (Diss. Münster. 90 pp.)

*1933. WICKARDT, W. *Die Formen der Perspektive in Charles Dickens Romanen; ihr sprachlicher Ausdruck und ihre strukturelle Bedeutung.* (Diss. Göttingen, unpublished; available as Bd. 22 of the series *Neue Forschung*, Berlin. 122 pp.)

*1936. SENNEWALD, C. *Die Namengebung bei Dickens, eine Studie über Lautsymbolik.* (Diss. Berlin, and as Bd. 203 of the series *Palaestra*, Leipzig. 121 pp.)

*1937. SELIGO, I. 'Charles Dickens.' (*Frankfurter Zeitung*, 26. Feb.)

1937. SCHIRMER, W. F. *Geschichte der englischen Literatur.* (Halle/Saale. Dickens, pp. 566–9.)

ABBREVIATION: *A.S.N.S.* = *Archiv für das Studium der neueren Sprachen.*

* Examined in Part III.   † Not seen by me.

APPENDIX I

LIST OF ARTICLES ON DICKENS IN GERMAN PERIODICALS, 1837–1870

ALL the periodicals referred to here are in the British Museum, but their indexes are frequently missing; that is one of the reasons for the inclusion of this list. The selection given is fairly representative, though the periodicals were of varied importance and influence.

The number and length of the articles on any one of the earlier books are not necessarily a true guide to that book's popularity; it must be noticed that much space is frequently devoted to synopsis and quotation apart from the criticism proper, which in one or two cases occupies only a fraction of the whole length, and also that, as the earlier books were often published in separate parts, a periodical might give a brief mention to each part as it appeared. This is the case with the articles on *Master Humphrey's Clock* in the *Blätter für Literatur und Bildende Kunst*.

Most of the articles of the first ten years are referred to in L. Sigmann's *Die Englische Literatur von 1800 bis 1850 im Urteil der zeitgenössischen deutschen Kritik*,[1] but for that period this list is more complete; only brief references and notes of no importance have been excluded. The *Grenzboten* was not included, because a list of its articles for 1848–61, drawn up by L. M. Price, is readily available,[2] and also because Julian Schmidt's views on Dickens are more easily studied in his published essays.

1. *Jenaische Allgemeine Literaturzeitung*.

As an *Organ für die Gelehrtenwelt*, this periodical usually confined itself to the study of learned works, and seldom considered the novel. When it did, the appearance of an article could be taken as a compliment to the writer of the book chosen, which must have become widely known. This paper ceased publication after 1848; these are the only articles:

1839   No. 138 (July): *Oliver Twist*.
          Ergänzungsblatt No. 28: *Pickwick*.
1841   No. 55 (March): *Master Humphrey's Clock*.

2. *Blätter zur Kunde der Literatur des Auslandes* (Stuttgart, Augsburg).

There is good and intelligent criticism to be found here; but the paper was of short life, and ceased publication after 1840.

1838   Nos. 104–9 (18 Nov. ff.): *Pickwick*.[3]

[1] *Anglistische Forschungen*, Heft 55, Heidelberg, 1918; Dickens, pp. 294–304.
[2] *The Attitude of Freytag and Schmidt to English Literature, 1848–1862*; Hesperia series, no. 7, Baltimore, 1915, pp. 113 ff. This list is of articles on English literature generally, but those on Dickens are easy to extract.
[3] As is so frequently the case in these articles, a large amount of the critic's space is here taken up by quotation and synopsis.

1839   Nos. 77/8–84 (7–24 July): 'Charles Dickens (Boz) und der englische humoristische und komische Roman'.[1]
       Nos. 116/17–23 (19 Oct.–7 Nov.): *Oliver Twist*.
1840   Nos. 18/19, 21/2, 23 (16, 22, 26 Feb.): *Nickleby*.

3. *Stuttgarter Literaturblatt* (supplement to the *Stuttgarter Morgenblatt für Gebildete Leser*), ed. Dr. Wolfgang Menzel.

Here again there is good criticism, and a wider range of Dickens' books is covered, for the *Literaturblatt* continued publication until the summer of 1849. This was an important paper of fairly wide influence.

1838   No. 22 (28 Feb.): *Pickwick*.
1839   No. 13 (4 Feb.): *Pickwick* and *Nickleby*.
       No. 14 (6 Feb.): *Nickleby* and *Oliver Twist*.
       No. 17 (13 Feb.): *Sketches* (Roberts' selection).
       No. 34 (1 April): *Oliver Twist*.
1840   No. 42 (24 April): *Nickleby* and *Sketches* (Diezmann's translation).
1842   No. 40 (15 April): *Master Humphrey's Clock* (complete).
1843   No. 26 (10 March): *American Notes*.
1845   No. 38 (11 April): *The Chimes*.
1846   No. 20 (17 March): *Cricket on the Hearth*.
       No. 65 (12 Sept.): *Pictures from Italy*.
1847   No. 34 (11 May): *Battle of Life*.

4. *Blätter für Literatur und Bildende Kunst* (supplement to the *Dresdner Abendzeitung*), ed. 'Theodor Hell'.[2]

In its earliest form, under Hell's editorship, this periodical contained good, but not always strict, articles on Dickens. Its praise is occasionally a very little too enthusiastic, perhaps because it was published for a local bookseller. In the main, however, it is reliable.

1837   No. 91 (15 Nov.): *Pickwick*.
1838   No. 35 (2 May): *Pickwick*.
       No. 53 (4 July): *Pickwick*.
       No. 68 (25 Aug.): 'Boz-Literatur': *Sketches* and *Nickleby*.
       No. 73 (12 Sept.): *Nickleby*.
       No. 100 (15 Dec.): 'Boz-Literatur': *Oliver Twist*.
1839   No. 24 (23 March): 'Boz-Literatur': *Oliver Twist* and *Nickleby*.
       No. 33 (24 April): *Sketches* and *Oliver Twist*.
       No. 94 (23 Nov.): *Sketches* and *Nickleby*.

[1] Much of this article is simply direct translation of English reviews from the *Literary Gazette*, the *Quarterly Review*, and the *Edinburgh Review*.
[2] Pseudonym of K. G. Theodor Winkler, a man of wide knowledge and powers, a great linguist and a well-known translator. He was also the editor of the main paper. — v. *Allg. Dte Biographie*, vol. xi, pp. 693–4, under 'Hell'.

1839 No. 99 (11 Dec.): *Nickleby*.
1840 No. 13 (12 Feb.): *Nickleby*.
     No. 75 (16 Sept.): *Master Humphrey's Clock*.
     No. 92 (14 Nov.): *Master Humphrey's Clock*.
1841 No. 40 (19 May): *Master Humphrey's Clock*.
     No. 59 (24 July): *Master Humphrey's Clock*.
     No. 97 (4 Dec.): *Barnaby Rudge*.
1842 No. 29 (9 April): *Barnaby Rudge*.
1843 No. 7 (25 Jan.): *American Notes*.

4a. The same, continued as *Literatur- und Kunstblatt*, ed. Robert Schmieder.

The articles on English literature become fewer and shorter in this, and are of much less interest.

1844 No. 14 (4 April): *Chuzzlewit*.
     No. 39 (26 Sept.): *Chuzzlewit* and *Christmas Carol*.

5. *Blätter für Literarische Unterhaltung* (Leipzig, 1826–98).

This long-lived and widely-known paper produced, in its earlier years, some excellent articles on Dickens; but its opinions changed with successive changes of editor, and it showed no interest in Dickens after the appearance of *Hard Times* in 1854. Its article on this book was the last on Dickens for the years studied (1837–70), and no mention was made of Dickens' death in 1870.

1838 Nos. 13–14 (13–14 Jan.): *Sketches, Pickwick*.
     No. 49 (18 Feb.): *Pickwick*.
     Nos. 252–3 (9–10 Sept.): *Sketches, Pickwick, Nickleby*.
1839 No. 95 (5 April): 'England über Dickens'.[1]
     Nos. 285–8 (12–15 Oct.): 'Boz und die gegenwärtige Gestaltung des Volksromans' (remarks based on *Oliver Twist*).
     No. 335 (1 Dec.): *Nickleby*.
1841 No. 244 (1 Sept.): *Master Humphrey's Clock*.
1842 No. 45 (14 Feb.): *Barnaby Rudge*.
     No. 79 (20 March): *Barnaby Rudge*.
1845 No. 204 (23 July): *The Chimes*.
     Nos. 221–5 (9–13 Aug.): 'Über Dickens' Romane.'[2]
1846 No. 115 (25 April): *Cricket on the Hearth*.
1847 No. 145 (25 May): *Battle of Life*.
1849 No. 61 (12 March): *Haunted Man*.
1851 No. 46 (22 Feb.): *Copperfield*.[3]

[1] Largely a translation of an article in the *Edinburgh Review*, but contains some interesting remarks by the German writer.
[2] The long essay by T. W. Danzel, discussed on pp. 32–3, above.
[3] Translated from an article in the *Athenaeum*.

ARTICLES ON DICKENS IN GERMAN PERIODICALS 183

1854 No. 49 (7 Dec.): 'Charles Dickens und der Materialismus'. (*Hard Times.*)

6. *Europa, Chronik der Gebildeten Welt*, ed. H. Lewald till 1846 (Stuttgart); 1846–59 by F. G. Kühne (Leipzig). After 1859 *Europa* was published by C. B. Lorck, the Leipzig publishing house.

This started life apparently as a drawing-room magazine, containing short stories and fashion plates; literary criticism was a secondary interest, and during Lewald's editorship the notes on Dickens were rare, brief, and not very important. Under Kühne the magazine reached a higher standard, and though its opinions on Dickens were occasionally too harsh, they are worthy of full attention.

1838 Vol. ii, p. 231: *Pickwick.*
1839 Vol. i, pp. 23–5: *Oliver Twist.*
      Vol. ii, pp. 37–40: *Oliver Twist* and *Nickleby.*
1840 Vol. ii, pp. 419–20: *Nickleby.*
1841 Vol. iii, pp. 183–4: 'Boz's Sämmtliche Werke, neue Ausgabe.'
1843 Vol. i, pp. 487–8: *American Notes.*
1852 No. 36 (29 April): A reference to the theme of *Bleak House.*
1855 No. 5, pp. 53–4: 'Boz = Dickens und die "Harten Zeiten" des englischen Romans' (*Hard Times*).[1]
1858 No. 10, cols. 337–9: Dickens, in 'Männer der Zeit'.[2]
1859 No. 19, cols. 641–52: 'Dickens und Thackeray.'[3]
1860 No. 10, col. 327: *Tale of Two Cities.*
1861 No. 51, cols. 2045–6: *Great Expectations.*
1864 *Europa-Chronik* (a supplement), No. 22, col. 324: *Our Mutual Friend.*
1870 No. 33, cols. 1045–56: 'Charles Dickens.'[4]

7. *Magazin für die Literatur des Auslandes* (Berlin, 1832 ff.).

Literatur was taken in a very catholic sense by the various editors of this periodical; they welcomed articles on politics, society notes, and pieces of pure gossip, as well as straightforward literary criticisms. In the earlier years translations of chapters of Dickens' books are frequent; in later years they found Dickens' *Household Words* a gold-mine for brief notes on political and social conditions in England. Personal notes on Dickens are also frequent. A selection of all these is given here, for general interest's sake, together with references to the direct

[1] A very bad-tempered article which called forth a reproof from the *Magazin für die Literatur des Auslandes* (1855, no. 27; 3 March).
[2] A short life of Dickens, apparently based on Julian Schmidt's *Charakteristik* of 1852.
[3] The long essay by Spielhagen referred to in Chapter VI of Pt. II.
[4] A long article on Dickens' death by 'Corvin' (= O. J. B. von Corvin-Wiersbitzki), who had worked for a time on *Household Words* and *All the Year Round*. — v. *Allg. Dte. Biographie*, vol. xlvii, pp. 531 ff.

APPENDIX I

criticisms of Dickens' books. The magazine was studied for the first twenty years of the period (1837–57).

- 1837   No. 126 (20 Oct.): A translation of 'Doctor's Commons' from *Sketches by Boz*.[1]
- 1838   No. 50 (25 April): Notices *Grimaldi*.
- 1842   No. 5 (12 Jan.): An account of an American's visit to Dickens.
  No. 8 (19 Jan.): Dickens' letter to Künzel of 13.9.1841.
  Nos. 143–4 (30 Nov.–2 Dec.): Extracts from *American Notes*.[2]
- 1844   No. 12 (27 Jan.): *Christmas Carol*.
  No. 110 (12 Sept.): '*Martin Chuzzlewit* und das Darstellungstalent des Herrn Dickens.'
- 1845   No. 5 (11 Jan.): *The Chimes*.
- 1846   No. 1 (1 Jan.): *Cricket on the Hearth*.
  Nos. 39–41, 51–2 (March–April): Translations from *Pictures from Italy*.[3]
- 1847   No. 15 (4 Feb.): *Battle of Life*.
- 1850   No. 15 (2 Feb.): *Copperfield*.
- 1852   Nos. 6–7 (13–15 Jan.): 'Bulwer und Dickens.'[4]
  Nos. 111–12 (14–15 Sept.): 'Literaturbrief aus England' considers Dickens, 'seine Lebensstellung, seine Wohnung und seine Persönlichkeit'.
  No. 118 (30 Sept.): A criticism of Julian Schmidt's *Charakteristik* of Dickens.
- 1853   No. 115 (24 Sept.): 'Literaturbrief aus England' discusses *Bleak House*.
- 1854   No. 112 (19 Sept.): 'Literaturbrief' discusses *Hard Times*.
- 1855   No. 27 (3 March): 'Kühne's *Europa contra* Dickens.'[5]
  No. 149 (13 Dec.): *Little Dorrit*.

Reference may also be made to the following:

Dresdner Abendzeitung, 1848, no. 1 (6 Jan.) *Dombey* (in the *Feuilleton* s.v. *London*).

Die Gartenlaube (Leipzig), 1856, no. 6: Biographical article on Dickens. 1861, no. 39: 'Eine Vorlesung von Dickens' by 'Corvin'.[6]

---

[1] The earliest reference to Dickens in these periodicals.
[2] The first of many to appear in the magazine in this and the next year.
[3] From the original form—letters appearing in the *Daily News*.
[4] By D. Asher; perhaps the David Asher who later published *On the Study of Modern Languages* (a pamphlet of 80 pages), London, 1859.
[5] See note 1, p. 183.   [6] For 'Corvin' see note 4, p. 183.

APPENDIX II

NOTES ON SOME EARLY GERMAN TRANSLATORS OF DICKENS' WORKS

LITTLE can now be discovered about the early translators of Dickens' books into German. Their work was frequently produced in a great hurry for an importunate publisher anxious to forestall his rivals (since there was in those years no question of a single authorized translation); and in such circumstances it is clear that the translators could rank little higher than publishers' hacks, and that their work could seldom have any pretension to artistry. They are, therefore, not considered in general literary or biographical encyclopaedias such as the *Allgemeine Deutsche Biographie* or Brümmer's *Deutsches Dichterlexikon*, and the few details of their activity still to be found have to be laboriously collected from catalogues and booklists or deduced from prefaces and contemporary criticisms. It is rare to discover any personal information about them.

In the case of H. ROBERTS, who produced the first German translations of Dickens, the information to be found is enigmatic. His version of *Pickwick*, the one published by Weber at Leipzig in 1837–8, has two forewords; one to the first, one to the fifth volume. The latter, though ostensibly written by 'the translator', and containing no sign that it is the work of any other person, is signed K. Jürgens, and Theodor Hell of the *Dresdner Abendzeitung* took this to be the real name of the translator.[1]

It is just possible that 'H. Roberts' is a pseudonym, for there is here a certain conformity in dates and places of appearance. K. Jürgens worked as a translator for Vieweg of Brunswick between 1833 and 1836; 'H. Roberts' did the same in 1835–6. Both names appear on translations published by Weber of Leipzig in and after 1837, in which year two appeared translated by 'Roberts' with a foreword by Jürgens—the fifth volume of *Pickwick* and the German version of W. Carleton's *Traits and Stories of the Irish Peasantry*. But there seems to be no sound reason for a writer to translate a book under a pseudonym and to add a preface in his own name, still less for him to use either name indiscriminately; and final identification is apparently impossible. Nor is there enough evidence to connect this K. Jürgens, who is most probably the K. H. Jürgens who translated Frederic Chamier's *Life of a Sailor* for Vieweg in 1835, with the theologian and politician K. H. Jürgens

[1] *Blätter für Literatur und bildende Kunst* (supplement to the *Dresdner Abendzeitung*), 1838, no. 53 (4 July). So, apparently, did the critic of the *Blätter für literarische Unterhaltung*: see no. 253 of 1838 (10 Sept.), p. 1026.

whose life is recorded in the *Allgemeine Deutsche Biographie*, although both had strong connexions with Brunswick.

Roberts, who had worked for Vieweg on Marryat's complete works and on miscellanies from Washington Irving, was employed by Weber from 1837 to 1839 on five of Dickens' books—a selection of the *Sketches*, *Pickwick*, *Oliver Twist*, the *Life of Grimaldi*, and *Nickleby*—as well as on several other authors' works. *Nickleby* seems to have been his last work for Weber, though he wrote a new foreword to his third edition of *Pickwick* which appeared in 1842. There then seems to have been a gap in his activity for a time until he reappears in 1844 as a translator for Westermann of Brunswick; but he was not employed on Dickens again.

His methods of translation are made clear in the second preface to *Pickwick* (vol. 5). He felt it his duty to reconcile Dickens' books as much as possible to his own conception of German taste, and consequently he did not scruple to use paraphrase or at times précis, or even to omit completely sentences and paragraphs which he considered obscure or over-long. Theodor Hell commented on Roberts' methods as seen in his translation of *Oliver Twist*:

> Man kann die Robert'sche Übersetzung mehr eine Bearbeitung nennen, da sie alles weggelassen oder wesentlich verkürzt hat, was in dem Originale nach englischer Sitte allerdings mitunter etwas breit auslief. Das Werk liest sich daher hier mehr als ein Original, und dies um so mehr, als der Übersetzer auf geschickte Art in mehrern der Anfangskapitel die Diebe, Räuber und Hehler, in deren Gesellschaft der arme Oliver gerät, sich der Ausdrücke der deutschen Gaunersprache bedienen läßt, und diese in hinzugefügten Noten erklärt, wodurch die Erzählung ein noch eigentümlicheres Kolorit erhält.[1]

Elsewhere Hell praises Roberts' translations highly:

> ... Der Übersetzer hat sich einer recht schwierigen Arbeit mit Geschicklichkeit, Kenntnis und Fleiß unterzogen.... Vortrefflich ist H. Roberts Übertragung, da sich eben in solchen Romanen die größten Schwierigkeiten für Aneignung zu deutschem Verständnis darbieten.[2]

But an opposite point of view is put forward by a modern writer, R. Freymond, who says in a brief comparison of Dickens' translators:

> Ungenauer und dem Originale wenig nachempfunden sind die Übersetzungen von H. Roberts...[3]

---

[1] *Blätter f. Lit. und bild. Kunst* (cit.), 1838, no. 100 (15 Dec.).

[2] Loc. cit., 1837, no. 91 (15 Nov.) and 1838, no. 35 (2 May). Hell was a competent linguist, but it is not clear if he spoke here from actual acquaintance with the English originals.

[3] *Dickens' Einfluß auf Freytag*, Prag, 1912, p. 18, footnote 2.

EARLY GERMAN TRANSLATORS OF DICKENS 187

and it is most probably to Roberts' version of *Oliver Twist* that R. H. Horne referred in 1844, when he wrote in an article on Dickens:

> The high reputation of the Germans for their faithfulness and general excellence as translators is well supported in some of these versions; and in others that reputation is perilled. Bad abbreviations, in which graphic or humorous descriptions are omitted, and the characteristics of dialogue unnecessarily avoided, are far from commendable. No one could expect that the Italian *Oliviero Twist*, of Giambattista Baseggio, published in Milan, would be, in all respects, far better than one of the most popular versions of that work in Leipzig. But such is the fact.[1]

CARL KOLB was a very productive translator of the period, who began this type of work in 1841, and was still employed on it in 1874, when he prepared the authorized German translation of John Stuart Mill's autobiography. No personal information about him can be discovered, but in view of his long connexion with Stuttgart, where almost all his work was published, it may be suggested that he was a relation of Gustav Eduard Kolb, editor of the *Augsburger Allgemeine Zeitung*, a man of a Stuttgart family whose life can be studied in the *Allgemeine Deutsche Biographie*.[2]

His long work on Dickens (he translated nearly every one of Dickens' books) began in 1841 with translations of *Oliver Twist*, *Nickleby*, *Pickwick*, and the *Sketches*, and continued almost without break during the two following decades. His publishers were Krabbe, and later Hoffmann, both of Stuttgart. At the same time, in 1841, he was employed by Liesching of Stuttgart on the translation of a large number of books by Fenimore Cooper; he also worked on Defoe in 1842 for Belser, of Stuttgart, and in 1843 and 1846 for Krabbe on various books by Marryat.

In reviewing the enormous list of books translated by Kolb during the eighteen-forties, one is tempted to doubt that work so crowded can have been of high standard. Confirmation of this doubt is given by a curious pamphlet, published at Berlin in 1880, entitled *Dickens und Daudet in deutscher Übersetzung*, by Louis Weizmann. The author, having demonstrated to his own satisfaction that it is highly patriotic to show the faults in German translations of foreign works (the relevance of the question of patriotism is not clear), reviews some versions of Daudet's novels and proceeds to Dickens, saying:

> Ist es nicht ein Unrecht gegen Dickens, daß seit Jahren seine Werke in deutschen Übersetzungen geduldet sind, die mit einem parlamentarischen Epitheton kaum bezeichnet werden können?

The translations he chooses for prolonged criticism are those of the

---
[1] In *A New Spirit of the Age*; 'World's Classics' edition, p. 52.
[2] Vol. xvi, pp. 457-9.

Sketches and of *Dombey* by Carl Kolb. Weizmann finds a large number of mistakes, some of them amusing, a few of them incomprehensible, and for all of them, with one exception, where Weizmann himself is at fault, Kolb must be blamed; whether one supposes that he was in too great a hurry, or that he was too casual in his study of the original; or, more widely, that he had a faulty knowledge of English syntax, and little acquaintance with colloquial English and with English manners and customs. This judgement must stand in spite of an appreciative criticism of his work to be found in the periodical *Europa*. Of Kolb's work on *Oliver Twist* the reviewer says:

[Dr. Kolb] scheint, nach dem ersten jetzt ausgegebenen Bändchen zu urteilen, sich dieser nicht leichten Arbeit mit Ernst und Umsicht zu unterziehen. Die Übersetzung liest sich gut und fließend, und die Eigentümlichkeiten des Autors in Auffassung und Ausdrucksweise sind getreu wiedergegeben.[1]

JOHANN AUGUST DIEZMANN was well enough known in other ways to find a place in the *Allgemeine Deutsche Biographie*,[2] and his life need therefore be only briefly described. Born near Pegau in 1805, he studied medicine and natural science at Leipzig from 1824 to 1828; later he turned to the study of language and literature, remaining in Leipzig for most of his life. He died at Chemnitz in 1869. He is now most remembered for his work on Goethe and Schiller (e.g. *Goethe und die lustige Zeit in Weimar*, 1857); his language studies produced a *Vollständiges Taschenwörterbuch der vier Hauptsprachen Europas* (2 parts, 1832–6), a German-French and a French-German dictionary (both in 1836), and his many translations. Of this branch of his activity the *Allgemeine Deutsche Biographie* says:

Als Übersetzer errang er sich überall Beifall, indem er nicht allein belletristische Werke aus dem Englischen und Französischen, sondern auch aus dem Französischen wissenschaftliche, namentlich naturhistorische, übertrug.

Diezmann was most active as a translator in the later thirties and in the forties of his century, during which time he was employed, mostly by Leipzig houses, on the works of Sterne, Warren, Marryat, Bulwer, Ainsworth, Dickens, George Sand, Dumas, Hugo, Mérimée, Sue, and many others. His first work on Dickens was the translation of *Nickleby* for Georg Westermann of Brunswick. Of this edition parts 1 and 2 were translated by K. H. Hermes;[3] the book was then completed in five more parts by Diezmann, who later also translated the *Sketches*, *Oliver Twist*, and the *Christmas Carol*.

[1] *Europa: Chronik der Gebildeten Welt*, Stuttgart, 1841, vol. iii, p. 184.
[2] Vol. v, p. 222.
[3] There is a biographical note on Hermes in the *Allg. Dte Biographie*, vol. xii, pp. 199–201.

In spite of his apparent speed in translation, the praise given by his biographer appears to be justified, and is supported by the testimony of Theodor Hell of the *Dresdner Abendzeitung*. Commenting on Diezmann's version of the *Sketches*, Hell refers to the translator:

... der hinsichtlich der Gewandtheit und Treue der Übersetzung keinem seiner Mitbewerber nachsteht. ...[1]

and, in a comparison of the methods employed by Roberts and Diezmann, he writes:

Mehr seinem Originale völlig treu bleibt Diezmann, gibt es aber auch mit Gewandtheit und Sprachkenntnis wieder.[2]

But to the critic of *Europa*, it must be admitted, Diezmann's translations were no more than *ziemlich*; the English colour, he felt, was unnecessarily destroyed by the complete substitution of German equivalents for names, coins, titles, and the like.[3] But in the case of *Nickleby*, some of this blame should probably go to Hermes, for here Diezmann did no more than continue a translation begun by him, and he would have been bound to the methods of his predecessor.

Diezmann had some correspondence with Dickens himself. He wrote to Dickens in 1840 (that is, after his translations of *Nickleby*, the *Sketches*, and *Oliver Twist* had appeared), apparently to ask for advance copies of future books for translation; perhaps he suggested himself for the position of authorized translator of Dickens' books. Dickens replied, on 10 March 1840:

My dear Sir
I will not attempt to tell you how much gratified I have been by the receipt of your first English letter: nor can I describe to you with what delight and gratification I learn that I am held in such high esteem by your great countrymen, whose favourable appreciation is flattering indeed.
To you, who have undertaken the laborious (and often, I fear, very irksome) task of clothing me in the German garb, I owe a long arrear of thanks. I wish you would come to England, and afford me an opportunity of slightly reducing the account.
It is with great regret that I have to inform you, in reply to the request contained in your pleasant communication, that my publishers have already made such arrangements, and are in possession of such stipulations relative to the proof-sheets of my new works, that I have no power

---

[1] *Blätter für Literatur und bildende Kunst* (supplement to the *Dresdner Abendzeitung*), 1838, no. 68 (25 August).
[2] Loc. cit., 1838, no. 100 (15 Dec.).
[3] *Europa* (Stuttgart), 1839, vol. ii, p. 40. The reference is to a Brunswick translation, which I take to be Diezmann's.

APPENDIX II

to send them out of England. If I had, I need not tell you what pleasure it would afford me to promote your views.[1]

It is known that some arrangements for translation, or at least publication, in Germany, had already been made; for Dickens, writing to G. Cattermole on 13 January 1840, mentioned that the early sheets of *Master Humphrey's Clock* had to be sent to America and Germany.[2] But Messrs. Chapman & Hall are unable to give details of these arrangements, and they appear not to be known.

EDWARD AUBREY MORIARTY[3] is the most interesting of the early translators. He was an Irishman, of good education and wide interests, whose command of German was so excellent that it brought him a reputation as author and editor in, and translator into, that language.

He was born in 1819, and entered Trinity College, Dublin, in 1834, where five years later he received the B.A. degree. In that year (1839) he went to Germany. He was then only twenty years old, and there is no record of his having studied German previously; but by 1840 he was already active as a translator for different publishers in Brunswick and Leipzig. His first work seems to have been on a book by P. E. Turnbull, which was published as *Oesterreichs Sociale und Politische Zustände* by J. J. Weber of Leipzig in 1840. In that year Moriarty edited the *British and Continental Examiner* for T. O. Weigel of Leipzig.[4] In 1840–1 he translated 'aus dem Yankee-Englischen' *Sam Slicks des Uhrmachers Reden und Thun*, and *Europa* speaks of this as an 'überaus gelungene und glückliche Übersetzung'.[5]

From this time until 1846, when he left Germany, Moriarty was a most productive and successful translator; chiefly of Dickens. His work on Dickens for J. J. Weber began in 1840 where that of H. Roberts ceased: with the translation of *Master Humphrey's Clock* in its complete form.[6] He then translated *American Notes* (1843); *Chuzzlewit* (1843–4); the *Christmas Carol* (1844); the *Chimes* (1845); and part of *Dombey*—

[1] *Letters*, Nonesuch edition, London, 1938, vol. i; March 1840.
[2] *Letters*, vol. i; January 1840.
[3] I am much indebted to Professor M. F. Liddell, of Trinity College, Dublin, for many details of Moriarty's life.
[4] Described as a 'political-literary-critical and commercial' weekly. The full 52 numbers were published. In 1841 the title was changed to *The German Examiner and Continental Advertiser*: this also lasted the whole year, but apparently no longer. Kayser's *Bücherlexikon* for 1841–6 also notes a *German and Continental Examiner* for 1841–2–3, published by Binder of Leipzig; this may also have been edited by Moriarty.
[5] *Europa* (Stuttgart), 1841, vol. iii, p. 327.
[6] The critic of the *Jenaische Allg. Lit.-Zeitung* (an important periodical) said of this book that 'die Übersetzung des Herrn Moriarty sich leicht und gefällig bewegt' (1841, no. 55). *Barnaby Rudge* appeared separately in 1841 (Weber, Leipzig).

presumably only the earliest part. All these translations were of good standard, and they show a surprising fluency of German; they were widely known and highly valued.[1] Much of Julian Schmidt's praise for the complete edition of Dickens in translation, published by Lorck of Leipzig from 1852 onwards,[2] must go to Moriarty, for all his translations were reprinted in that edition.

A few further notes on Moriarty's career may find a place here.[3] His work on Dickens was far from occupying his whole time. From 1842 to 1844 he collaborated with Julius Seybt on a translation of selected books by Theodore Hook (published by Weber, Leipzig); in 1843 he published his own German biography of Daniel O'Connell (whom he knew personally), and also, in collaboration with J. F. Neigebaur, a guidebook entitled *London: Ein Handbuch für Reisende*.[4] He was the editor of *Selections from British Authors in Prose and Poetry* (Leipzig, 1844), and the translator (into English) of F. T. Kugler's *History of Frederick the Great* (London, 1844). From 1843 to 1846, when he left Germany, he was professor of English literature at the Royal Academy of Trade in Berlin.

After these remarkably active seven years he returned to London to read for the Bar as a student of the Inner Temple; he was not yet twenty-eight years old. He was called to the Bar in 1849. In 1851 he translated the catalogue of the Great Exhibition into German as the *Amtlicher Katalog der Ausstellung der Industrie-Erzeugnisse aller Völker*; his knowledge of German must have been known and appreciated in London for him to have been chosen, possibly by Prince Albert himself, for such a responsible task.

He died in London on 13 July 1874. He had other interests besides those noticed above; he was known as a contributor to the *Edinburgh Review*, and had been Director-General of the Cologne and Frankfurt railway. He may have had interviews with Dickens during his period of work as a translator; there appears to be no evidence of this from English sources, but the *Magazin für die Literatur des Auslandes*, reviewing his translation of *American Notes*, says:

Zu Herrn Moriarty sagte Dickens wenige Tage, ehe er sich nach Amerika einschiffte: 'Ich gehe mit einem lebhaften Vorurteil *für* die Amerikaner über den Ozean. . . .'[5]

This information was probably drawn from a foreword to the translation, which was unfortunately not available. There seems to be no other confirmation of it.

[1] According to R. Freymond's short note on Dickens' translators—op. cit., p. 18, footnote 2.   [2] *Die Grenzboten*, 1853, vol. iii, p. 437.
[3] Some details here from F. Boase, *Modern English Biography*, Truro, 1897, vol. ii, p. 970.   [4] Published Berlin and Leipzig respectively.
[5] *Mag. f. d. Lit. des Auslandes*, 6 Jan. 1843.

APPENDIX II

JULIUS SEYBT was one of the best-known and most successful of the early translators of Dickens, and one whose occupation with Dickens' books was second in duration to that of Carl Kolb alone. His full name was apparently Julius Bernhard Seybt, for it seems probable that he is to be identified with the writer of that name who translated Mariotti's *Italy* for Lorck of Leipzig in 1846.

He worked mainly for Weber, Lorck, and Wiedemann, all of Leipzig, and seems to have started as a translator in 1840, when he prepared a successful German version of Shelley's poems.[1] From 1842 to 1844 he collaborated with Moriarty on a translation of selected novels of Theodore Hook, published in twenty parts by Weber of Leipzig. His first work on Dickens was a translation of the *Cricket on the Hearth* for Lorck in 1846; in the same year he made the German translation of *Pictures from Italy* for the same publisher. When Moriarty's services were no longer available, Seybt became the regular translator of Dickens for Weber and Lorck: he completed *Dombey* (begun by Moriarty) and from then translated every one of Dickens' books up to, and including, *Great Expectations*. He was the general editor of the complete edition of Dickens in German translation published by Lorck of Leipzig in and after 1852; this edition, which included the new work of Seybt, also incorporated all the earlier work of Roberts and Moriarty, and part of Seybt's work was to revise their translations. This may have induced him to prepare versions of his own; translations of *Oliver Twist* and of *Nickleby*, announced to be by him, are known, but it is not clear whether these are original translations or Roberts' versions rewritten by Seybt. Neither was available for study.

Seybt was well known to Freytag and Spielhagen, who have left descriptions of him and his work in their memoirs. Spielhagen describes him as:

Der kleine, kugelrunde, behagliche Herr mit der jovialen Miene und dem ausgesprochenen sächsischen Dialekt. . . .[2]

and Freytag describes his work:

Seybt war ein gewandter, zuweilen flüchtiger Schriftsteller, am Morgen ebenso schnell und regelmäßig bei seinem Werke, wie abends beim Becher. Er übte den Brauch, seine Übertragungen aus dem Englischen einem Stenographen zu diktieren und wußte so in wenigen Wochen einen starken Roman zu bewältigen. Blieb bei diesem Verfahren auch Vieles für die Übersetzung zu wünschen übrig, sie war immer noch besser, als die große Mehrzahl ähnlicher behender Leistungen.[3]

---

[1] *P. B. Shelley: Poetische Werke*, pt. 1, 1840; pts. 2 and 3, 1842. Republished in one volume, 1844 (Leipzig, Engelmann).
[2] *Finder und Erfinder*, Leipzig, 1890, vol. ii, p. 384.
[3] *Erinnerungen*, Leipzig, 1887, p. 233.

EARLY GERMAN TRANSLATORS OF DICKENS

Spielhagen supplements this by mentioning that Seybt called the use of a dictionary 'eine große zeitraubende Unvorsichtigkeit'; and he adds: 'in der Tat hatte er selbst seit Jahren alle Lexika aus seiner Wohnung verbannt und behauptete, sich dabei ganz vortrefflich zu stehen.' This is a very interesting light on Seybt's methods. Though they seem a little haphazard, there is praise for them from Julian Schmidt to confirm that of Freytag. Schmidt twice refers to Seybt's work on the complete Lorck edition of Dickens, and says:

Wir glauben nicht zu viel zu sagen, wenn wir Julius Seybt als den besten Übersetzer derartiger Werke bezeichnen[1],

and in another article on the merits of the translations:

Wenn man also auch hie und da einem Fehler der Flüchtigkeit begegnet, so wird dadurch der Totaleindruck nicht im geringsten gestört, und Herr Seybt verdient ein nicht gemeines Lob, sich so ganz in seinen Dichter eingelebt und ihn verstanden zu haben.[2]

[1] *Die Grenzboten*, 1852, vol. iv, p. 189.
[2] Loc. cit., 1853, vol. iii, p. 437.

GENERAL BIBLIOGRAPHY

ONLY the more useful books and articles are mentioned here. Dickens' books and, wherever possible, the better-known German novels considered in the text, are quoted by section or chapter; any edition of them can consequently be used for reference, and they are not included in this list for that reason. Less important works used are described in the footnotes. Part III has its own list, and the periodicals studied are described in Appendix I.

Allgemeine Deutsche Biographie. Leipzig, 1875–1912, 56 vols.
ALTVATER, F. *Wesen und Form der deutschen Dorfgeschichte im 19. Jahrhundert.* (Germ. Studien, Hft. 88.) Berlin, 1930.
AUERBACH, B. *Briefe an Jakob Auerbach.* Frankfurt a/M., 1884, 2 vols.
BENNETT, E. K. *The German Novelle.* Cambridge, 1934.
BETZ, J. *Otto Ludwigs Verhältnis zu den Engländern.* Diss. Frankfurt, 1929.
BIEBER, H. *Der Kampf um die Tradition.* (Epochen der deutschen Literatur, vol. v.) Stuttgart, 1928.
BRÜMMER, F. *Deutsches Dichterlexikon.* Eichstätt, Stuttgart, 1876–7, 2 vols.
Cambridge Modern History, vol. xi (*The Growth of Nationalities*). Cambridge, 1909.
CHURCH, H. 'Otto Babendiek and David Copperfield.' *Germanic Review* (Columbia Univ.), Jan. 1936, pp. 40–9.
DANZEL, T. W. *Gesammelte Aufsätze*, hrsg. O. Jahn. Leipzig, 1855. (Dickens, pp. 99–117.)
Deutsches Bücherverzeichnis. Leipzig, Verein der deutschen Buchhändler, 1911 ff.
DICKENS, C. *Letters*, Nonesuch edition, ed. W. Dexter. London, 1938 (3 vols.).
The Dickensian, publication of the Dickens Fellowship. 1905 ff.
DOERNENBURG, E., and FEHSE, W. *Raabe und Dickens.* Magdeburg, 1921.
DRESCH, J. *Le Roman social en Allemagne, 1850-1900.* Paris, 1913.
ECKHOLT, H. A. *Untersuchungen über die Romantechnik F. Reuters.* (Diss. Münster.) Haselünne i.H., 1912.
ENSLIN, T. C. F., and ENGELMANN, W. *Bibliothek der schönen Wissenschaften.* Leipzig, 1846.
FEHSE, W. 'Dickens *Pickwickier* und Freytags *Journalisten.*' *Die Neueren Sprachen*, vol. xxxv, pp. 138–40. (1927.)
—— *Wilhelm Raabe, sein Leben und seine Werke.* Braunschweig, 1937.
—— and see DOERNENBURG, E.

FLIESS, S. *Wilhelm Raabe*. Grenoble, 1912.
FORSTER, J. *The Life of Charles Dickens*. Everyman's edition, London, 1927, 2 vols.
FRENSSEN, G. *Grübeleien*. Neue Ausgabe, Berlin, 1934.
—— *Möwen und Mäuse*. Berlin, 1928.
—— *Vorland*. Berlin, 1937.
FREYMOND, R. *Der Einfluß von Charles Dickens auf Gustav Freytag*. (Prager deutsche Studien, vol. xix.) Prague, 1912.
FREYTAG, G. 'Ein Dank für Charles Dickens.' (*Ges. Aufsätze*, vol. ii, pp. 239–44.)
—— *Erinnerungen aus meinem Leben*. Leipzig, 1887.
—— *Gesammelte Aufsätze*. 2 vols., Leipzig, 1888.
FÜRST, R. 'Literarische Verwandtschaften.' (Dickens and Ebner-Eschenbach.)' *Die Zeit*, Wien, 27 Dec. 1902. (= Vol. xxxiii, no. 430.)
GAEDERTZ, K. T. *Reuterstudien*. Wismar, 1889.
GEISSENDOERFER, J. T. 'Dickens' Einfluß auf Ungern-Sternberg, Hesslein, Stolle, Raabe und Ebner-Eschenbach.' (*Americana-Germanica*, vol. xix.) 1915.
GEIST, H. *Fritz Reuters literarische Beziehungen zu Charles Dickens*. Diss. Halle, 1913.
GELLER, M. F. *Spielhagens Theorie und Praxis des Romans*. Diss. Bonn, 1917. (Complete only in *Bonner Forschungen*, Neue Folge, Band 10.)
HART, H. and J. *Kritische Waffengänge*, Heft 6: *F. Spielhagen und der deutsche Roman der Gegenwart*. Leipzig, 1884.
JUNGE, H. *Wilhelm Raabe. Studien über Form und Inhalt seiner Werke*. (Schriften der literarhistorischen Gesellschaft, Bonn, no. 9.) Dortmund, 1910.
KAYSER, C. G. *Vollständiges Bücherlexikon, 1750–1910*. Leipzig, 1834–1911. (Continued as the *Deutsches Bücherverzeichnis*, q.v.)
KOHN-BRAMSTEDT, E. *Aristocracy and the Middle Classes in Germany. Social Types in German Literature, 1830–1900*. London, King, 1937.
KRÜGER, H. A. *Der junge Raabe, Jugendjahre und Erstlingswerke*. Leipzig, 1911.
KUMMER, F. *Deutsche Literaturgeschichte des 19. Jahrhunderts*. Dresden, 1909.
LAUBE, H. *Erinnerungen*; as vols. 1 and 16 of his *Gesammelte Schriften*, 16 vols., Wien, 1875–82.
LOHRE, H. 'Otto Ludwig und Charles Dickens.' *A.S.N.S.*, 1910, vol. 124, pp. 15–45.
LÜDER, F. *Die epischen Werke Otto Ludwigs und ihr Verhältnis zu Charles Dickens*. (Diss. Greifswald) Leipzig, 1910.

GENERAL BIBLIOGRAPHY

LUDWIG, O. *Epische Studien.* (The only full printing of these is in vol. vi of the edition of his works by A. Stern and E. Schmidt, Leipzig, 1891, from which they are here quoted.)
MAYNC, H. *Immermann, der Mann und sein Werk.* München, 1921.
MAYRHOFER, O. *Freytag und das junge Deutschland.* (Beiträge zur deutschen Literaturwissenschaft, 1.) Marburg, 1907.
MERKER, P., and STAMMLER, W. *Reallexikon der deutschen Literaturgeschichte.* Berlin, 1925/6–1931, 4 vols.
MEYER, R. M. 'Zu Reuters Stromtid; zwei Quellennachweise.' (*Jahrbuch des Vereins für Niederdeutsche Sprachforschung*, vol. xxii, 1896, pp. 131–2.)
MIELKE, H., and HOMANN, H. J. *Der deutsche Roman.* Dresden, 1920, 7. Auflage.
MÜLLER-EMS, R. *Otto Ludwigs Erzählungskunst.* Berlin, 1905.
MUNDT, T. *Die Literatur der Gegenwart.* Berlin, 1842.
PRICE, L. M. 'The Attitude of Gustav Freytag and Julian Schmidt to English literature, 1848–1862.' *Hesperia*, no. 7, Göttingen, Baltimore, 1915.
—— *English > German Literary Influences.* Part I, bibliography; Part II, survey. (University of California Publications in Modern Philology.) Univ. Cal. Press, 1919, 1920.
—— *The Reception of English Literature in Germany.* Univ. Cal. Press, Berkeley, Cal., 1932.
REUTER, F. *Briefe*, hrsg. O. Weltzien. Leipzig, n.d.
RICHTER, H. *Untersuchungen zum Stil W. Raabes.* (Diss. Greifswald.) Stettin, 1935.
RÖMER, A. *Fritz Reuter in seinem Leben und Schaffen.* Berlin, 1896.
SCHLÖSSER, A. *Die Englische Literatur in Deutschland, 1895–1934.* (Forschungen zur englischen Philologie, no. 5.) Jena, 1937.
SCHMIDT, J. *Boz (Dickens), eine Charakteristik.* Leipzig, 1852.
—— *Übersicht der englischen Literatur im 19. Jahrhundert.* Sondershausen, 1859.
—— *Bilder aus dem geistigen Leben unserer Zeit:*—Neue Folge. Leipzig, 1871.
—— Ibid. —Neue Bilder. Leipzig, 1873.
—— *Charakterbilder aus der zeitgenössischen Literatur.* Leipzig, 1875.
SIGMANN, L. *Die Englische Literatur von 1800 bis 1850 im Urteil der zeitgenössischen deutschen Kritik.* (Anglistische Forschungen, Heft 55.) Heidelberg, 1918. (Dickens, pp. 294–304.)
SKINNER, M. 'The Indebtedness of Spielhagen to Dickens.' (*Journal of Eng. and Germ. Philology*, 1910, pp. 499–505.)
SPIELHAGEN, F. *Beiträge zur Theorie und Technik des Romans.* Leipzig, 1882.

—— *Neue Beiträge zur Theorie und Technik der Epik und Dramatik.* Leipzig, 1898.
—— *Finder und Erfinder, Erinnerungen aus meinem Leben.* Leipzig, 1890, 2 vols.
—— *Vermischte Schriften.* Leipzig, 1872.
STIRK, S. D. *Kritiken von H. Laube, 1829–35.* Breslau, 1934.
STONEHOUSE, J. H. *Catalogue of the Library of Charles Dickens, from Gadshill.* London, 1935.
ULRICH, P. *Freytags Romantechnik.* (Beiträge zur deutschen Literaturwissenschaft, 3.) Marburg, 1907.
UNGERN-STERNBERG, A. VON. *Erinnerungsblätter*, Teil 2. Berlin, 1856.
VÖLK, V. *Dickens' Einfluß auf Freytags Soll und Haben.* (4. Jahresbericht, Salzburger Mädchenlyzeum.) Salzburg, 1908.
WARNCKE, P. *Fritz Reuter; woans hei lewt un schrewen hett.* Leipzig, 1899.
WEIL, E. *Alexander von Sternberg.* (Germanische Studien, Heft 130.) Berlin, 1932.
WILBRANDT, A. Biography of Reuter as foreword to *Reuters Sämtliche Werke*, Volksausgabe, 7 vols. Wismar, Hinstorff, 1877. (First published 1874.)
WYZEWA, T. DE. 'Jörn Uhl, par Gustav Frenssen.' *Revue des deux Mondes*, 15 sept., 1902, pp. 457–68.

CHRONOLOGICAL LIST OF DICKENS' MAJOR WORKS

Sketches by Boz	1836
Pickwick Papers	March 1836–Oct. 1837
Oliver Twist	Jan. 1837–March 1839
Nicholas Nickleby	April 1838–Oct. 1839
Master Humphrey's Clock	April 1840–Nov. 1841
Old Curiosity Shop	April 1840–Jan. 1841
Barnaby Rudge	Jan. 1841–Nov. 1841
Christmas Carol	Christmas 1843
Martin Chuzzlewit	Jan. 1843–July 1844
The Chimes	Christmas 1844
The Cricket on the Hearth	Christmas 1845
Pictures from Italy	1846
The Battle of Life	Christmas 1846
Dombey and Son	Oct. 1846–April 1848
The Haunted Man	Christmas 1848
David Copperfield	May 1849–Nov. 1850
Bleak House	March 1852—Sept. 1853
Hard Times	April–August 1854
Little Dorrit	Dec. 1855–June 1857
A Tale of Two Cities	April–Nov. 1859
Great Expectations	Dec. 1860–Aug. 1861
Our Mutual Friend	May 1864–Nov. 1865
Edwin Drood	April–Sept. 1870

INDEX

Addison, 146-7, 152, 156-7.
American Notes, 8, 29, 31, 33, 97, 190-1.
Auerbach, B., 47, 52-3, 57-8, 117.

Balzac, 57, 125-6, 135.
Banner, A., 12.
Barnaby Rudge, 8, 29, 31-2, 41, 45, 82, 95, 111, 117, 132, 143, 147, 153, 172, 190.
Battle of Life, 33-4, 172.
Behn-Eschenburg, H., 52.
Bleak House, 43, 46-8, 50, 71, 98-9, 118, 148-9, 151, 170, 172.
Bohnstedt, Dr., 52.
Borchardt, R., 79.
Brandl, A., 146-7, 152-4, 159, 162-3.
Bulwer-Lytton, 8, 113, 135, 184, 188.
Busch, M., 13.

Carlyle, 25, 103, 143, 145, 149, 152-3, 163.
Chimes, 8, 22, 33, 91, 111, 145, 172, 190.
Christmas Carol, 8-9, 12, 22, 24, 33, 95-6, 111, 145, 153, 161, 163-4, 169-70, 172, 188, 190.
Corvin-Wiersbitzki, O. J. B. von, 53, 183-4.
Cricket on the Hearth, 13, 22, 29, 33-4, 85, 96, 170, 172-3, 192.
Czarnowski, O. von, 7-8, 170.

Danzel, T. W., 32-3, 35.
David Copperfield, 37, 40, 42-3, 45, 48, 63-4, 68, 71, 74, 76-80, 91, 95, 97-9, 102, 114, 117-34, 143-4, 148-9, 151, 161, 168-70, 172.
Devrient, E., 2.
Dibelius, W., 146-7, 153-63, 167.
Diezmann, J. A., 2, 7-8, 188-90.
Dombey and Son, 8, 34-5, 37, 42, 45, 51, 82, 85, 88, 91, 95, 99, 107-8, 117, 143, 148, 151, 170, 172, 188, 190, 192.
Dresch, J., 68-9, 119.
Droste-Hülshoff, A. von, 60.
Dubois, L., 12.

Ebner-Eschenbach, M. von, 124, 128, 136-9.
Edwin Drood, 13, 52, 149, 162, 172.
Engel, E., 14, 53, 168.

Fielding, 19, 24, 85, 113-14, 146-7, 152-7.

Fontane, 5, 125.
Forster, J., 1, 54, 142-5.
Freiligrath, 2, 53-4, 113.
Frenssen, 63-4, 124-34.
Freytag, 14-15, 27, 37-8, 47, 55-8, 61-4, 66-81, 105, 117, 124, 192-3.

Geissendoerfer, J. T., 10-11, 94, 136-7, 171.
Glasbrenner, A., 25, 30, 58.
Goethe, 4, 64, 86, 102, 108, 117, 125, 127, 129, 188.
Goldmark, K., 173.
Great Expectations, 13, 51, 82, 132, 162, 172, 192.
Gutzkow, K., 38-9, 60.

Hackländer, F., 59, 94.
Hard Times, 43-4, 48-51, 71, 82, 84-6, 111, 118, 145, 148-9, 152, 159, 170, 172.
Hart, H., 14, 20, 120-3.
Haunted Man, 34, 97, 172.
Heichen, P., 145, 170.
Hell, T., 181, 185-6, 189.
Hermes, K. H., 7, 188-9.
Herrig, L., 11.
Hesslein, B., 11.
Hippel, T. G., 24-5.
Hoffmann, E. T. A., 24-5, 33-4, 58, 65, 91.
Hoffmann, P. T., 171.
Holtei, K. von, 59.
Hook, T., 154-7, 191-2.
Horne, R. H., 24, 187.
Household Words, 3, 43, 59-60, 183.

Immermann, 21, 24-6.

Jean Paul, 23-5, 32, 65, 75, 114.
Jürgens, K., 185.

Kaufmann, J., 71.
Keller, G., 64, 124-5, 127-8.
Kinkel, G., 3.
Kolb, C., 8, 11-12, 170-1, 187-8, 192.
Künzel, H., 2.

Laube, H., 17, 26.
Lehmann, E., 13.
Lehmann-Haupt, C., 53.
Letters of Charles Dickens, 2-4, 145, 148, 189-90.
Life of Our Lord, 169.
Little Dorrit, 44, 50-1, 54, 82, 85, 149, 162, 172-3.

INDEX

Lobedan, H., 170.
Ludwig, O., 25, 47, 57, 60–2, 82–93, 109, 124.

Marryat, F., 154–7, 172, 187–8.
Martin Chuzzlewit, 8, 24, 31–3, 40, 42, 45, 68, 82, 95, 97, 99, 148, 172, 190.
Master Humphrey's Clock, see *Barnaby Rudge* and *Old Curiosity Shop*.
Memoirs of Joseph Grimaldi, 11, 184, 186.
Meyrink, G., 171.
Mielke, H., 75, 119, 136.
Moosthal, E. von, 8.
Moriarty, E. A., 8, 13, 190–2.
Mundt, T., 23.

Nicholas Nickleby, 7–8, 20, 28–32, 40–1, 45, 65, 68, 77–8, 91, 95–8, 101, 107, 117, 136–9, 143, 148, 150–1, 170, 172, 186–9, 192.
Niemann, W., 173.
Notovich, O. K., 173.

Old Curiosity Shop, 8, 29, 31, 41, 65, 71, 82, 95, 98, 107, 136, 147, 151, 170, 172, 190.
Oliver Twist, 7–9, 22, 28–32, 35, 41, 45, 68, 75, 77, 91, 95, 97, 117, 137–8, 148, 151–2, 155, 157, 161, 170, 172, 186–9, 192.
Our Mutual Friend, 51–2, 82, 88, 149, 162, 172.

Pickwick Papers, 7–11, 14–20, 24, 29–30, 32, 40–1, 45, 55, 63, 66, 71–2, 75, 79, 82, 95, 97–8, 101, 104–5, 107, 110–11, 113, 117, 121, 126, 129, 132, 143, 145, 147–8, 151–2, 156–7, 161, 167–8, 170, 172–4, 185–7.
Picnic Papers, 11–12.
Pictures from Italy, 29, 34, 192.
Price, L. M., 38, 46–7, 59, 70–1, 180.
Prutz, R., 18, 59, 77.

Raabe, 24, 63–4, 93, 94–102, 124–5, 127–8.
Rabener, G. W., 25.
Reuter, F., 47, 63–4, 94, 103–12, 127.

Reynolds, G. W. M., 11.
Richter, J. P. F., *see* Jean Paul.
Roberts, H., 7–8, 11, 13–14, 170, 185–7, 190, 192.

Sand, G., 16, 22, 114, 188.
Scheibe, A., 170.
Schlösser, A., 171–2.
Schmidt, J., 13–14, 17, 20, 37–50, 55, 57–66, 71, 105, 119, 121–3, 143, 180, 191, 193.
Schönthan, F. von, 173.
Scott, M., 13.
Scott, W., 39, 66, 68, 70, 73, 79, 86, 89, 101, 103–4, 108–9, 113, 154–5, 172.
Seybt, J., 13, 66, 71, 170, 191–3.
Shakespeare, 25, 66, 85–6, 103, 108, 113, 125–6, 158, 163.
Sigmann, L., 28, 35, 37, 180.
Sketches by Boz, 7, 28–30, 33, 40, 117, 146–7, 151, 170, 172, 184, 186–9.
Smollett, 19, 24, 85, 113, 146–7, 152–7.
Spielhagen, 15, 57, 63–4, 113–23, 168, 192–3.
Sternberg, A. von, *see* Ungern-Sternberg.
Sterne, 24, 113, 154, 188.
Stolle, F., 10–11.
Sue, E., 12, 18, 23, 46, 57, 59, 188.

Tale of Two Cities, 13, 50–1, 78, 82, 149, 153, 161, 170, 172.
Tauchnitz, B., 3, 8–9, 142.
Temme, J. D. H., 59.
Thackeray, 18, 94–5, 113–17, 150.
Thümmel, M. A. von, 25, 114.

Ungern-Sternberg, A. von, 26, 58, 60, 135–6.

Weizmann, L., 14, 187–8.
Wessely, J. E., 12.
Wilding, K., 170–1.
Willkomm, E., 59.
Winter, A., 12.

Zoller, E., 12.
Zoozmann, R., 170.